ROUTLEDGE LIBRARY EDITIONS:
PSYCHOLOGY OF EDUCATION

Volume 14

THE SCHOOL PSYCHOLOGIST IN NONTRADITIONAL SETTINGS

THE SCHOOL PSYCHOLOGIST IN NONTRADITIONAL SETTINGS

Integrating Clients, Services, and Settings

Edited by
RIK CARL D'AMATO AND RAYMOND S. DEAN

Routledge
Taylor & Francis Group
LONDON AND NEW YORK

First published in 1989 by Lawrence Erlbaum Associates, Inc.

This edition first published in 2018
by Routledge
2 Park Square, Milton Park, Abingdon, Oxon OX14 4RN

and by Routledge
711 Third Avenue, New York, NY 10017

Routledge is an imprint of the Taylor & Francis Group, an informa business

British Library Cataloguing in Publication Data
A catalogue record for this book is available from the British Library

ISBN: 978-1-138-24157-2 (Set)
ISBN: 978-1-315-10703-5 (Set) (ebk)
ISBN: 978-0-415-79208-0 (Volume 14) (hbk)
ISBN: 978-1-315-21189-3 (Volume 14) (ebk)

The School Psychologist in Nontraditional Settings

Integrating Clients, Services, and Settings

Edited by

Rik Carl D'Amato
Mississippi State University

Raymond S. Dean
Ball State University and
Indiana University School of Medicine

LAWRENCE ERLBAUM ASSOCIATES, PUBLISHERS
1989 Hillsdale, New Jersey Hove and London

Lawrence Erlbaum Associates, Inc., Publishers
365 Broadway
Hillsdale, New Jersey 07642

Library of Congress Cataloging-in-Publication Data

The School psychologist in nontraditional settings : integrating clients, services, and settings / edited by Rik Carl D'Amato, Raymond S. Dean.
p. cm.
Includes bibliographies and indexes.
ISBN 0-89859-996-2
1. School psychologists—United States. 2. Educational psychology. 3. School psychology—United States. I. D'Amato, Rik Carl. II. Dean, Raymond S.
[DNLM: 1. Psychology, Clinical. 2. School Health Services. LB 3013.6.S372]
LB3013.6S28 1989
371.2'022—dc19
DNLM/DLC
for Library of Congress

88-30076
CIP

Printed in the United States of America
10 9 8 7 6 5 4 3 2 1

To Marcia for her support and love
R.C.D.

To Heather and Whitney for their love and patience
R.S.D.

Contents

Preface

This book is for applied psychologists and school psychologists-in-training who are interested in meeting client needs notwithstanding the setting of service. Thus, we agree with Lightner Witmer's original notions, and like him, have tried to lay a foundation for what we have called the field of school psychology in *nontraditional* settings. When school psychology is considered free of the setting, the emphasis becomes a melding of client needs with appropriate services. From this view comes a model of school psychology services that can be applied to medical facilities, residential treatment centers, businesses, private practices, community agencies, and the like. This reconceptualization stresses that school psychology is an approach to problem solving and not a setting-specific profession.

Such a nontraditional model flows from data showing that school psychologists display skills and abilities that can be successfully applied to a variety of clients in numerous settings. Indeed, it is our hope that after considering this book the reader will come to appreciate the *promise* of school psychology.

We are grateful to the many talented authors who have contributed to this volume.

Rik Carl D'Amato
Raymond S. Dean

Contributors

Jack I. Bardon, Ph.D.
Excellence Foundation Professor of Education
School of Education
The University of North Carolina at Greensboro
Greensboro, NC 27412

Jane Close Conoley, Ph.D.
Associate Professor
Buros Institute of Mental Measurements
Department of Educational Psychology
University of Nebraska-Lincoln
Lincoln, NE 68588-0348

Rik Carl D'Amato, Ph.D.
Director, Programs in School Psychology
Assistant Professor, Department of Educational Psychology
Post Office Box EP
Mississippi State University
Mississippi State, MS 39762-5670

Raymond S. Dean, Ph.D.
Distinguished Professor of Neuropsychology
Director, School Psychology Program and
Neuropsychology Laboratory
Teachers College 524
Ball State University
Muncie, IN 47306

Jeffrey W. Gray, Ph.D.
Associate Director
Neuropsychology Laboratory
Assistant Professor
Department of Educational Psychology
Ball State University
Muncie, IN 47306

Patti Harrison, Ph.D.
Chair, School Psychology
College of Education
Post Office Box Q
The University of Alabama
Tuscaloosa, AL 35487-9782

George McCloskey, Ph.D.
Senior Research Associate
American Guidance Service
Circle Pines, MN 55014

Richard J. Morris, Ph.D.
Professor and Director, School Psychology Program
Department of Educational Psychology
College of Education
University of Arizona
Tucson, AZ 85721

Yvonne P. Morris, Ph.D.
Department of Educational Psychology
College of Education
University of Arizona
Tucson, AZ 85721

Steven I. Pfeiffer, Ph.D.
Director, Clinical Training and Research
Institute of Clinical Training and Research
19 South Waterloo Road
Post Office Box 400
The Devereux Foundation
Devon, PA 19333

Walter B. Pryzwansky, Ed.D.
Professor and Chair
Psychological Studies
Peabody Hall 037A
University of North Carolina at Chapel Hill
Chapel Hill, NC 27514

Brian J. Stone, Ph.D.
Assistant Director
Neuropsychology Laboratory
Ball State University
Muncie, IN 47306

David L. Wodrich, Ph.D.
Clinical Director of Child Psychology
Division of Behavioral Pediatrics
Post Office Box 2989
Phoenix Children's Hospital
Phoenix, Arizona 85062

1

The School Psychologist as an Applied Educational Psychologist

JACK I. BARDON
The University of North Carolina at Greensboro

Education takes place in many ways and in many contexts. Schooling does not just occur in schools. Knowledge and methods of psychology applied to education and schooling, subsumed under the title "educational psychology," need not be confined to schools alone. The professional specialty of school psychology is not only for schools. When practiced at the highest levels, school psychology has much to offer those in nontraditional settings.

A reconceptualization of the way school psychologists think about their purposes and services can increase the usefulness of this specialty by helping others to understand how school psychologists differ from other human service providers. This chapter traces the development of school psychology, explains why school psychological services in nonschool settings makes sense, and illustrates why the title "school psychologist" need not be viewed narrowly. This chapter offers a model for practice that may help school psychology clarify its particular contributions as a human service provider specialty of psychology.

THE IMPORT OF HISTORY AND DEVELOPMENT

School psychology is a product of the 90-year development of psychology, particularly clinical psychology, and education, especially special education (Fagan, 1986). Its development cannot easily be traced to significant and clear lines of theory or research, nor does it have national or international progenitors who are identified as its founders. Rather, it is best considered as having derived from an accumulation of services (Bardon, 1983) based originally on the schools' need for classification and management of children with educational and behavior problems. It originated during a time when immigration policies created a large population of children who, for various reasons, contributed to the range of individual differences in school achievement and behavior, while universal and compulsory education were concurrently taking root (Levine & Levine, 1970).

It was stimulated by the innovation of tests of mental ability. The mental health movement and the influx of psychoanalytic thought in the United States provided further incentive for the provision of psychological services in the schools by offering additional innovative ways to conceive of the causes and treatment of problem behavior. Thus, the influence of the testing movement in education, the mental health movement in psychology and related disciplines served to furnish the major ingredients for the formation of modern day school psychology, at least through the 1970s (Bardon & Bennett, 1974). As new specialties in psychology based on further refinements of knowledge and thought (especially in clinical psychology) developed, school psychology also benefited. There is virtually no area of clinical psychology innovation that has not been tried by school psychologists.

Borrowing someone else's ideas and methods to use in your own work does not lead to clarification of what you are that "they" are not. The struggle for separate identity, dating back to 1953 at least (Cutts, 1955), has never stopped and continues to be a major preoccupation of the specialty. School psychologists' bifurcated title has presented it with a special problem. Education in schools and psychology practiced in academic and professional settings are not isomorphic. Controlled through certification by bureaucratic state education establishments, its expansion often hampered by rules, regulations, and limited views of what psychologists have to offer, school psychology has not often enough been able to become what it purported to be, or wished to be. The gap between its literature and its practices is wider than desired. To be a psychologist and to be in schools is what Shulman (1982) described as being a "border provincial" required to speak the language of both psychology and education while often regarded by each as belonging to the other. One of the major problems of school psychology has been its need to determine how to function most productively in someone else's house—to become recognized as part of the household while continuing to function as psychologists who bring new and different ideas and approaches to the resolution of problems that occur in school buildings.

School psychologists, out of necessity, were forced to consider as part of their professional survival how to appraise the setting in which they worked. They paid attention to formal and informal ways to function productively in a place where acceptance is neither automatic or easily predictable. In effect, school psychology became "street wise" to an extent not found in most other professional specialties. In the absence of a professionally acceptable and clear definition of what school psychology is, and faced with about as many definitions as there were textbooks in the field, school psychologists were led to devise their own definitions of who and what they are, based on how they used ideas from other specialties (Reynolds, Gutkin, Elliott, & Witt, 1984). The result has been great diversity in practice and orientation among school psychologists. The negative side of this lack of professional identity is the nonconceptual aspect of the field; the impression of its being a collection of techniques used by a group of heterogeneous persons who have in common only their intelligence tests and classificatory powers in special education. The positive side has been school psychology's ability to exercise ingenuity in resolving problems and the potpourri phenomenon which has characterized much of school psychology in the past: "Try it if it exists. What have you got to lose?" School psychology may well have experimented with as many ways to deal with human problems as any psychological specialty. It has been a living laboratory for methods, techniques, and both good and bad ideas and schemes. Out of this mix of hit-and-miss attempts to deal with difficult problems has come a richness of background that, over the years, has produced practitioners of uncommon and varied skills with the ability to adjust and accommodate to other settings in which their services might be useful.

What Might Have Been

In anticipation of my thesis that there may be better ways to think about school psychology than are currently in vogue, I want to speculate on what professional psychology might have become if certain events in the history of psychology and education had been different. It is generally acknowledged that both school and clinical psychology can trace their beginnings to Lightner Witmer's establishment of a psychological clinic at the University of Pennsylvania in 1886, primarily to work with children with learning difficulties (Reynolds, Gutkin, Elliott, & Witt, 1984). What is especially noteworthy about subsequent events is the branching off of the two specialties, one to become the major psychological practice specialty, and the other to remain with schools and, in some respects, to be co-opted by the schools through their rigid arrangements for certification and job assignments.

The importance of education and concern for learning in the early years of the psychology profession was not confined to the University of Pennsylvania clinic. At the turn of the century, psychologists studying how people learn and how instruction influences learning were among the most prominent persons in the new science of psychology. Shulman (1982) described the bitter and long-standing controversies in the field over the relative merits of science versus common sense, with G. Stanley Hall serving as a major spokesperson for a position, which involved teachers and parents in the collective interpretation of data, with others seeking to use laboratory methods to understand problems of teaching and learning. One of the earliest journals in psychology, founded by G. Stanley Hall, was titled *The Pedagogical Seminary*. Edward Thorndike "ushered in decades of educational research and theory development pertinent to the ways individuals learn, and the influence of instruction on learning and individual differences" (Lambert, 1983, p. 1). Shulman (1982) concluded that education and schools more than clinical psychology and psychopathology were the original foci for applied psychology as psychology developed during the late 1880s and early 1890s.

A turning point—perhaps *the* turning point—was the introduction of Freudian theory and the appeal of the medical model in psychology. Psychoanalytic theory led to the movement away from an educational/psychological emphasis and toward the psychopathology/mental health emphasis in psychological research and theory in practitioner psychology today.

A fascinating account of the 1909 Psychology Conference at Clark University called by G. Stanley Hall makes the point that at the turn of the century psychology and education lived reasonably and comfortably side by side, with concern for pedagogy very much within mainstream thinking in psychology (Evans & Koelsch, 1985). It was at the Clark conference that Sigmund Freud, Carl Jung "and others of the psychoanalytic movement were introduced to an American audience" (Evans & Koelsch, 1985, p. 942).

The conference was sponsored jointly by the Clark Departments of Experimental and Comparative Psychology and the Department of Pedagogy and School Hygiene. Topic presentations included "Problems of Schoolroom Sanitation and School Work," "The Teaching of Psychology in Normal Schools," "School Hygiene in Courses for the Training of Teachers," as well as Adolf Meyer's talk on "The Dynamic Factors in Dementia Praecox and Allied Psychoses" and "The Opportunity and Need for Research in the Field of Education." Carl Jung lectured on "Studies of Association and Mental Hygiene," and Edward Bradford Titchner spoke on "The Experimental Psychology of the Thought Processes." Freud's talk on the psychopathology of everyday life was followed by "Education as a School Subject" (Evans & Koelsch, 1985). At these meetings Freud received the degree of Doctor of Laws and was introduced as follows: "Sigmund Freud of the University of Vienna, founder of a school of *pedogogy* (italics added) already rich in new methods and achievements, leader today among students of the psychology of sex, and of psychotherapy and analysis, doctor of laws" (Evans & Koelsch, p. 946). The conference, often called the "Freud Conference," has historical importance because all that took place there was overshadowed by the introduction to America of Freudian thought. From that time on clinical concerns dominated American practitioner psychology.

It is possible to conceive of a different direction for American practitioner psychology based on the relatively easy and natural cohabitation of psychology and pedagogy in the formative years of American psychology. Given the central position of learning in psychology, the melding of learning and teaching might well have moved toward the creation of what Witmer appeared to have in mind when he began his laboratory: How do people learn? What can be done when learning goes wrong or does not come easily? If Freud had not come along when he did with the force of his ideas and the dominance of physicians in the psychoanalytic movement, it is likely that something like an applied educational or pedogogical psychology might have development from the confluence of research and theory on individual differences, the testing movement, and experiment work on memory, sensation, brain function, self consciousness, attention, association, imagination, perception, reasoning, emotion, and will, the topics of the field as early as 1890 when William James wrote the famous book *Psychology* (1948).

The Reality

History cannot be wished away or changed. Present day school psychology began when education and mainstream psychology began to move apart. School psychology developed within the public schools. It then benefited in its further development by finding a place for itself in American Psychology in 1945 when the present American Psychological Association was formed and the Division of School Psychology was organized (Fagan, 1986). The ensuing development of the specialty and its struggle to become a major practitioner specialty in psychology through raising standards, encouraging doctoral status, the formation of the National Association of School Psychologists, and the creation of its own literature, attest to the vibrancy of the field (Fagan, 1986; Reynolds & Gutkin, 1982).

School psychology is composed of a heterogeneous group of professionals. They use many theories, varied methods, and hold diverse views about the nature, purposes, and priorities of school psychology, seeking to reconcile its dual allegiance to education and to psychology, constrained by the setting of the school yet involved in figuring out how to solve problems within that setting without loss of integrity or professionalism. They have learned to rely most often on clinical psychology skills, thinking, and language to carry out their varied responsibilities. The field's major claim to separate professional status is on the basis that its practices are modified to some extent by the setting in which it functions—the schools (Bardon, 1976). Although reliance on clinical psychology's nomenclature and points of view have served the specialty well, it has not helped to clarify what it is that school psychology has to offer that cannot be achieved by other clinical or child clinical psychology practitioners.

UNIFYING AND DIVERGING FORCES INFLUENCING SCHOOL PSYCHOLOGY

Altman (1987) has presented a cogent analysis of trends influencing psychology. Using principles derived from "transactionalism/contextualism" and "dialectic philosophies," he traced the history of psychology from the pre-1900 period until the present time. I would like to use his approach to examine what aspects of school psychology hold it together and what factors have served to keep it from becoming what many of us believe it can be.

A transactional/contextual view conceives of psychological phenomena as linked to and actually defined by the physical and social contexts within which they are embedded. Hardly controversial, this view suggests that school psychology is influenced by the settings in which it is carried out and is changed by the social contexts, both local and far reaching, in which it exists.

The concept of "dialectics" is based on the assumption that phenomena are composed of oppositional features. They exist in a state of dynamic tension, with oppositional features more descriptive than value laden. Psychological phenomena are not unidimensional; rather, they are characterized by polarities which best describe the range within which one functions, (e.g., conformity and independence, love and hate, etc.). Also, the oppositional processes form a whole, the oppositional poles offering meaning to each other. One side does not exist without the other. Altman (1987) characterized these oppositional forces as centripetal (consolidating, unifying) and centrifugal (separating and diverging). The relationship between consolidating and diverging forces interact differently, assuming different strengths at different times. There are periods of time in which stability and unity are desirable for the development of a field. There are other times in which change and experimentation may lead to the exploration of new conceptual, philosophical, and methodological approaches that enrich and stimulate thinking. These concepts—a transaction/contextual view and dialectics—are useful in understanding the development of school psychology and also provide bases for the argument that school psychology is not only for schools but has something special to offer in nontraditional settings as well.

During the formative years of modern school psychology, approximately 1950 to 1970, the need for consolidation was great. School psychology was represented by disparate groups of people at many levels of functioning, not closely related either to psychology or educational professional groups, coming from a wide variety of training programs and state certification routes. The need was to "join the club;" to become part of the psychology establishment so that the standards, prestige, and organizational benefits available to more mature and better established professional specialties in psychology could also be provided to school psychology. Uniformity of state standards (Bardon, Bindman, Hill, Rosebrock, & Scott, 1963), training program accreditation, and state and national organization of school psychologists held high priority. The polarities existing during this period were concerned mainly with allegiance to education versus psychology, doctoral versus nondoctoral education, separate profession versus specialty of psychology, and meeting immediate school needs versus expanding to meet broader educational needs.

Although unification did occur along with increasing acceptance of school psychology as one of the major areas of professional psychology within the American Psychological Association, counter forces were operating that rejected the APA view of psychology practice and entry requirements and, instead, opted for even great unity. These forces led to the formation of the National Association of School Psychologists (Farling & Agner, 1979), an organization that succeeded in uniting school psychologists at the local level throughout the United States into what it conceived of as a *profession* of school psychology, creating some distance from the rest of American professional psychology, but, nevertheless, serving a centripetal purpose.

The pull toward involvement in nonschool services provided an additional oppositional force, adding to the diverging (centrifugal) forces within the field. Some believed school psychology should be a service to schools. Others thought school psychology could serve a distinctive role in many settings (Bardon, 1976). Related to both ends of these oppositional views of the field was the problem of whether school psychology had centripital properties that could help distinguish it from the services offered by other specialties in or out of psychology. The strong influence of clinical psychology on the field and the emphasis on mental health concerns and clinical approaches to problem solution (e.g., psychotherapy, medical model diagnosis), served to raise questions about what school psychologists have offer in or outside of the school setting that cannot be offered by others.

For some practitioners what school psychologists uniquely offered was not an issue, as they made no important distinction between school psychology and child clinical psychology. In schools they primarily offered assessment services, using clinical instruments and skills. If they also engaged in private practice, their services were likely to be identical or very similar to the services offered by clinical psychologists of different persuasions. But, the counter argument went, "If this is so, why bother to have school psychology training programs?" A pragmatic response in the past was a bureaucratic one: "The schools won't let us in unless we are certified by a state department of education. They require that we have education courses and demonstrate that we know something about schools. School psychology training programs provide assurance that we will fit into the system."

With further developments in the field and with unification of the field through national organization, the position that school psychology is a distinct service *within schools* moved to a higher level of rationale. The case was made that the distinctiveness of the field offered school-related services not duplicated by other pupil personnel services workers. These oppositional forces—the need for unification of the specialty around its association with schools versus the need to define the specialty in such a way that it is more than and different from other specialties in and out of psychology—remain as critical dynamic tensions within the field.

This book represents a formal attempt to delineate one pole of this dialectic: that school psychology can be something of distinct merit apart from its school context. The creative tension involved in having a specialty, which serves schools but also is of such constitution that it can usefully and differentially serve other settings as well, is one that can be anticipated from study of the way the specialty has grown and developed over many years. We appear at this time in the specialty's history to be in the process of reconciling the need for unity at the same time that we are promoting divergence of setting and expansion of function. As Altman (1987) pointed out, such counterforces can be salutary even though they create debate and dissension. Change and experimentation are needed as field tests of what school psychology has to contribute to human welfare; as ways to enrich, stimulate, and further develop the discipline.

UNIQUE ATTRIBUTES OF SCHOOL PSYCHOLOGISTS

A necessary tension in the formation of any specialty of any profession is the extent to which it is similar to and different from other specialties in that profession. In school psychology, this particular polarity—similarity and difference—is especially important. The very existence of the specialty is dependent on the extent to which it is part of the profession of psychology and, at the same time, also so distinct that it merits separate status. In considering whether school psychology is applicable to nonschool settings, knowledge about this particular polarity is especially useful. If school psychologists are to be employed outside of schools *as school psychologists,* they and their employers need to understand what it is they can offer; what potential employers or clients might expect that will lead them to want to use school psychologists rather than other professionals. If the basis for nonschool employment of persons educated or trained in school psychology is because they are no different from some other kind of professional (clinical, counseling, industrial/organizational psychologists, learning disability specialist, or special educator) a case can be made for the competency of the *person* but not for the *specialty* call school psychology.

Common Core Knowledges and Functions

A job analysis of licensed psychologists in the United States and Canada was carried out by the Center for Occupational and Professional Assessment of the Educational Testing Service (ETS) for the American Association of State Psychology Boards (1983). This analysis, based on a 63% return rate of 2,994 inventory booklets mailed to licensed psychologists in clinical, school, counseling, and industrial/organizational psychology, had as its goal the identification of a common structure of the job of psychologists that could be used to evaluate the knowledge and technique areas important to all four major practice areas. Thirty-eight core knowledges and techniques were identified by a majority of license psychologists in the four practice areas and considered by those in all areas to be at least moderately important in carrying out their responsibilities related to intervention, research and measurement, organizational applications, and problem definition/diagnosis.

This impressive amount of knowledge and functions held in common among the four specialties lends credence to the idea that there is similarity among professional psychologists. This leads to the view that differences among them may not be as important as the various professional psychology specialties have indicated. It has been argued that professional (practitioner) psychology really is or should be a single entity, with the differences in specialized knowledges and techniques relatively unimportant (Bardon, 1976; Fox, 1982; Levy, 1984). In the ETS report (1983) the investigators noted that a negative aspect of specialty practice is that "such groups take uniqueness so seriously that they argue that competence to practice rests not on a common core of psychological knowledge, but on the specialized techniques they have developed for dealing with the problems of their practice domain" (p. IX-2).

A different interpretation can be placed on the data from the ETS study. The fact that there is a common core of knowledge and methods offers support for the belief that there is such a thing as professional psychology practice reasonably distinct from the practice of other human service providers. However, the data do not speak to the differences among the specialties that provide uniqueness. Although it may be argued that commonality is greater in importance than uniqueness, no clear evidence for placing such a weighting on commonality currently exists. Instead, a case can be made, albeit it without hard evidence, that there is or can be useful and necessary differences among specialties which justify differences in education, orientation, and function; that some kinds of psychologists can do some things better than or different from other specialists in psychology.

Available information about crossover of specialties appears related to a particular specialty assuming the functions of another without changing its name. The best documented example is in counseling psychology where job function and professional intention often are so similar to that of clinical psychologists that, it is claimed, it is often not possible by role or intent to differentiate the two specialties (Fitzgerald & Osipow, 1986; Watkins, 1987). It is suspected that some practitioners and training programs in school psychology also may have difficulty in justifying differences in knowledge, methods, and intent from those in clinical psychology but, it is held here, they do not constitute the main thrust of the specialty.

Differences From Other Specialties in Psychology

School psychology has been forced to recognize, whatever the demands made upon it, that ultimately it is involved in indirect service delivery, working with third parties who themselves offer direct service to clients (Conoley & Gutkin, 1986). Although still called upon at times to offer direct service such as counseling or psychotherapy, school psychologists more typically help other people who bear direct responsibility for resolving problems. Broadly, this role is educative. It requires particular skills and approaches to help people help other people, most often school-age children and youth. The advantage and special opportunity in such a role is that "indirect service leads to the real possibility of ripple effects, that may extend further the service impact of professionals" (Conoley & Gutkin, 1986, p. 398).

The problems involved in offering services in which outcomes cannot be *directly* attributable to the work of the psychologist are many. Conoley and Gutkin (1986) listed among these problems that such services are, of necessity, more complicated and cumbersome; reliance on others to carry out treatment or assistance depends on *their* motivation and willingness to expend the time and energy necessary to offer help; and the resources needed in order to help others offer appropriate assistance may be lacking.

It is believed that these extra and particular demands on the school psychologist, among others, have tended to produce certain qualities of attitude, orientation, and approaches to working with others which have not received sufficient attention in the literature (Bardon, 1986). They do not deal with knowledge and techniques in the ordinary sense. Instead, they speak to adaptive mechanisms, special proficiencies, insights, and emphases that appear to be characteristic of many successful school psychologists. Directly or indirectly (most often indirectly) these qualities are taught or encouraged in school psychology training programs or learned on the job. These differences from other psychology professionals provide important information about those attributes that lend themselves well to school psychologists practicing in nontraditional—that is, nonschool—settings.

During an era in which psychotherapy is the growing, dominant function in professional psychological services, school psychology has continued to highlight assessment services. Its concern with classification for special education and assistance with differentiating among a variety of poorly defined categories of handicapping conditions has kept school psychology involved in assessment issues and knowledge about testing and measurement to a greater extent than is true in clinical and counseling psychology. Concerns about the fairness of intelligence tests and the effects of cultural differences for minority groups (Reschly, 1980) has made school psychology especially sensitive to issues of cultural diversity. Further, assessment in schools inevitably is linked by good sense and by federal rules and regulations (Reynolds & Birch, 1982) to educational programming and interventions. School psychologists have sought to find ways in which their assessment findings relate usefully to management and teaching of children who, by the nature of their handicaps, are more likely to be difficult both to manage and teach.

School psychologists have learned that they must struggle to serve schools other than as narrow psychometric technicians. They have been led by their graduate training programs to aspire to broad functioning (Bardon, 1982). As a result, they are willing to assist schools in every conceivable way, using whatever knowledge they can get and whatever methods appear useful and respectable. A consequence of this attempt to reach out to serve schools is the need to rely on many different bodies of knowledge and methods in psychology and other fields as the bases for practice. Trachtman (1980) in his keynote address at the Spring Hill Symposium on the Future of Psychology in the Schools discussed recent developments in theory and practice in fields on which school psychology relies. Without attempting to be all-inclusive, he was able to present recent findings in such areas as learning theory, developmental psychology, human ethnology, environmental psychology, ecological psychology, social/personality psychology, behavioral psychology, social problem solving, learning disabilities, school consultation, interactional assessment, nondiscriminatory assessment, adaptive behavior, educational technology, program evaluation, education of the gifted, reading, and networks. He suggested some ways in which these areas may relate to an understanding of schools, children, and the interactive relationships among community, home, school, and child.

Of course, no one person can possibly be expert in all these areas, but the vast array of areas which impinge on the responsibilities of the school psychologist (the questions asked of them) are often different from those of other specialists in psychology. Schools are complex places. Once the school psychologist is freed from psychometric responsibilities alone, the breadth and depth of knowledge required to deal with presenting problems is awesome.

One consequence of this need to draw on many areas of psychology and other disciplines, tempered by the specific interests and concerns of the particular school system in which the psychologist is employed, is a mixture of specialization and generalization of unusual quality. School psychologists often become specialists in virtually every conceivable aspect of psychological practice applicable to school-related problems while, at the same time, they tap diverse areas of psychology in order to be prepared for additional questions and problems presented to them. Also, they come to understand the system in which they function. They try to understand what schools are about, what teachers do, how schools are organized, how people who work in schools function, the politics of education, and the opportunities and constraints of the system. In other words, they strive to learn what systems are like, and they come to understand well a particular place called school. They live daily with the knowledge that, although needing to know all these things, they really do not and cannot possibly be everything to everyone. Therefore, it is difficult to identify school psychologists by their specific areas of expertise, as these vary with program, career development, and opportunities for specialization based on needs and happenstance.

School psychologists, if they are successful, learn to work in other peoples' territories. Schools employ few school psychologists and many teachers and administrators. A favorable ratio of school psychologist to pupils is typically one to several thousand. School psychologists make their way in situations where the potential for being seen as foreign and different is always present. Learning to get along with others while being different from them and learning to know what others need and helping them get it while finding professional solace and identity outside of the workplace are special problems of school psychologists, which, if successfully resolved, become useful qualities that can carry over into other work settings as well.

Although school psychologists are not all of one kind, there do seem to be certain qualities and attitudes that help them to overcome professional isolation and to work well within systems. An attitude of positive skepticism (Bardon & Bennett, 1974) is useful. Skepticism reflects an understanding of the imperfections of the current state of knowledge and tools. School psychologists are primarily involved in immediate life situations. They often act without the benefit or the security offered by exact knowledge and precision instruments available to other disciplines. If they remain open to change and benefit from their own successes and failures, they tend to develop a critical, cautious, skeptical approach to the assessment of their findings and deliberations. The adjective "positive" is added to indicate that, along with skepticism there is a willingness to try new approaches and to persist even in the face of disappointments, lack of immediate results, apparent lack of cooperation, and sheer frustration.

Another characteristic of successful school psychologists is believed to be what Wallace (1966) called response capability. This term suggests that people respond differently under different circumstances and that it is important to examine the conditions under which certain behaviors occur. It is the opposite of the belief that there is a response predisposition; that people are defined by certain properties that describe their "essence." Despite the bad image school psychologists have received because of their involvement in classification of children as mentally retarded through IQ labeling (IQ 75 you are in; IQ 76 you are not), it is held here that "successful" school psychologists as compared with employable school psychometricians know better and in truth operate, regardless of theoretical orientation, with full knowledge of the interaction of person, circumstances, and setting.

Successful school psychologists operate as problem solvers (Burke, Haworth, & Brantley, 1980). To reconcile differences in situations (like classrooms) loaded with confounding and extraneous as well as pertinent variables, they must weigh evidence and come to decisions through a distillation of all they know and all they can learn about the situation at hand. To the data they bring experience, a past history of trial-and-error behavior, the personality and attitude attributes previously mentioned, and a profound respect for the scientific method. When they make recommendations or prescribe a course of action or help others to make decisions, they judge the probability of the validity of their actions against their data.

In sum, school psychology as a specialty when practiced successfully may require certain qualities of personality and attitude and certain intentions, interests, and proficiencies not as often seen, in totality, in the practitioners of other specialties in psychology. They include:

- An orientation to working in complex systems
- Knowing how to work with others dissimilar from oneself personally and professionally
- Ability to serve others indirectly—assisting those who work with others
- Ability to deal with complex variables without ignoring the import of their complexity
- Tolerance of ambiguity
- Working in teams as well as alone
- Consideration both of individual and group differences and similarities
- Understanding organizational hierarchies, rules, and regulations and knowing how to maneuver among them in order to accomplish goals
- Persisting despite frustration and resistance
- Dealing with interaction while concentrating on particular persons
- Seeking broad knowledge in many areas of psychology and related areas with application to problems peculiar to particular situations, the nature of the questions asked varying across the broad spectrum from individual concerns to system and community problems
- Possession of competencies and special proficiencies in many different areas
- Special skill in assessment linked to how assessment influences intervention
- Special skill in how teaching and learning take place and the relationship between teaching and learning and sociopersonal variables.

So that there is no misunderstanding, successful school psychologists are not paragons of virtue, nor should arguments be raised about their being better than other professional psychologists. The purpose of this summary of characteristics believed to emanate from the particular functions related to working in schools is to try to identify those qualities not captured by the 38 core knowledges and methods common to all four psychology specialty areas. I am certain that an assessment of the work conditions and special problems typical of other specialties could also result in groupings of hypothesized qualities. The point made here is that school psychologists are not only understood by their common functions with others, but also by what differentiates them from others. The attributes listed are likely to be in operation when persons educated as school psychologists or who have experience as school psychologists are employed in nonschool settings.

APPLIED EDUCATIONAL PSYCHOLOGY AS A WAY TO CHARACTERIZE SCHOOL PSYCHOLOGY PRACTICE IN ANY SETTING

School psychology, at least in the United States, has been susceptible throughout its development to society's changing conceptions of education and also to movements in psychology which directly influence how psychologists think about human problems. School psychology's early involvement in special education was a function of the belief that separation of children with handicapping conditions is educationally beneficial; that heterogeneous classes serve children and youth well (Reynolds & Birch, 1982). Recently, a major shift in opinion about how to serve the needs of children with special educational problems has taken place. This view is based on the principle of "normalization" (Wolfensberger, 1972) translated in our country through legislation into the concept of the least restrictive alternative or environment, often termed "mainstreaming" (Reynolds & Birch, 1982). In special education, the mission has become one of educational integration more than separation, with attention shifted to ways of teaching exceptional children in regular classrooms and buildings. School psychologists have been influenced by these changes in perception of how special needs are to be met. Consideration of teaching and learning has become an increasingly important part of their responsibilities as assessors, recommenders, and interveners in the schools.

Profound changes have taken place in our society's view of education; how and where people are taught and the value placed on education as compared with other societal issues. What have been termed "electronic learning" (White, 1981) and "the computer age" (Gutkin & Elwork, 1985) are now part of everyday living for all (e.g., television, computer programs and games, video discs, VCRs, films). Print learning is but one way in which education takes place. Teaching and learning are no longer confined to formal schools and the family as much as in the past. Nonschool learning at all ages is a part of everyday life (Landers, 1987). Preschool care and education are accepted parts of life for many families and are usually based on educational and developmental considerations (Barnett, 1986). The importance of education in our society as necessary for economic gain and as a way to improve society has become common currency. There has not been a period of time since the late 1940s and 50s when teaching and learning have been so prominently a part of our society's highest priorities (National Commission on Excellence in Education, 1983).

With these changes have come changes in educational psychology. That field, which, like school psychology, lives in two worlds—education and psychology—is undergoing dramatic changes in the way it conceives of its role (Wittrock & Farley, in press). Over at least the past decade, educational psychology has redeveloped a psychology of instruction; moved out into a larger world in which its knowledge is applicable to a wide range of problems having to do with teaching and learning; is exploring how it can be more useful in more ways to more people; and is seeking flexibility while maintaining rigor in the modes of disciplined inquiry applicable to different educational questions (Bruner, 1985; Glaser, 1983; Resnick, 1981; Shulman, 1982; Wittrock, 1979). All this has been happening while behavioral psychology with its emphasis on learning, and cognitive psychology with its emphasis on information processing, have become major ways of conceiving of how learning and teaching take place (Glover & Ronning, 1987).

The mental health movement too has changed as it has struggled with its polarities. It has been influenced, on the one hand, by increasing emphasis on primary prevention, the view that attention to a variety of societal ills prior to the time they result in person problems will lessen the need for secondary and tertiary treatment (Albee, 1986). On the other hand, clinical psychology has had to fight for parity with psychiatry for the right to engage in psychotherapeutic treatment. It has been influenced by market-place considerations concerned with third party payments and competition from new and potent competitors such as social work, marriage counselors, mental health counselors, and others. A psychology industry of great important to its practitioners has developed (Dörken & Associates, 1986).

These changes in education emphasis and in psychology have influenced school psychology in ways that are completely understandable given school psychology's predeliction to respond to movements in human service delivery and to the needs of the schools. For example, when school psychologists began to engage in private practice, leaving the schools as their sole work setting, they too were caught up in clinical psychology's concerns with private practice issues and problems. It is believed they moved easily into the practice of diagnosis and psychotherapy in ways that did not distinguish them as *school psychologists* in independent practice. That they could do so is a tribute to their broad background and training, but it did not help the field to identify itself to ensure its specialty status.

The polarities of education versus mental health as emphases of the specialty were extenuated with the widening of differences between school needs and clinical psychology's involvement in psychotherapy and private practice issues. The common bond that made it possible for school psychology to bridge the gap was primary prevention. The schools were seen as ideal settings in which to help children resolve problems and decrease their chances of having problems as adults (Alpert, 1985). But primary prevention is not the provence of school psychology alone and has not served to make the specialty distinctive (Bardon, 1986).

Beginning in the early 1980s, the literature in school psychology began to reflect an educational orientation in addition to the predominant mental health orientation that characterized the field during most of its professional development since the 1950s, reflecting reemphasis on educational values and educational purposes at the local, state, and national levels (Bardon, 1983; Berliner 1985; Cancelli & Kratochwill, 1981; Deno, 1986; Elliott & Piersel, 1982; Lentz & Shapiro, 1986; Tidwell, 1980). Acknowledged leaders in school psychology articulated positions which attempted to change the focus of school psychology toward education rather than or more than mental health as a way to conceptualize what school psychology is about that defines its distinctiveness (Meyers, 1985; Myrick 1986; Rosenfield, 1985; National School Psychology Inservice Training Network, 1984; Reilly, 1984; Ysseldyke & Algozzine, 1983).

The idea that learning and teaching should be the key concepts in defining a practice specialty in psychology is not unique to school psychology (Authier, Gustafson, Guerney, & Kasdorf, 1975). As early as 1970, Guerney, Stollack, Guerney, & Stover (1970) proposed that clinical psychology should follow an educational model, teaching interpersonal skills to solve present and future problems and to enhance satisfaction with life. What is different about the current literature about school psychology's focus on teaching and learning is its reliance on educational psychology research and theory and on the view that teaching and learning are not simply other techniques or treatment modalities in a repertoire of many others methods of offering "therapy," but a significant shift in perception about what the specialty can represent (e.g., systematically helping people learn and teach others in schools and other settings in which teaching and learning take place). As Ysseldyke and Algozzine (1983) put it "a shift from the presumption that academic problems result from pupil problems to a recognition that students exhibit academic problems in an educational context under a set of conditions" (p. 192).

It is this perceptual shift that is referred to here as "applied educational psychology." It reflects a deliberate effort to reorient the specialty of school psychology toward application of psychological knowledge primarily derived from the field of educational psychology to the solution of problems concerned with education wherever they may occur. The rationale for such a shift has been discussed in detail elsewhere (Bardon, 1983), but certain features especially applicable to its use in nonschool settings are presented here.

The Importance of Words, Assumptions, and Intentions

All school psychologists are familiar with the problems of using of labels in special education. It matters greatly to many parents that their child be called learning disabled rather than mentally retarded or emotionally disturbed because of the connotations (attributions) assigned to these labels (Palmer, 1983). Zucker (1986) in describing the process a school psychologist uses in thinking through a case noted that "The words the psychologist used in thinking about these issues might have affected his choice of procedures. . . The words we choose in framing questions to ourselves involve subtle professional judgments that have an important influence on the assessment procedures chosen and resulting determinations" (p. 2).

Salomon (1983) reminded us that "what really matters are people's perceptions of the world rather than anything that may exist in 'objective reality.' These perceptions guide people's communicational activity, both as receivers and as senders, leading to certain interpersonal attributions of intent and to various amounts of effort invested in the processing of messages" (p. 31).

Witt, Moe, Gutkin, & Andrews (1984) examined the "supposition that teacher judgments pertaining to the acceptability of an intervention are partially a function of the way in which the intervention is described and the rationale provided" (p. 361) with findings of differential results based on jargon type and case severity.

The importance of these comments is to stress that we not only influence others by the words we use when we function as school psychologists, but that our words—our terms—reflect attributions and assumptions that influence process and outcomes of our professional efforts.

It is for these reasons that what we call ourselves, how we conceive of our purposes and goals, and what we believe are the reasons we act as we do when we attempt to help others solve problems are of great importance. Over the past 40 years school psychology has been guided philosophically by the underlying assumptions of the mental health movement based on its adaptations of mental health concerns in the practice of clinical psychology (Bardon & Bennett, 1974). The major concern of the mental health movement is the prevention and treatment of psychological pathology (Albee, 1986; Lentz & Shapiro, 1986). Even if mental health is considered as the opposite side of mental illness, (positive mental health) it is intervention for the purpose of preventing pathology later in life. It involves thinking about maladjustment, looking to find it, or seeking to keep it from happening. Invariably, it involves some form of therapy or therapeutic-like intervention. In the mental health approach to helping resolve problems, attention is on the future; on signs of maladjustment and on the causes of problem behavior. Behavioral "therapists" are indeed involved in teaching and learning but for the purpose of preventing or treating maladaptive behavior. Even though they are behavioral psychologists, they still are using a mental health–mental illness model as one aspect of their conceptualization of the problem at hand along with a particular treatment approach to therapeutic intervention. As long as prevention, treatment, therapy, illness, wellness, and even "clinical" are the terms of choice, they are likely also to reflect purpose and philosophy that influence attitude and behavior and may determine communication process and outcomes. When nonclinical terms such as coping, competence, and development are considered as means to ameliorate maladjustment as *purpose,* they carry the messages of a mental health model. The dialectic involved in primary versus secondary prevention is a limited one of wellness–illness and tends to limit or preclude other ways of thinking and acting about problem resolution.

There is nothing wrong with primary, secondary, or tertiary mental health approaches. They are powerful means to consider and act on human problems. However, they are not in themselves ways of offering assessment, intervention, and evaluation that distinguish one specialty from another. Many professions use a mental health model. But, as Jahoda (1958) reminded us years ago, there are many human values, including mental health. It is not the only useful way to be concerned about human well-being and progress.

It should be recognized that it is possible within a mental health model to have different perspectives about its implementation. For instance, community psychology has tried with mixed results to differentiate itself from other areas of psychology by its perspective, strategies, and values (Glenwick, 1982). Shinn (1985) pointed out that community psychologists are distinguished from other groups not by where they work, but by what they do when they are there. For community psychology, primary prevention and empowerment within an ecological approach involving both action and research appear to be important purposes and values. So, presumably, when community psychologists come to schools they come to prevent problems of pathology, bringing with them their special understanding of community needs and interactions and knowledge of how sociopolitical power operates to make systems and persons work well or poorly.

It is useful to consider community psychology's attempts to articulate special attributions, because, like school psychology, it is characterized by multimethod, multispecialty practices, and must seek ways to identify what it is that goes beyond both method and proficiencies involved. Within a medical model that stresses primary prevention (Swift, 1982) it makes a reasonably good case that a community psychologist is something other than a clinical or counseling psychologist, although there are skills in common to all of these specialties. A community psychologist holds to values and purposes that lead to thinking differently; asking different question, highlighting different influencing factors, and seeking to influence different people for different reasons. Tools may not be different but they are used differently and, in addition, tools and approaches are added that other specialists in psychology might not think to use. The knowledge base is extended to use of different areas of psychology and related disciplines in different configurations. Thus, by this analysis, community psychologists, although varying among themselves in method and still functioning broadly at the wellness end of the medical model continuum, appear to know what they want to achieve. Within a mental health model they have established the basis for the use of language, thought, and theory in ways which hold promise of serving the public usefully and uniquely.

As is clear from the literature on community psychology, their attempts to seek separate identity has been a difficult one. The terminology of the field remains unclear; purposes still vary among its members, the curriculum by which one learns to be a community psychologist remains controversial. Although the field in its short history, since its formal inception in 1965 (Bennett, Anderson, Cooper, Hassol, Klien, & Rosenblum, 1966) has led to some research and practice not clearly identified with other specialties, it continues to overlap and subsume other specialties. Many persons who consider themselves to be school, clinical, and counseling psychologists *also* consider themselves to be community psychologists by virtue of their ideals, values, orientation, and emphases. Community psychology has not extricated itself from its association with the medical model and is unlikely to do so as long as mental health is its major goal.

In the primary prevention literature, it has been noted that "neither the public at large nor the educational establishment appears fully to have accepted these goals (mental health goals) as *prime* responsibilities of the school . . . nor do they seem ready to do so" (Baker & Shaw, 1987, p. 14). It could be added that the public at large has not readily accepted mental health goals in other settings or as viable goals applicable to them in general. It has been a special problem of the mental health movement that even when it has stressed wellness and prevention it tends to be confused in the public mind with illness and stigma.

In contrast, at one level or another the public at large *does* understand that people must learn a lot of things and, if they do, they can better manage their affairs right now as well as in the future. The public also knows that good teaching matters, it is a good thing to be able to learn, and one learns differently depending on what is being taught and why one needs to know something. It is also generally recognized that motivation helps learning. It may be easier for most people to understand that emotional factors get in the way of learning than that "mental health variables" must be taken into account. In other words, alternate ways of thinking about helping others than those involved in mental health conceptions of health-illness may be more compatible with the ways most people think about themselves and about how they go about resolving problems.

Schooling is More Than What Happens in Schools

Both formal and informal education occur in many ways and in many settings throughout the life span. It is no longer appropriate to use the noun "schooling" only to describe what takes place in those institutions we call schools. If we accept Cremin's definition of education as "the deliberate, systematic, and sustained effort to transmit, evoke, or acquire knowledge, values, attitudes, skills, or sensibilities, as well as any learning that results from the effort, direct or indirect, intended or unintended" (1980, p. ix), we must also accept that education takes place in schools, homes, public places, business and industry, between persons, between persons and instruments, and in groups (White & Duker, 1973).

To clarify terminology, it may be useful to divide Cremin's definition into two parts. Education describes the knowledge and development resulting from an instructional process—the intended outcomes. Schooling describes the process itself—the nature of the most appropriate activities and interactions between persons and setting or instruments that lead to effective outcomes.

Schooling and education are clearly differentiated conceptually from primary, secondary, and tertiary prevention or treatment. Schooling is for now as well as for the future. It is intended to achieve specific educational goals. It is generalizable; it carries over into other settings. It is cumulative, as what is learned now forms the basis for subsequent learning. It relies heavily on knowledge from educational, developmental, and social psychology. Schooling is concerned with how to teach and includes attention to the interactions among behavior, cognitions, and other internal events, and the external environments—what Bandura (1978) refers to as reciprocal determinism.

Of course, schooling occurs in schools. In schools all kinds of schooling take place so that intended educational outcomes include more than academic learning. Schools have taken on many forms of education as society, in its complexity, has been unable to find satisfactory means to provide other kinds of education and other kinds of services needed by children and youth. Schooling also takes place wherever education is needed. A psychologist who knows how to help others achieve educational goals may have something to offer that is perceived as useful and germane to institutional and societal ends, perhaps more so in many instances than psychologists of other persuasions.

So far, no human service specialty in psychology has used schooling and education as a major orientation to the provision of psychological services. School psychology gradually has been moving in this direction. It is conceivable that the title "applied educational psychologist" is one which may help to delineate such a specialty in professional psychology, one which can participate in the delivery of human services with improved chance of warranting separate status from other specialties by virtue of goals, values, and methods. Use of education as outcome and schooling as method may lead to the development of "alternative proficiencies, technologies, and strategies that enhance psychological practice without detraction from other ways of offering assistance to those in need" (Bardon, 1983, p. 190).

Within this conception of a revised specialty, practitioners certainly are human service providers. They may also be "health service providers" as defined by the Council for the National Register of Health Service Providers in Psychology as psychologists "duly trained and experienced in the delivery of direct, preventive, assessment and therapeutic intervention services to individuals whose growth, adjustment, or functioning is actually impaired or is demonstrably at high risk of impairment" (1987, p. xv). The difference is not necessarily in the problem to be solved but in the approaches taken to resolve it, how the expected outcomes are described, and differences in the methods and techniques used.

The Educational Psychology Knowledge Base

All professional psychologists are encouraged to be educated in the basic substantive areas of psychology: the biological, cognitive, affective, social bases of behavior, and individual behavior, as well as scientific and professional ethics and standards, research design and methodology, statistics, psychological measurement, and history and systems of psychology (American Psychological Association, 1986). These are core knowledges that help differentiate the profession of psychology from other professions.

In addition to this common background, professional psychologists derive additional knowledge from intermediate or specialized bodies of knowledge that help them apply knowledge to the problems they intend to work on. Community psychologists derive specialized knowledge from areas in and out of psychology that help them focus on ecological consideration, power politics, and social climate. Clinical and counseling psychologists, depending on their particular orientations, concentrate on areas of psychology concerned with personality, abnormality, applied behavior analysis, or physiological psychology. Particular techniques and methods are based on research and theory in these specialized areas of psychological knowledge.

The National School Psychology Inservice Training Network (1984) recommended that the following knowledge domains be considered for leadership and function by school psychologists: class management, interpersonal communication and consultation, basic academic skills, basic life skills, affective/social skills, parental involvement, classroom organization and social structure, systems development and planning, personnel development, individual differences in development and learning, school–community relations, instruction, legal/ethical and professional issues, assessment, multicultural concerns, and research. These areas indicate both commonalities and differences in school psychology knowledge bases from other specialties in psychology. They suggest that at least major portions of psychology function derive from knowledge in educational psychology. Although these domains are school-specific, it is easy to see how each might be translated so as to be applicable in other settings in which teaching and learning take place.

As indicated, school psychology has increasingly relied on, or at least added to its background, knowledge from educational psychology, Educational psychology, like school psychology, is a hybrid. Both are intermediate specialties. Educational psychology attempts to serve as a linking science (Grinder, 1980) concerned with understanding and thinking systematically about educational phenomena in order to bring about educational improvement (Snow, 1981). School psychology has been described as a professional specialty serving a "coupling function" concerned with translation, transformation, and transfer of knowledge especially to resolve real-life problems in education (Bardon, 1968). Although school psychology has borrowed generously from areas basic to clinical psychology more than any other practice specialty, it has also looked to educational psychology as a source of knowledge.

Educational psychology is not a unified discipline that can precisely define either its content or its methods. Like school psychology, it is better defined by its intentions and on what aspects of knowledge in psychology it choses to concentrate its attention. Below are some selected examples of topics of interest in educational psychology not ordinarily found in other areas of psychology. The list deliberately excludes broader topics likely to find expression through research and practice not only in educational psychology but in many psychological fields, for example, modeling, skill training, role playing, behavior analysis, attribution theory. It may be instructive to consider the extent to which these selected topics are directly applicable as areas of psychological knowledge leading to practice considerations in all the various professional specialties. It is my assessment that they are most applicable to school psychology as currently taught and practiced and are illustrative of knowledge leading to practice competencies that can form the basis for consideration of even more pertinent education and training of school psychologists as applied educational psychologists.

Achievement motivation (Snow, 1986)
Aptitude-treatment interaction (Phillips, 1985)
Categories of learning (Gagné, 1977)
Characteristics of instructional methods (Wittrock, 1979)
Computer assisted instruction (Tobias, 1984)
Creativity (Snow, 1986)
Educational assessment of learners (Howell, 1986)
Effective teaching (Brophy, 1986)
Engaged time of learners (Gettinger, 1986)
Group instructional and behavioral management (Woolfolk, 1986)
Information processing analysis of mental abilities (Sternberg, 1981)
Instructional assessment (Englemann, Granzin, & Severson, 1979)
Instructional planning (Woolfolk, 1986)

Intrinsic and extrinsic motivation and learning (McCombs, 1984)
Mastery learning (Block, 1978)
Preparation for learning (DiVista, 1974)
Student learning strategies (Weinstein, 1985; Wiener, 1986)
Teaching style as it influences learners' attention, motivation, understanding, and behavior (Wittrock, 1979)
Test anxiety (Tobias, 1985)
Thinking, reasoning, and problem solving (Bransford, Sherwood, Vye, & Rieser, 1986)
Transfer of learning (VanderZanden & Pace, 1984)
Writing instruction (Hayes & Flower, 1986)

To say that these are knowledge areas well established in school psychology practice is untrue. It is also an overstatement to say that there already is sufficient established knowledge even in these particular examples of educational/schooling areas so that valid movement from research to practice is possible. Rather, they illustrate concerns and intentions that permit alternative assessment, intervention, and evaluation strategies to take place on a host of human problems. Problems now characterized as pathological, or "at risk" or within the realm of primary prevention can benefit from being conceptualized in language and context clearly related to an important intermediate scientific knowledge base not now well used as the basis for the delivery of human services in psychology; what is being called here applied educational psychology.

IMPLICATIONS OF APPLIED EDUCATIONAL PSYCHOLOGY FOR PRACTICE IN NONTRADITIONAL SETTINGS

A change in emphasis in school psychology from mental health to schooling and education (teaching and learning) with greater use of educational psychology research and theory as bases for practice permit reappraisal of both the centripital (consolidating) and centrifugal (diverging) forces influencing the dialectics (polarities) involved in practice, training, and research in school psychology. Greater stability is brought about through a better match between the practices of school psychology and the goals, language, and methods of education. It is no longer education *versus* psychology but psychology in the service of education (Bardon, 1983).

What is likely to happen if an applied educational psychology emerges in school psychology is the creation of a new set of dialectics, this time based less on education versus psychology and more on polarities intimately related to the issues faced by a revised view of what problems are to be resolved and what approaches are most suitable to their resolution. For instance, an applied educational psychology will undoubtedly find differences within its own researchers and practitioners on such issues as whole person versus person as student only, emphasis on teacher or on learner, teacher versus learner control, knowledge as content versus knowledge as process, intrinsic versus extrinsic motivation, learning as holistic versus learning as molecular, learning as social versus learning as individual (Berlak & Berlak, 1981), and setting emphasis versus person emphasis. Differences among researchers and practitioners about behavioral, cognitive, or dynamic theory preferences will continue to exist. All theoretical/research approaches are applicable to applied educational psychology as they are to all other practitioner specialties. But the major concerns and questions raised and the debates and differences among those involved will be different from those raised in other human service provider specialties in psychology. That difference is what can make a difference!

Applied educational psychologists need not delete mental health approaches to problem solving from their repertoires. The change in approach is akin to the current mental health model using teaching as one modality within a mental health model of prevention and treatment. The applied educational psychologist would consider use of mental health modalities (e.g., well recognized mental health counseling approaches) as one way among others to help a person develop knowledge or skills needed in order to deal with the difficulty at hand.

What in actuality would an applied educational psychologist do that is different from what would be done by any other human service provider in psychology? Any psychologist in any setting will be asked to deal with problem behavior. The answer is in what the applied educational psychologist *as instrument* brings to the problem; the personality characteristics, attitudes, values and special knowledges already discussed in this chapter derived from what is currently believed to be the special attributes of school psychology training and practice. The answer also is in the awareness of those in settings where it is possible to ask questions unlike the questions one asks other human service professionals. It is envisioned that the applied educational psychologist will be involved in "assessment that leads to effective interventions, that is, interventions that enhance skills and expand opportunities" (Reschly, 1980, p. 842); service as a translator, developer, educational engineer, designer (Short, 1973); training and goal setting (Fletcher, 1987); evaluating, case managing, and serving as a team member (Pfeiffer, Dean, & Shellenberger, 1986), consulting with others on teaching and learning as a way to resolve personal, social, and institutional problems; intervention concerned with how people can learn both knowledge and skills to use in solving their personal, professional, and social problems.

From the Present to the Future

Until fairly recently, school psychology's struggles—its particular dialectics—have centered on its place in schools. School psychologists have strived to find balance in their allegiance to psychology and education and to the extent to which they draw sustenance from each. Perhaps more than any other specialty in psychology, school psychology has been concerned with role, especially with the discrepancy between its aspirations and potential and the limitations placed on it by rules, regulations, and limited expectations of those responsible for how school psychologists are employed and can function in the public schools.

Many school psychologists have been able to stretch the boundaries of expectation within the schools so that their roles have become comprehensive. They have been able to do so by proving their worth and by their intent to be more than others thought they were. School psychologists also have found that their education, training, and experience in schools provided excellent preparation for work in other settings. School psychologists have become administrators in schools, colleges, and universities; teachers in higher education; and have a found a place for themselves in virtually every setting in which human service psychologists are employed. When they moved out of schools, they brought with them the professional competencies held in common by all well educated and trained professional psychologists and the competencies, values, attitudes, and special wisdom that accrued from being involved in a specialty that has constantly had to prove itself while trying to solve problems in that complex, community-based, multidimensional multi-age, highly political, problem rich, undervalued, overused place called school.

The chapters in this book describe how school psychologists are now serving in other settings and how they are using their skills and special attributes to augment and enhance the services of others. The roles and responsibilities described are not necessarily commensurate with the model of an applied educational psychologist presented in this chapter. Applied educational psychology is a way of conceptualizing the future of school psychology. There are few who practice it, but there are many who subscribe to its tenets and would like to move the field in its direction. It will not be the preferred model for all school psychologists. It does offer an approach to unifying the field so that it is distinctively different from other professional psychology specialties. It moves school psychology in the direction of offering its services in any setting in which psychological services based on an approach dedicated to assisting with instruction and learning are seen as useful. It can serve schools but is not confined to schools. Like all specialties in practitioner psychology, it has a common core of knowledge and methods but, in addition, benefits from having a specialized intermediate body of knowledge in educational psychology and training, perspective and purpose that can lead to fresh techniques, approaches, and services related to helping people solve problems; that is, to teach and to learn.

REFERENCES

Albee, G. W. (1986). Toward a just society: Lessons from observations on the primary prevention of psychopathology. *American Psychologist, 41,* 891–898.

Alpert, J. L. (1985). Change within a profession: Change, future, prevention, and school psychology. *American Psychologist, 40,* 1112–1121.

Altman, I. (1987). Centripetal and centrifugal trends in psychology. *American Psychologist, 42,* 1058–1069.

American Psychological Association. (1986). *Accreditation handbook.* Washington, DC: Author.

Authier, J., Gustafson, K., Guerney, B. Jr., & Kasdorf, J. A., (1975). The Psychological practitioner as a teacher: A theoretical-historical and practical review. *The Counseling Psychologist, 5,* (2), 31–50.

Baker, S. B., & Shaw, M. C. (1987). *Improving counseling through primary prevention.* Columbus, OH: Merrill.

Bandura, A. (1978). The self-system in reciprocal determinism. *American Psychologist, 33,* 344–358.

Bardon, J. I. (1968). School psychology and school psychologists: An approach to an old problem. *American Psychologist, 23,* 187–194.

Bardon, J. I. (1976). The state of the art (and science) of school psychology. *American Psychologist, 31,* 785–791.

Bardon, J. I. (1982). The psychology of school psychology. In C. R. Reynolds & T. B. Gutkin (Eds.). *The handbook of school psychology* (pp. 3–14). New York: John Wiley.

Bardon, J. I. (1983). Psychology applied to education: A specialty in search of an identity. *American Psychologist, 38,* 185–196.

Bardon, J. I. (1986). Psychology and schooling: The interrelationships among persons, processes, and products. In S. E. Elliott & J. C. Witt (Eds.). *The delivery of psychological services in schools: Concepts, processes and issues* (pp. 53–79). Hillsdale, NJ: Lawrence Erlbaum Associates.

Bardon, J. I., & Bennett, V. C. (1974). *School psychology.* Englewood Cliffs, NJ: Prentice-Hall.

Bardon, J. I., Bindman, A., Hill, P., Rosebrock, A., & Scott, W. (1963). Proposals for state department of education certification of school psychologists. *American Psychologist, 18,* 711–714.

Barnett, D. W. (1986). School psychology in preschool settings: A review of training and practice issues. *Professional Psychology: Research and Practice, 17,* 58–64.

Bennett, C. C., Anderson, L. S., Cooper, S., Hassol, L., Klein, D. C., & Rosenblum,

G. (1966). *Community psychology: A report of the Boston conference on the education of psychologists for community mental health.* Boston, MA: Boston University.

Berlak, A., & Berlak, H. (1981). *Dilemmas of schooling: Teaching and social change.* London: Methuen.

Berliner, D. C. (1985). The clinical educational psychologist: scientist and practitioner. In J. R. Bergan, *School psychology in contemporary society: An introduction* (pp. 378–393). Columbus, OH: Merrill.

Block, J. H. (1978, February). The "C" in CBE. *Educational Researcher,* pp. 13–16.

Bransford, J., Sherwood, R., Vye, N., & Rieser, J. (1986). Teaching thinking and problem solving: Research foundations. *American Psychologist, 41,* 1078–1089.

Brophy, J. (1986). Teacher influences on student achievement. *American Psychologist, 41,* 1069–1077.

Bruner, J. (1985, June/July). Models of the learner. *Educational Researcher, 14,* 5–8.

Burke, J. P., Haworth, C. C., & Brantley, J. C. (1980). Scientific problem solving model: A resolution for professional controversies in school psychology. *Professional Psychology, 11,* 823–832.

Cancelli, A. A., & Kratochwill, T. R. (1981). Advances in criterion-referenced assessment. In T. R. Kratochwill (ed.), *Advances in school psychology, Volume I* (pp. 217–254). Hillsdale, NJ: Lawrence Erlbaum Associates.

Center for Occupational and Professional Assessment (1983). *Job analysis of licensed psychologists in the United States and Canada.* Princeton, NJ: Educational Testing Service.

Conoley, J. C., & Gutkin, T. B. (1986). School psychology: A reconceptualization of service delivery realities. In S. N. Elliott & J. C. Witt (Eds.), *The delivery of psychological services in schools: Concepts, processes, and issues* (pp. 393–424). Hillsdale, NJ: Lawrence Erlbaum Associates.

Council for the National Register of Health Service Providers in Psychology (1987). *National register of health service providers in psychology.* Washington, DC: Author.

Cremin, L. A. (1980). *American education: The national experience, 1783-1836.* New York: Harper & Row.

Cutts, N. E. (Eds). (1955). *School psychologists at mid-century.* Washington, DC: American Psychological Association.

Deno, S. L. (1986). Formative evaluation of individual student programs: A new role for school psychologists. *School Psychology Review, 15,* 358–374.

DiVista, F. J. (1974). Cognitive structures and symbolic processes. *Teachers College Record, 75,* 357–370.

Dörken, H., & Associates. (1986). *Professional psychology in transition.* San Francisco, CA: Jossey-Bass.

Elliott, S. N., & Piersel, W. C. (1982). Direct assessment of reading skills: An approach which links assessment to intervention. *School Psychology Review, 11,* 267–280.

Englemann, S., Granzin, A., & Severson, H. (1979). Diagnosing instruction. *The Journal of Special Education, 13,* 355–363.

Evans, R. B. & Koelsch, W. A. (1985). Psychoanalysis arrives in America: The 1909 psychology conference at Clark University. *American Psychologist, 40,* 942–948.

Fagan, T. K. (1986). School psychology's dilemma: Reappraising solutions and directing attention to the future. *American Psychologist, 41,* 851–861.

Farling, W. H., & Agner, J. (1979). History of the National Association of School Psychologists: The first decade. *School Psychologist Digest, 8* (2), 140–152.

Fitzgerald, L. F. & Osipow, S. H. (1986). An occupational analysis of counseling psychology: How special is the specialty? *American Psychologist, 41,* 535–544.

Fletcher, J. D. (1987, June). Training research and educational psychology. *Newsletter for Educational Psychologists,* Division 15, APA, pp. 4–5.

Fox, R. E. (1982). The need for a reorientation of clinical psychology. *American Psychologist, 37,* 1051–1057.

Gagné, R. M. (1977). *The conditions of learning* (3rd ed.). New York: Holt, Rinehart & Winston.

Gettinger, M. (1986). Issues and trends in academic engaged time of students. *Special Services in the Schools, 2,* 1–17.

Glaser, R. (1983, June). *Education and thinking: The role of knowledge.* (Tech. Rep. No. PD5-6). Pittsburgh: University of Pittsburgh, Learning Research and Development Center.

Glenwick, D. P. (1982, Summer). Community psychology in the 80's: A discipline for all seasons or one whose time has passed? *Division of Community Psychology Newsletter, APA,* pp 4–6.

Glover, J. A., & Ronning, R. R. (Eds.). (1987). *Historical foundations of educational psychology.* New York: Plenum.

Grinder, R. E. (1980, November). The growth of educational psychology as reflected in the history of Division 15. *Newsletter for Educational Psychologists,* Division 15, American Psychological Association, pp. 5–9.

Guerney, B. Jr., Stollak, G., Guerney, L., & Stover, L. (1970). The practicing psychologist as educator—An alternative to the medical practitioner model. *Professional Psychology, 2,* 276–282.

Gutkin, T. B., & Elwork A. (1985). The behavior sciences in the computer age. *Computers in Human Behavior, 1,* 3–18.

Hayes, J. R., & Flower, L. S. (1986). Writing research and the writer. *American Psychologist, 41,* 1106–1113.

Howell, K. (1986). Direct assessment of academic performance. *School Psychology Review, 15,* 324–335.

Jahoda, M. (1958). *Current concepts of positive mental health.* New York: Basic Books.

James, W. (1948). *Principles of psychology.* Cleveland OH: Fine Editions Press (Original work published 1892).

Lambert, N. M. (1983). *The developmental acquisition of the ability to apply educational psychology to school psychology.* Paper presented at the meeting of the American Psychological Association, Anaheim, CA.

Landers, S. (1987, February). Poll explores non-school learning. *APA Monitor,* pp. 8–9.

Lentz, F. E. Jr., & Shapiro, E. S. (1986). Functional assessment of the academic environment. *School Psychology Review, 15,* 346–357.

Levine, M., & Levine, A. (1970). *A social history of helping services: Clinic, court, school, and community.* New York: Appleton–Century–Crafts.

Levy, L. H. (1984). The metamorphosis of clinical psychology: Toward a new charter as human services psychology. *American Psychologist, 39,* 486–494.

McCombs, B. L. (1984). Process and skills underlying continuing intrinsic motivation to learn: Toward a definition of motivational skills training interventions. *Educational Psychologist, 19,* 199–218.

Meyers, J. (1985). *School psychology: The current state of practice of the specialty.* Paper presented at the meeting of the American Psychological Association, Los Angeles, CA.

Myrick, C. C. (1986). An emerging consensus on school psychology's future. *Professional Psychology, 1,* 291–294.

National Commission on Excellence in Education (1983). *A nation at risk: The imperative for educational reform.* Washington, DC: U.S. Government Printing Office.

National School Psychology Inservice Training Network (1984). *School psychology: A blueprint for training and practice.* Minneapolis, MN: University of Minnesota.

Palmer, D. J. (1983). An attributional perspective on labeling. *Exceptional Children, 49,* 423–429.

Pfeiffer, S. I., Dean, R. S., & Shellenberger, S. (1986). The school psychologist in medical settings. In T. R. Kratochwill (Ed.), *Advances in school psychology, Volume V* (pp. 177–202). Hillsdale, NJ: Lawrence Erlbaum Associates.

Phillips, B. N. (1985). New directions in aptitude-treatment research: Concepts and methods. In C. Reynolds & V. L. Willson (Eds.), *Methodological and statistical advances in the study of individual differences* (pp. 241–273). New York: Plenum.

Reilly, D. H. (1984). School psychology: The continuing search. *Psychology in the Schools, 21,* 66–70.

Reschly, D. J. (1980). School psychologists and assessment in the future. *Professional Psychology, 11,* 841–848.

Resnick, L. B. (1981). Instructional psychology. In M. R. Rosenzwieg & L. W. Porter (Eds.), Annual review of psychology (Vol. 32). (pp. 659–704). Palo Alto, CA: Annual Reviews.

Reynolds, C. R., & Gutkin, T. B. (1982). *The handbook of school psychology.* New York: John Wiley.

Reynolds, C. R., Gutkin, T. B., Elliott, S. N., & Witt, J. C. (1984). *School psychology: Essentials of theory and practice.* New York: John Wiley.

Reynolds, M. C., & Birch, J. W. 1982). *Teaching exceptional children in all America's schools (2nd ed).* Reston, VA: . he Council for Exceptional Children.

Rosenfield, S. (1985, August). *Classroom intervention techniques for children with learning problems.* Paper presented at the meeting of the American Psychological Association, Los Angeles, CA.

Salomon, G. (1983). *Toward a theory of communication and education in reciprocal relations: Learners' active role.* Invited address presented at the meeting of the American Psychological Association, Anaheim, CA.

Shinn, M. B. (1985, Summer). Expanding community psychology's domain. *Division of Community Psychology Newsletter, APA,* p. 9.

Short, E. C. (1973). Knowledge production and utilization in curriculum: A special case of the general phenomenon. *Review of Education Research, 43,* 237–301.

Shulman, L. S. (1982). Educational psychology returns to school. In A. G. Kraut (Ed.). *G. Stanley Hall lecture series,* (Vol. 2). (pp. 73–117). Washington, DC: American Psychological Association.

Snow, R. E. (1981). On the future of educational psychology. *Newsletter for Educational Psychologists, Division 15, APA, 5* (1), 1.

Snow, R. E. (1986). Individual differences and the design of educational programs. *American Psychologist, 41,* 1029–1039.

Sternberg, R. J. (1981). Testing and cognitive psychology. *American Psychologist, 36,* 1181–1189.

Swift, C. (1982, Summer). Community psychology: Riding the crest of the third wave. *Division of Community Psychology Newsletter, APA,* pp. 6–7.

Tidwell, R. (1980). Informal assessment to modify the role and image of the school psychologist. *Psychology in the Schools, 7,* 210–215.

Tobias, S. (1984). *Implications of wellness models for educational and school psychology.* Paper presented at the meeting of the American Psychological Association, Toronto, Canada.

Tobias, S. (1985). Test anxiety: Interference, defective skills, and cognitive capacity. *Educational Psychologist, 20,* 135–142.

Trachtman, G. (1980). *On such a full sea.* Paper presented at the Spring Hill Symposium on the Future of Psychology in the Schools, Spring Hill, Minnesota.
VanderZanden, J. W., & Pace, A. J. (1984). *Educational psychology in theory and practice (2nd ed.).* New York: Random House.
Wallace, J. (1966). An abilities conception of personality: Some implications for personality measurement. *American Psychologist, 21,* 132–137.
Watkins, C. E. Jr. (1987). On myopia, rhetoric, and reality in counseling psychology. *The Counseling Psychologist, 15,* 332–336.
Weinstein, C. E. (1985). Learning strategies: The flip-side of teaching strategies. *Innovation Abstracts,* VII (19), 2 pp.
White, M. A. (1981, April). *The electronic learning period vs. the print learning period.* Speech given at the Preschool Assessment Workshop, Teachers College, Columbia University, New York, NY.
White, M. A., & Duker, J. (1973). *Education: A conceptual and empirical approach.* NY: Holt, Rinehart & Winston.
Wiener, J. (1986). Alternatives in the assessment of the learning disabled adolescent: A learning strategies approach. *Learning Disabilities Focus, 1,* 97–107.
Witt, J. C., Moe, G., Gutkin, T. B., & Andrews, L. (1984). The effect of saying the same thing in different ways: The problem of language and jargon in school-based consultation. *Journal of School Psychology, 22,* 361–367.
Wittrock, M. C. (1979, February). The cognitive movement in instruction. *Educational Researcher,* 5–11.
Wittrock, M. C., & Farley, F. (in press). *The future of educational psychology.* Hillsdale, NJ: Lawrence Erlbaum Associates.
Wolfensberger, W. (1972). *The principle of normalization in human services.* Toronto, Canada: National Institute on Mental Retardation.
Woolfolk, A. E. (1986). *Educational psychology (3rd ed.).* Englewood Cliffs, NJ: Prentice-Hall.
Ysseldyke, J. E., & Algozzine, B. (1983). On making psychoeducational decisions. *Journal of Psychoeducational Assessment, 1,* 187–195.
Zucker, K. B. (1986). *Issues in professional judgment in school psychological practice.* Paper presented at the meeting of the American Psychological Association, Washington, DC.

2
The School Psychologist as a Community/Family Service Provider

JANE CLOSE CONOLEY
University of Nebraska, Lincoln

Historically, school psychologists have been in public or community service. They tended to work in public school buildings and their practice has focused on individual children. In recent years, however, many school psychologists have broadened their professional repertoire to include family consultation, parent training, and brief family therapy modes. These activities, although vitally important in schools, are also very critical contributions to community mental health centers (CMHCs) and social service agencies, especially those concerned with child protective services. The movement of school psychologists into family-centered treatment modalities outside of school buildings, represents another aspect of the nontraditional practice of school psychology.

To explore this innovative element of school psychology practice, this chapter will develop several themes.

1. The professional, theoretical, and community forces creating the context for this shift among school psychologists
2. The interface between traditional school psychology knowledge and skills and the demands of family service
3. Family interventions with divorcing and abusive families
4. Challenges faced by school psychologists who offer community service outside of the school building

FORCES SUPPORTING NONTRADITIONAL SERVICE

Professional Forces

The last decade has seen a dramatic shift in how and where psychologists spend their professional time. Universities, once the largest employers of psychologists, have become less common choices for post-doctoral employment. The majority of newly graduated psychologists (in clinical, counseling, and school psychology) intend to be practitioners rather than professors (Committee on Employment and Human Resources, 1985).

This shift in the balance between the professional ideal of scientist/practitioner has fueled school psychologists' interest in the delivery of health services outside of the school building. School employment has not grown very rapidly since the explosive growth following the passage of federal legislation guaranteeing a free appropriate education to all children (P.L. 94-142). In contrast, employment in organized human service settings has increased dramatically. With their increasing numbers and more comprehensive graduate preparation, school psychologists have become more likely to see family therapy as an effective way to serve children and to seek employment in settings that emphasize family treatment. Although such service can be practiced in schools, as well as in community agencies, this chapter focuses on family intervention outside of the school building.

Theoretical Support

Availability of employment settings has not, however, been the major force moving school psychologists toward family intervention. School psychologists have been interested in influencing families to improve the adjustment of children, and so have been eager consumers of and contributors to theory about family intervention. Several prevailing family therapy models are based on general systems theory. Recent work has made the constructs associated with systems theory available to school psychologists (e.g., Plas, 1986; Wendt & Zake, 1984). A brief overview of important concepts is provided as a basis for understanding family therapy techniques. Following the review of general systems theory, other theoretical approaches to family intervention are described.

General Systems Theory

Originally developed in theoretical biology, general systems theory (GST) is a metatheory concerned with the general properties and laws of all living or open systems (von Bertalanffy, 1981). A system is a complex of elements with some shared activity and expectations. Every part of a system is so related that change in one part will cause a change in the total system (Watzlawick, Beavin, & Jackson, 1967).

Open systems live by a continuous import and export of materials with their environments. An open system is active in its use of (interpretation of) input. This interpretation is defined in terms of a system's preexisting arrangement. The Piagetian constructs of assimilation/accommodation capture the active nature of an open system in its contexts. An open system does not merely await a stimulus from the environment but actively stimulates, is stimulated by, and changes its context.

General systems theory is both a parsimonious and useful theory when applied to human behavior. The theory uses similar descriptions of patterns appearing in divergent fields including biology, chemistry, physics, mathematics, psychology, sociology, history, and politics. In pursuing the similar characteristics of differing systems, a simpler, more internally consistent pattern of science emerges (Miller, 1972).

General systems theory supplies a framework for understanding the meaning of things. Not merely a collection of facts, it is an overarching model that "makes sense" of many content areas. Many consider GST to be a counter toward somewhat reductionistic views of human behavior (e.g., classical psychodynamics and radical behaviorism). Several basic constructs of GST are useful for psychologists in their work with families and so will be outlined below.

Wholism. Despite the fact that systems are made up of separate elements, they are not mere collections, that is, knowledge of the constituent parts does not completely explain a system. All the parts of a system are interactive, creating both the "ripple effect" phenomenon (i.e., change in one part of a system can spread to other parts) and a uniqueness to the system that is due to the system members, their interaction, their own internal developmental experiences and that of the system, and the particular context in which the system is embedded.

Experts in family intervention use the system property of wholism to plan small changes in family patterns with the hope that any small change (i.e., any difference that makes some difference) will affect the family complaint. They also see families as examples of micro-cultures, sharing values, understandings, and behaviors. These similarities exist over time and space making explorations of the family of origin useful. Patterns present in one's family of origin are likely to reappear when a person builds new relationships and becomes a parent. In addition, families' shared cultures permit them to identify goals with overlapping segments.

Centralization and differentiation. All systems have some sort of executive decision-making subsystem. This might be the nucleus of a single-celled organism, the brain in the human, or the parliment or congress of a political system. In families, the parental or marital subsystem is looked upon as the executive subsystem and is, therefore, of particular importance when planning family interventions. This decision-making unit should be the trigger mechanism of the family, that is, a small change in the parents should wield significant influence with the rest of the family. Family therapists almost always make, at least, initial attempts to strengthen, inform, or adjust the parental unit when a child is identified as troubled in some way. When children are the trigger mechanisms of the family, the therapist is immediately aware of a disordered hierarchy. The wrong subsystem is "in charge."

A companion process to centralization in a human system is differentiation. As systems grow and become more complex, there is a predictable tendency for separate subsystems to assume particular tasks and, more importantly, to seek identities separate from the family system. Not everyone does everything. Some people pay bills, while others take out trash, fix dinners, do laundry, and make decisions. Family therapists look for instances in which appropriate differentiation has not occurred (e.g., the teenage children never go for recreational activities without the parents present and vice-versa or grown children have difficulty leaving home) and for evidence that differentiation of functions has been based on some irrelevant dimension, (e.g., gender) and some family members have complaints about how tasks are assigned.

The assignment and reassignment of tasks are potentially powerful interventions. This is true because each subsystem should have a unique agenda. Assigning tasks can promote healthy differentiation (e.g., parents should go out once per week alone to enjoy each others company; children should handle some school problems without assistance from their parents; parents who divorce should communicate directly with one another rather than using the children as communication conduits). The assignment of the task affects not only those who actually perform the task, but has potential effects on the differentiation of each subsystem in the family.

Regulation. Of considerable practical and therapeutic interest is the fact that all living systems have regulators. These may be autonomic physiological responses that govern temperature, blood pressure, and respiration; behaviors that create distance or closeness among system members; psychological processes such as selective attention, defensiveness, anxiety, or needs to dominate or be submissive; or societal behaviors related to population dispersal and growth, caste systems, or economic systems. A therapist may see the identification of the problem regulator as the most important therapeutic task, that is, what keeps a family behaving in a way uncomfortable for it? Who or what condition is allowing some behaviors, but not others, to be used in problem solving?

Summary. Constructs from GST provide the building blocks of modern family therapy. The few concepts outlined above are among the most important for family therapists to grasp.

There is a tendency among many mental health specialists (and, perhaps, traditional school psychologists in particular) to see client complaints as evidence of individual psychopathology. The important paradigmatic shift suggested by GST is to see people's problems as products of unique formulas in which individual attributes are but one contributing variable. In some cases, the individual attribute (e.g., autism) is so dramatic that it eclipses the importance of other variables in explaining behavior. More often, however, a family member's behaviors are intricately connected to the behaviors and expectations of all the other family members. Merely diagnosing the individual is insufficient and ineffective.

Other Approaches to Family Intervention

Although GST has been extremely influential in family intervention conceptualizations, school psychologists are probably more familiar with Adlerian and behavioral approaches. The notion of providing educative or guidance services to families is not new. In fact, it predates the publication of information about GST. Adlerian child guidance centers have been available in certain parts of this country since the 1940s. This approach emphasized intervention with normal, fairly well-functioning families who were experiencing difficulties with the developmental stresses and strains of child rearing. From this perspective children are seen as having "mistaken goals," that is, occupying a dysfunctional role in the family. Parents are educated in ways to counteract the child's abuse of power, attention, revenge, or inadequacy (Dinkmeyer & McKay, 1976; Dreikurs & Stolz, 1964).

More recently, parent training approaches have appeared based on behavioral technology, teaching parents more effective ways to interact with their children. Many of these programs have been adopted and adapted by school-based practitioners for implementation through the public schools. The principles and approaches are also commonly used in behavior therapy with children in community or private practice settings. Although these approaches (as parent training packages) have limited empirical support, they are extremely popular (Abidin, 1980; Atkenson & Forehand, 1978, 1979; Fine, 1980; Patterson, Reid, Jones, & Conger, 1975; Reid, 1978).

The common thread running through GST, Adlerian guidance, and behavioral parent training is the importance of adult-focused service. The systems therapists see the executive subsystem as critical as do the Adlerians and the behaviorists. Each group tries to increase the skills, change the tasks, or improve the information available to parents. Practitioners who intervene with families conceptualize parents and children as in a delicate and intricate balance with each other. When the balance is marred by poor communication, ineffective problem solving, serious internal or external stress, or poor role definition and clarity, the vulnerable children are likely to serve as the evidence of problems. They are the "identified patients" in a troubled family system (Hobbs, 1975, 1982).

Psychologists who embrace this understanding of children's difficulties consider family intervention as the treatment of choice. In fact, many assume that an over-reliance on individual service is doomed to failure.

Although some of the family systems literature seems abstruse because of family theorists' penchant for a new jargon, most psychologists can recognize the basic premises of family systems therapy to be very similar to Bandura's (1978) exposition of reciprocal determinism. Some valuable additional contributions from the family systems literature are focuses on roles, irrational behavior, family-of-origin influences, family secrets, and models of healthy family functioning. Family therapy practitioners have suggested new and promising techniques and brief models of therapy. These will be examined in detail in a subsequent portion of this chapter.

The overarching conceptual umbrella of GST (Apter & Conoley, 1984) is a useful device to organize information about family interaction, developmental phases, and position in the larger society. General systems theory allows an analysis of each human system level (i.e., micro, meso, macrosystems) searching for intervention points likely to begin helpful change processes (Anderson, 1983). Throughout this chapter, illustrations of systems theory's important theoretical and practical insights into families will be explored.

Community Forces

Armed with new theories and techniques, psychologists have found many families in serious need of help (Bronfenbrenner, 1984; Levitan & Belous, 1981; Moynihan, 1986; Yogman & Brazelton, 1986). From a position of relative invisibility just a few decades ago, families' needs are now very apparent. Community members recognize the incidence of and effects of divorce, poverty, physical and sexual abuse, family patterns of substance abuse, and neglect on children's current and long-term adjustment. Adolescent pregnancy, suicide, delinquency, substance abuse, and learning problems are rampant and are increasingly considered signs of family dysfunction—not evidence of merely "bad" or "mad" children.

Despite these very real needs, the resources available to children and families have been diminishing. Poverty is a particular problem for the young. Twenty-two percent of children live below the poverty line, making them the poorest group in America. One out of every six preschoolers live in poverty and 10 million children receive no regular health care (Children's Defense Fund, 1982; Miller, 1983; U.S. Bureau of the Census, 1985).

Children and families are among our lowest national priorities. Miller (1983) reported that AFDC, Medicaid, and Food Stamps accounted for 5.2% of the federal budget but took 10% of the 1982 cuts. These programs are for children. In the same year 21.3 billion dollars were available for tobacco products, 2 billion in write offs for oil drilling and development, and 3 billion in oil depletion allowanced (Miller, 1983; Edelman, 1981).

The economic situation of many families makes CMHC or social welfare agency services the only available options. The school psychologist's historical mission to engage in the public practice of psychology is continued in these agencies making psychological care available to the broadest spectrum of community members.

Psychologists who operate at macro-levels can have some influence on public policy and, thus, funding priorities (DeLeon, VandenBos, & Kraut, 1984). In addition, communities are clamoring for direct, therapeutic assistance from psychologists. Some preventive (e.g., parent education) and many remedial and crisis interventions (e.g., family therapy and child protective services) are now recognized as vital for community health. These approaches are promising, and demand that school psychologists integrate new knowledge and skills with traditional ones.

NEW AND OLD SKILLS

Many of the school psychologist's traditional skills are useful in delivering high quality family treatment. Psychologists who have been effective in facilitating behavior change in classrooms (which have many of the same system characteristics as a family) will find family therapy a natural extension of their work (Anderson, 1983; Conoley, 1987a). Psychologists who have emphasized individual diagnostics as their speciality, however, will need some new information and supervision before embarking on a family practice.

Because family therapy is probably least familiar to traditionally trained psychologists (i.e., in contrast to parent training), the following sections will elaborate on three related approaches to family therapy. The three models are examples of brief therapy approaches making them most useful in community service settings and in crisis situations such as child abuse cases.

Family Therapy

Originally based on work from the Mental Research Institute at Palo Alto, California, family therapy comes in several "brand names" (Hoffman, 1981). These include structural (Minuchin, 1974), problem solving/strategic (Haley, 1967, 1973, 1976, 1980; Madanes, 1981; Watzlawick, Weakland, & Fisch, 1974), historical (Bowen, 1978; Boszormenyi–Nagy & Sparks, 1973), systemic (Selvini-Palazolli, Cecchin, Boscolo, & Prata, 1974, 1978), and solution-focused (deShazer, 1985).

In keeping with the systems orientation of this chapter, structural, strategic, and solution-focused therapies will be highlighted. In practice, these are far more similar than different. None depend on insight or the interpretation of historical family dynamics. Both insight and exploration of a nuclear family's families of origin are very helpful in certain situations, however, and readers should consult Hoffman (1981) for an overview of all the family therapy schools.

Strategic Therapy

Strategic family therapy tends to be problem-focused. That is, the therapist attempts to formulate the current problem the family is experiencing and the strategies-in-use by the family to solve the problem. Interventions are designed that reframe the problem, prescribe behaviors quite different from the current family problem solving attempts, or prescribe behaviors that are exaggerations of current strategies (for indepth study of these techniques, consult: Andolfi, 1980; Haley, 1973, 1976; Hare–Mustin, 1975; Hoffman, 1981; Madanes, 1980; Papp, 1980; Raskin & Klein, 1976; Selvini-Palazzoli, Boscolo, Cecchin, & Prata, 1978; Soper & L'Abate, 1977; Weeks & L'Abate, 1979).

Assumptions. The expert use of family interventions depends on a thorough knowledge of their basic assumptions. Foremost among these assumptions is a rejection of a pathology model of human behavior. The problems experienced by families are not seen as signs of illness, but rather as attempts to adapt to normal developmental challenges faced by all families or to particular stresses that challenge the usual problem solving capacity of a family.

Many family practitioners assume that insight is not necessary for behavior change. Using a systems theory approach to family organization, they suggest that any small change in a problem behavior has the potential to change the uncomfortable pattern. In fact, strategic therapists avoid teaching a particular model of optimal family functioning and assume that change does not depend entirely on rational processes.

Change. The terms, first and second order change, are often used to describe the degrees of change in family functioning. First order change refers to change that is an adjustment to a situation. For example, a father may be told to be "more involved" in delivering contingencies to a noncompliant child. The change is a do-more-of-the-same adjustment.

In contrast, second order change refers to change that is outside of the usual, expected transactions in a system. In essence, a change that alters the rules governing the problematic situation is a second order change. A mother may be told to stop saving her children from the father's discipline. She should, rather, allow the children to face the father's reactions to their misbehavior, and his reactions to their successes. This directive might mean the mother stops covering up the children's misbehaviors, stops threatening the children with the father but never following through, or stops intervening for the children with the father. In this way, the children experience more consequences from their behaviors than does the mother, and the father is brought into closer contact with his children. This is a change from the former rule by which mother enjoyed the status of person in charge of the children and deprived father of interaction with the children.

Paradoxical techniques. So-called paradoxical techniques are considered hallmarks of strategic family therapy. These techniques may appear paradoxical (i.e., not moving a family toward its stated goal), but are actually used to facilitate problem resolution. They may be best understood by calling them restraint-from-change strategies rather than paradoxical interventions.

For example, prescribing strategies, restraining strategies, and positioning all suggest to the client that change, at this moment, may not be the best alternative. The prescribing strategies usually involve the therapist in telling the client to engage in the behaviors that are targets for elimination. Often, the prescription contains a qualifier, however, for example to engage in the behavior at an accelerated rate, or during particular time periods, or to pretend to be engaging in the behavior, or, perhaps, to continue at the same rate but note the rate and the situations surrounding the behavior (Conoley, 1987b).

Restraining strategies are used when the therapist tells the client not to change or to go very slowly toward the desired goal. A therapist may also tell the client the dangers of the change the client is contemplating. These dangers are, by the way, very real possibilities if problematic behaviors are considered to be serving some adaptive purposes in a system.

Finally, positioning refers to strategies a therapist uses to avoid the usual complementarity of a "symptom." If, for example, a therapist recognizes a parent's pattern is to ask for and then disregard advice, the therapist can avoid advice giving and wait for the recalcitrant parent to suggest possible interventions. When the parent has been manuvered into suggesting strategies, the parent's usual nonproductive pattern may be avoided. Other family members can be advised to interact in the same way.

One of the most vital skills needed by practitioners interested in using strategic interventions is that of positive connotation or reframing. Because blaming and criticism tend to reduce client cooperation (and because most clients have already been criticized and blamed for their inappropriate behaviors with no positive result) a therapist must be expert at ascribing new meanings to the behaviors of the family. The positive connotation identifies the therapist as accepting and as convinced that all the members are motivated for a positive resolution. Most families find this stance surprising as they have identified each other as blameworthy and labeled each others' motivations as destructive. A therapist may, for example, connote the rebelliousness of a teenager as experimentation with adulthood or the intrusiveness of a mother as signs of excellent parenting skills when the child was an infant. Understanding the same behavior differently can cause changed reactions because defensiveness and anxiety may be reduced by the more positive connotation.

Skills in reframing or positive connotation are not mere semantics or tricks. They should reflect the therapist's belief that most members of a family are doing their best and that motivations are not absolutes, but can be legitimately perceived very diversely.

Summary. This mode of therapy may not be appropriate for all families having an "identified patient" child, but it does hold promise for certain problems and in situations where one to three family meetings are possible. Expert use of strategic family therapy provides the practitioner with frameworks to facilitate family cooperation in carrying out child interventions. The use of the family's own problem definition and acceptance of each member's positive work for the family may enhance treatment acceptability and compliance.

Strategic therapy can seem a "bag of tricks" to people not aware of the theoretical frameworks guiding well-trained practitioners. It is a difficult therapy to learn and should not be practiced without careful study and live supervision opportunities (Garrigan & Bambrick, 1977).

Structural Family Therapy

The very special contribution of structural family therapy is Minuchin's (1974) description of a healthy family. The therapist conceptualizes a family "map" examining membership in the marital, child, parental, and extra-familial subsystems, and the qualities of the boundaries demarcating these subsystems. Interventions are designed that re-align the family subsystems (e.g., remove a child from overinvolvement with a parent).

Most characteristic of structural family therapy is attention to family subsystems, roles, boundaries, and triangles. Minuchin (1970, 1974) articulates a model of optimal family functioning. He sees a strong executive/parental subsystem and clear boundaries as critical for successful coping. Structural therapists are likely to shore up a faltering parental system by emphasizing the parents' obligation to guide the children. This system is also supported by trying to draw the parents closer to one another and disentangle any child who has been inappropriately put in a parental role.

Boundaries. Structural therapists notice the transactions in a system and describe subsystem boundaries as enmeshed, rigid, or clear. A boundary is a metaphorical demarcation between systems. A boundary is enmeshed when the roles, functions, and experiences between members of two systems are unclear. For example, a father who gets angry and depressed when his son is disciplined at school, may be illustrating an enmeshed boundary. The father is suffering for the son.

In contrast, a rigid boundary creates too much distance between systems so the normal feedback mechanisms that operate are ineffective in keeping each system informed as to the other system's needs. A family that does not react to a child's school failure, drug use, disregard for curfews, and so forth, may have boundaries that are too rigid. The child's calls for help or indications of distress do not trigger appropriate problem solving.

Finally, clear boundaries operate so that age-appropriate interaction takes place among subsystems. People understand each other's roles and can exchange information, attention, affection, and influence. Family therapists notice, for example, that appropriate supervision of children changes dramatically as they grow older. A good mother or father of an infant is quite "enmeshed" with the infant; anticipating the child's needs, keeping continual contact, and making decisions about each minute aspect of dress, food, medical care, and so on. Appropriate supervision when the child is 17 is quite different. Clear boundaries allow the parents to recognize their roles must change, and the child to understand the meaning or goals inherent in the parents' behaviors.

Triangulation. Triangles (or coalitions) are important to structural therapists. These triangles refer to a tendency for people to divert their communication or interaction through a third party, rather than deal directly with another. Parents, for example, often use their children in coalitions. When mother is disatisfied with father, she may complain of the father's ineptness to the son. The son, understanding the father is somehow peripheral, may ignore the father's requests or openly rebel. Mother is horrified at the son's actions, and blames father for handling discipline situations badly.

In other cases, the children's misbehavior is all the parents have in common. Without the child to concern them, their marriage would fail. In these classic triangles, the child's "symptom" becomes acute whenever the parents begin to directly engage with one another, thus diverting their attention away from a miserable relationship and toward a needy child.

Triangles to be avoided in families are ones that take on rigid and long-lasting qualities. Temporary alliances between and among family members are natural, but consistent detouring of genuine encounters between people robs family members of important system information and connections.

Restraint-from-change strategies. It should be noted that Minuchin, himself, does not approve of the use of so-called paradoxical techniques as structural family therapy interventions. Despite this assertion, however, structural and strategic therapists often suggest the same intervention, but understand it (as paradoxical or not) differently. Hoffman (1981) describes Minuchin's rejection of paradoxical techniques as a weakness in his approach.

Summary. School psychologists may find Minuchin's model especially appealing. Working in a school is a lesson on the effects of organizational variables on individual behavior. A perceptive psychologist notices that children's behaviors change depending on the skills of those adults who care for them; that schools with strong, skilled principals have better morale and productivity; and that confusion among the adults about roles and functions inevitably damage children's abilities to learn.

Solution-Focused Therapy

Although sharing basic theoretical similarities with much of structural and strategic therapies, solution-focused therapy (deShazer, 1985) has an interesting slant useful to psychologists who treat families. deShazer's work is not well known in the school psychology literature, so a fairly comprehensive discussion is provided.

Solution-focused therapists adopt a brief therapy model that sees the client's problem as the "patient." Brief therapists are not merely practitioners who do therapy quickly (Garfield, 1971; Koss, 1979), rather they have a particular understanding of how people conceptualize and maintain the problems or complaints brought to therapy. Brief therapists use the family's problem definition to construct solutions to problems. No attempts to understand or ameliorate "underlying" or causative factors are made (Erickson, 1954a, 1954b, 1964).

In contrast to other therapy systems, deShazer emphasizes that a solution to a complaint need not be uniquely constructed to match the problem. Although substantial research in problem-solving (e.g., Mayer, 1983) highlights how elements of a solution must match elements of the problem, deShazer suggests that "fit" is much more important than match. Von Glasersfeld (1984a) has the same orientation:

> A key fits if it opens the lock. The fit describes a capacity of the key, not of the lock. Thanks to professional burglars we know only too well that there are many keys that are shaped quite differently from our own but which nevertheless unlock our doors. (p. 21)

From this perspective, there is no one perfect answer, but rather information that enables family members to think or act differently. In fact, brief therapists like deShazer attempt to adjust some element of the family's complaint without concern about which might be the most important element. The therapist's task is to introduce some noticeable change in the problem pattern (von Glasersfeld, 1984b).

Assumptions. deShazer (1985) suggests some assumptions about the complaints people bring to therapy:

1. Complaints involve behavior brought about by the client's world view. A client can see an event as normal or as problematic. If the behavior is seen as problematic, then the client may see it as having a medical cause or a psychological cause. If the complaint is thought to be due to a psychological cause, the client can label the problem as an example of either "bad" or "mad" behavior. If the bad connotation is given, then punishment is the likely response. In contrast, if a behavior is judged to be mad, then treatment may be sought. Obviously, a decision-tree of sorts is used as people evaluate their own and their family members' behaviors. For example, informing the parents of a three-year-old boy that enuresis is so common as to be normal at that age, can drastically change their subsequent behaviors. Instead of punishing or medicating the child, they might simply allow him to "grow out of it."

2. Complaints are maintained by clients' ideas that what they decided to do about the original difficulty was the *only* right and logical thing to do (e.g., once having decided the behavior is "bad," they cannot entertain anything but punishment as a possibility). Therefore, clients behave as if trapped into doing "more of the same"

because of the rejected and forbidden half of the either/or premise. When embroiled in an emotional situation, most people find it difficult to shift to new understandings. The special flexibility in problem formulation possessed by a therapist may be the most effective element in psychotherapy. Therapists should be prepared for the fact, however, that people do not give up their problem formulations easily, even when they've been dismally ineffective in changing their situations.

3. Minimal changes are needed to initiate solving complaints and, once the change is initiated (this is the therapist's task), further changes will be generated by the client (the ripple effect; Spiegel & Linn, 1969). Brief therapists tend to give primary importance to the systemic concept of wholism. A change in one element of a system or in one of the relationships between elements will affect the other elements and relationships that together comprise the system.
4. Ideas about what to change are based on ideas about what the clients' view of reality might be like without the particular complaint. The "crystal ball" technique described later in this chapter can be used to generate this alternate reality.
5, A new frame or new frames need only be suggested, and new behavior based on any new frame can promote clients' resolution of the problem.

Duncker's (1945) study about "frames" provides a classic example of the problem of getting stuck in a particular understanding of reality. The subjects in the study were given matches, candles, tacks, and boxes. Some of the subjects received the matches, candles, and tacks *in* the boxes, while others were given the materials separately. Both groups were asked to construct free-standing lights. The subjects who first saw the boxes as containers had trouble seeing boxes as anything but containers, while the other group had no difficulty in using the boxes in the completion of the task.

Complaints. Despite the wide array of problems families bring to therapy, deShazer (1985) describes how all complaints have similar properties. Complaints are constructed of:

1. a bit or sequence of behavior
2. the meanings ascribed to the situation
3. the frequency with which the complaint happens

4. the physical location in which the complaint happens
5. the degree to which the complaint is involuntary
6. significant others involved in the complaint directly or indirectly
7. the question of who is to blame
8. environmental factors such as jobs, economic status, living space, etc.
9. the physiological or feeling state involved
10. the past
11. dire predictions of the future
12. utopian expectations.

A solution-focused therapist asks questions about each of these factors. This is done to define the problem in such a way that a solution can develop. A change in any of these 12 complaint elements has the potential to improve a family's situation.

Solutions. Complaints (understood according to their basic elements) can be transformed into solutions by using an array of techniques. deShazer commonly assigns tasks, uses reframing statements, points out exceptions to the rule that the problem occurs all the time, prescribes the symptom, emphasizes past successes, builds new expectations, suggests only minimal changes, asks the problem be scheduled for a new location, or has the client imagine how the disappearance of the problem will affect others.

Solution-focused therapists frequently assign tasks or homework. The first homework assignment is diagnostic because the therapist learns how the family responds to attempts to introduce a change or difference into the family.

DeShazer (1985) describes his responses to family task performance by a discussion of the well-known prisoner's dilemma game. In the prisoner's dilemma, the game can be mutually beneficial (i.e., most points earned) if the partners cooperate. If the partners compete, however, attempting winner-take-all strategies, the highest point totals cannot be achieved. The best game strategy is to begin by cooperating, and then do to your partner what he or she does to you—a tit-for-tat program.

Therapists must assume change will happen and, in fact, be surprised if it does not occur. Families who perform their homework should continue to receive direct tasks. In contrast, if a family performs the homework, but modifies it in some way, the therapist may be more successful with indirect or modifiable tasks (i.e., stories). If the family does just the opposite as was suggested by the therapist, then the next tasks should include the potential for opposite performance. Families who seem vague about remembering what they were told to do or unclear about what they did, should be assigned vague tasks. Finally, families who make no response to the tasks should either not be given anymore or have their homework optional—A tit for a tat.

For families who have difficulty organizing around a concrete plan of action, deShazer describes the crystal ball technique. Family members are asked to identify a pressing problem or complaint. The family member must be able to visualize the problem in a crystal ball and pay attention to his or her own behavior and the behavior of others. The client must be able to imagine how change in the complaint will affect other people in his/her life.

A second crystal ball is visualized to remember some success in life, particularly one that is an exception to the rules surrounding the complaint. While visualizing this crystal ball, the client is asked to notice his or her own behavior and the behavior of the other people who are involved.

In the third step, the client is oriented toward the future. The therapist introduces this third crystal ball by talking about the passage of time. Time is described, at first, in detail but then the description becomes increasingly vague. When the client is asked to look into the crystal ball no clues are being given about a specific date or hour. The therapist asks the family member to remember returning to tell the therapist about the successful resolution of the problem.

In the fourth and final step, the client looks into the crystal ball to remember the manner in which the problem was solved, his her reactions to the process, and the reactions of the other people involved. The therapist always asks the family member, "What will things be like for you and others when the problem is solved?"

I have used this technique successfully with adults and some adolescents. Predictably, only a few children under 12 have been able to do much elaboration of a hypothesized condition of change. That is, they have trouble imagining details about how their lives would be different if the family complaint was solved.

Skeleton keys. In keeping with his view of the importance of "fit" deShazer (1986) has evaluated the effectiveness of certain interventions he calls, "skeleton keys." These are strategies that are effective in many situations.

1. For example, in cases where a person is obsessively depressed over some event or situation, he tells the client to write down all his/her depressive thoughts, read the list very carefully, and then burn it. The

client is instructed to set aside time every day for this activity. It doesn't matter what the client is upset about. The solution is meant to fit, not to match, the complaint.

2. For couples who are concerned about their frequent and damaging arguments, deShazer recommends a structured fight. The couple is instructed to toss coin to decide who goes first. The winner gets to speak for 10 uninterrupted minutes. After that the other person get a 10 minute turn. Following both turns there must be 10 minutes of silence before another round is started with a coin toss. Structured fighting can be done by children, too, although 10 minutes may be too long for their "rounds."

3. Another effective strategy is to tell family members to "do something different." The parents are told to stop the usual consequences they apply to the problematic behavior and just do something different.

For example, One couple was in conflict over their different problem-solving styles. The woman would obsess and want to talk over minute details of interpersonal dilemmas, while the man preferred to ignore what seemed out of his control. She would demand he talk to her and he would demand that she stop talking. Arguments would inevitably ensue. They were told to "do something different." Following her next frantic description of some problem, he kissed her and said he loved her. She laughed at this incongruous reaction, and decided not to worry but try to enjoy the family outings.

4. Many families believe their problems are out of their personal control. A family member may say his or her problem is involuntary or the urges to behave inappropriately are too strong to resist. Most people, however, do not continuously engage in problematic behavior. There are exceptions. An assignment that can be used quite universally with family members with so-called involuntary problems is to ask them to, "Pay attention to what you do when you overcome the urge to . . . ."

When the client describes situations or behaviors that seem linked to control, the therapist can ask the client to spend more time in such situations or use those behaviors more often. For example, a family with a 15 year old daughter was in crisis over her curfew violations and her withdrawal from them when she was in the home. The therapist noticed the girl talked more openly when the father was absent and that the parents seemed willing to tolerate much of her behavior if only she would inform them in advance. For example, they would allow her to spend evenings with friends if she would just call to tell them. The daughter said she "just couldn't talk" to the father because he would become too angry and that she would "just forget" to call home on most nights when she'd decided to stay with a friend. She would, however, call if she was sure the father would not answer the phone. The therapist asked the family to use their answering machine on the evenings when the daughter was out. An informative phone call guaranteed the girl would not be in trouble with the father upon returning home. The girl learned she could control the father's anger and that remembering to call home was a voluntary decision.

5. A final skeleton key is the first session formula used by deShazer (1985) and his colleagues at the Brief Therapy Center in Milwaukee. The task given to almost every client at the end of the first session is this, "Between now and next time we meet, we would like you to observe, so that you can describe to us next time, what happens in your (family, life, marriage, relationship) that you want to continue to have happen."

DeShazer reports a very high percentage of clients who return with very specific descriptions and a surprising number who report their family functioning is inexplicably better since the last therapy session. Apparently the family's focus on strengths can have the effect of increasing the frequency of such desired behaviors or situations.

Summary. Solution-focused therapy is a somewhat novel approach squarely based on the functional analysis of behavior. Some of its appealing elements are:

1. its focus on a family's past successes, that is, both family strengths and exceptions to the rules governing the complaint
2. the acceptance of several problem formulations while challenging people's tendency to see situations as "either/or" (both of you are right but the results are wrong)
3. the simple but profoundly important mandate to insert doubt about any element of the complaint, so the family members have a way to change their behaviors
4. the insistence that therapists must have no doubt that change will occur.

Assessment

There are several additional "keys" to successful family intervention. Most of these are already well known to school psychologists. The first one is assessment skills. Although there may be particular situations that call for traditional psychoeducational assessment (Goh, Teslow, & Fuller, 1981), skills in behavioral assessment are far more useful. The assessment challenge when working with families is to identify the patterns of behaviors among family members that maintain dysfunctional situations. Each family member must change to improve communication, make roles clearer, establish a helpful hierarchy (i.e., parents are in charge of the children and children are not expected to function in parental or marital roles), and provide a nurturing balance between family interdependence and autonomy.

Goals

Family assessment is necessary to both determine the changes that must be made and the leverage points in the family system. Knowing what to do is easier than getting the family to agree to change. Ideally, careful assessment uncovers a family's stumbling blocks and suggests a strategy to use in suggesting change or facilitating new interactions.

Methods

Many familiar and innovative methods are useful (Patterson, Reid, Jones, & Conger, 1975; Reid, 1978). Carlson (1988) provides a comprehensive review of family assessment devices. Her chapter should be consulted by practitioners for indepth information about instruments. Parent interview formats have been described by several authors (Aponte, 1976; Fine & Holt, 1983; Friedman, 1969; Olson & Killarin, 1985; Olson, McCubbin, Barnes, Larsen, Muxen, & Wilson, 1983; Olson, Russell, & Sprenkle, 1983; Olson, Sprenkle, Russell, 1979; Pfeiffer & Tittler, 1983; Treffinger & Fine, 1979; Wise & Ginther, 1981). The goals of such interviews are usually to obtain information regarding:

1. Is the problem in question of chronic or acute duration? What does it look like at home and in other settings?
2. What problem solving steps have this family been able to accomplish in the past?
3. Is there one member of this family who has sufficient skill or motivation to be the ally of the psychologist?
4. What is the quality of the family communication (e.g., clear, direct, triangulating, blaming)?

Child administered. When an entire family is not available for interviewing, some child-administered assessments can be instructive (Anderson, 1981). For example, the California Test of Personality (Thorpe, Clark, & Tiegs, 1953), Mooney Problem Checklist (Mooney & Gordon,

1953); Offer Self-Image Questionnaire for Adolescents (Offer, 1979); Self-Concept and Motivation Inventory (Farrah, Milehus, & Reitz, 1977) are all general personality tests with scale scores reflecting family processes.

More specific devices to administer to children include the Behavior Rating Profile (Brown & Hammill, 1978); Child Report of Parent Behavior Inventory (Schaefer, 1965); Child's Attitude toward Mother and Father Scales (Guili & Hudson, 1977); and the Family Relations Test (Bene & Anthony, 1978).

Parent respondent. A number of instruments can also be completed by parents to derive information about their child. Some of these include the Becker Adjective Checklist (Patterson, et al, 1975); Behavior Problem Checklist (Quay & Peterson, 1967); Child Behavior Profile (Achenbach & Edelbrock, 1983); and the Parent Daily Report (Patterson et al, 1975).

Family measures. Hypotheses concerning family functioning and environment may be supplied by using devices such as the Family Adaptability and Cohesion Evaluation Scales (Olson, Bell, & Portner, 1978; Olson & Killarin, 1985); Family Environment Scale (Moos, 1974); and the Family Pre-Counseling Inventory (Stuart & Stuart, 1975).

Another very simple, but useful assessment, goal setting, and monitoring device is an ecomap (Hartmen, 1975; Holman, 1983; Newbrough, Walker, & Abril, 1978). The ecomap graphically represents each system involved with the identified child (e.g., family, church, YWCA, peers, probation) and notes the quality of the relationships among all of the systems. Goals to make the system supportive of change are set and monitored by updates of the ecomap. Essentially, the ecomap turns attention to the qualities of the boundaries surrounding clients as well as to their individual experiences.

Child Assessment

The most meaningful assessment of the child from the ecological perspective is called a profile analysis (Apter, 1982). Planning for the child depends on his or her individual strengths and weaknesses, points of discordance (i.e., areas where the child does not match the environment either academically, behaviorally, or emotionally), reactions to interventions, and specific needs. Short and long range objectives must be identified, as well as the methods and materials to be used and the persons involved with specific responsibilities assigned. A method of evaluation must also be specified.

School psychologists will recognize this as an individualized educational plan. It has particular relevance to family therapy because the profile analysis process highlights a child embedded in his or her own attributes (skills, attitudes, history) and embedded in a context that can be modified to be less or more demanding or supportive.

Interventions with Divorcing Families

The divorce rate has nearly tripled since 1960 (Report of Select Committee on Children, Youth & Families, 1983). The current divorce rate is almost 50% (Furstenberg & Spanier, 1984). About one child in four is growing up with more than two parents in a blended family. One out of four households with children under 18 are headed by single parents (U.S. Bureau of the Census, 1982; Gelman, et al, 1985) One million children experience divorce every year. These children have an increased probability of experiencing adverse psychological outcomes (Emery, 1982; Felner, Farber, & Primavera, 1983; Guidubaldi, Cleminshaw, Perry, & McLoughlin, 1983; Hetherington, 1979; Kurdek, 1981; Wallerstein & Kelly, 1979).

As one of the most striking phenomena in modern American society, divorce precipitates many requests for service from psychologists. Divorce is a process (not just an event) often exposing children to acrimonious battles between the parents, disrupted family communication and roles, and neglect prior to the actual separation of the parents. All of these present many opportunities for negative learning to occur and to generalize to other spheres of the child's life.

Following the divorce, most children's economic situations deteriorate and their access to adult supervision is reduced. Post-divorce children are likely to suffer a range of symptoms including learning problems, impaired interactions with one or both parents, anger control issues, self esteem and self control losses, and generalized feelings of depression. They are often inappropriately embroiled in their parents' continuing controversies and so are not given opportunities to resolve their own child agendas for mental health.

Although primary prevention of these negative outcomes would be most desirable, such prevention appears to be practically impossible (because such prevention would involve a change in social mores, laws, parenting skills, the status of women and children, etc.). Treatment has become a priority (e.g., Stolberg & Cullen, 1983; Stolberg, Cullen, Garrison, 1982; Stolberg & Garrison, 1985). Stolberg and his associates have developed a Divorce Adjustment Project that incorporates relaxation, communication, and anger control training. These researchers noted their program was more successful when child and parent groups met separately. Separate meetings may have been more therapeutic because so many child issues are related to the parents' difficulties with each other that children need a separate forum to sort out their own needs.

Divorce groups are uniquely suited to CMHCs because they are structured and cost effective. School psychologists have the advantage of a thorough preparation in normal child development as well as child–clinical concerns. A grasp of what should be typical of children at different ages is especially important in this work.

Pedro-Carroll (1986) and Pedro-Carroll and Cowen (1985) reported on a children of divorce intervention program (CODIP). Relying in part on Wallerstein's (1983) work identifying the need for children to become disengaged from their parents' conflict and resume their child agendas, these researchers make extensive use of role playing, self-talk, and training in skills for resolving interpersonal problems (with children's parents, friends, and teachers) for children of divorce. The program has been tailored for 7 through 11 years olds in both urban and suburban areas. Pedro-Carroll highlights the school as a natural arena for delivering CODIP because of the many hours children spend in school and the existence of supportive groups. The program can also be delivered, however, in child guidance centers and CMHCs.

Although poverty, abuse, neglect, and substance abuse occur in non-divorced families, the single parent family is in need of special support and attention from psychologists. In these families, one parent must succeed at a challenge that is very taxing, even for two parents. The mobility rate of Americans is high, frequently leaving these single parents far from the potentially helpful contributions of extended families (Lindblad–Goldberg & Dukes, 1985). The economic situations of most single-parent families make low-cost community care their only option.

Home And School Collaboration

Many children brought to therapy are referred because of problems at school. Frequently, school problems reflect some family difficulty as well. Many families find it problematic to communicate with their children's school. They experience the school as an adversary rather than as a partner in helping the child. School psychologists in community practice will be especially useful to families in coordinating planning efforts between the home and school. Helping a family establish a problem-solving relationship with the school creates therapeutic consistency for the child (Ayllon, Garber, & Pisor, 1975; Lightfoot, 1978).

School and families can cooperate at several levels. The most frequent collaboration sought from a community-based psychologist is that of developing and monitoring cooperative programs to improve a child's learning or behavior. The programs might include instructions for actually tutoring a child, teaching prosocial skills, or implementation of solutions or rewards. Hallmarks of successful collaborative efforts are as follows:

1. All parties understand exactly the changes expected of each. Everyone, teacher, parent, child, etc., needs to agree to a change.
2. A feasible communication system between parents and teachers must be established.
3. Consistent follow through on the parts of teachers and parents in terms of their behaviors and any rewards that have been agreed upon must be facilitated.

Often, cooperation is aimed at fairly discrete child behaviors, but can be the vehicle for classroom and family change if all parties live up to their contracts. For example, parents who follow through with positive attention to a child who performs well at school, are likely to improve ont only the child's school work, but also the parent/child relationship. Analogously, a teacher who communicates frequently with parents is likely to both be more successful with individual children and feel more supported by parents in doing difficult work (Conoley, 1987a).

The community-based school psychologist can use familiar consultation skills with teachers and principals. Often consultants outside of the school system are granted a measure of respect and cooperation withheld from within-the-system psychologists. This expert power dimension can prove useful in facilitating cooperation between the family and the school (Martin, 1978).

Lusterman (1984, 1985) suggested the fascinating hypothesis that the organization of schools and families along the dimensions of cohesion, communication, and adaptability suggests different intervention strategies. For example, chaotic families need more pressure from the school to force them to act with some purpose, whereas overly rigid families may need a mediator between them and the school in order to reorder unproductive patterns toward their children. A psychologist, sophisticated in family assessment, could test Lusterman's observations by shifting intervention strategies to match family characteristics.

Child Protective Services

Although the prevalence and incidence of child abuse has become a national scandal (Finkelhor, 1979; National Center on Child Abuse and Neglect, 1982), there is suprisingly little research done in the area. This is true despite the large number of programs currently in use to teach children abuse prevention skills. It may be the history of such efforts explains the lack of research evidence on effectiveness. Hazzard and Angert (1986) cite rape crisis centers and social service agencies as the original providers of information and intervention on abuse. These were locally funded efforts. Abuse prevention programs did not receive federal funding until 1980. This grass roots history led, of course, to an emphasis on service not evaluation. Research was not reported in academic journals, but rather exists in hard-to-access program reports or not at all.

Most programs focus on elementary school children and usually have the goal of increasing children's information about abuse. Only a few programs report targetting skills development (Downer, 1984; Finkelhor, 1986; Poche, Brouwer, & Swearingen, 1981). Such a knowledge focus is ironic because those who have already been abused seem to be least prepared to avoid it in the future. Merely knowing about abuse is not a sufficient innoculation against its occurrence (Toal, 1985).

The skill programs teach assertiveness, communication, specific behavioral skills to avoid abuse (e.g., run away from a stranger, scream if someone tries to grab you, seek the help of a mother with children or a grandmother if you are lost) as well as providing a cognitive context for the child to use in understanding abuse. This context usually involves teaching children their rights to privacy, differences between good and bad touching, their right to report abuse and keep reporting if not believed the first time, and their blamelessness for abusive events. As staggering as the abuse problem is, evaluation of skills programs is difficult because abuse is a relatively low frequency event and ethical concerns make analogue evaluations impossible.

Many of the families who receive treatment from CMHCs and social welfare agencies because of abusive situations are court-ordered to seek services. They can be difficult clients who are suspicious of mental health professionals. Psychologists must be prepared to deal with abusive parents with empathy and acceptance (no small accomplishment), but with significant strength and purpose. In these cases, the child's vulnerability makes the child the primary therapeutic client. Fortunately, many parent training programs exist that emphasize anger control, positive management strategies, stress reduction, and parent self development (Forehand & McMahon, 1981).

Even when physical abuse has been the referral problem, psychologists must stay alert to signs (often less apparent than bruises and broken bones) of possible sexual abuse. The behavioral signs that alert a psychologist that abuse may have occurred are well known to school psychologists. They include indications the child is:

1. overly compliant
2. pseudomature
3. hinting about sexual activity
4. arriving at school early and leaving late
5. unskilled at peer relationships or unable to make friends
6. lacking in trust; many secrets about even trivial matters or talking about having some special secrets
7. unable to concentrate in school
8. suffering from sleep disturbance: nightmares, bedwetting, fear of sleeping alone, needing a nightlight, sleeping under the bed or under pieces of furniture or rugs
9. withdrawn
10. clinically depressed
11. aggressive, especially random, unprovoked attacks
12. acting out sexually or engaging in seductive behaviors
13. reluctant to go to a particular place or be with a particular person
14. unusually interested in the genitals of other people or of animals—expressing affection in inappropriate ways, such as "french kissing" or fondling of another's genitals
15. regressive or showing babyish behavior
16. experiencing vaginal infections, frequent bladder infections.

The following are excerpts from a clinic-based school psychologist's report concerning an abused child. The child's name and other identifying information have been altered to protect confidentiality.

Presenting Problems

Thomas (age 4) was referred to me for evaluation because his foster parent was experiencing increasing uneasiness over behaviors he would exhibit upon returning from his twice weekly visits with his biological father. The problems and concerns she described were as follows:

1. *Unusual sexual interest.* For example, he tries to make each kiss very long, he lays on top of people sometimes simulating intercourse, attempts to feel the breasts of his foster mother and her daughters (frequently using the expression "boobs"), frequent masturbation, frequent requests that others in the family touch his penis, attempts to run his hands up women's dresses, resistance to leaving rooms where women are undressing. Although he asks for assistance in toileting from his foster

mother, he now always requests the door be shut and says, "Don't let Rick in." Rick is a nickname for his stepmother's brother. He has also said that Rick undressed him and urinated on him.

2. *Hygiene.* Although Thomas has been toilet trained by his foster mother, he always returns from a visit to his biological father "untrained." He often returns with urine soaked clothes, sometimes these clothes are wet other times the clothes are dry but badly smelling of urine.

3. *Aggressiveness.* After a visit, Thomas's behavior is quite regressed. He is noncompliant, uses obscene language, and acts quite aggressively (especially toward a usually much-loved kitten). When corrected by his foster mother for noncompliant behavior after a visit he often says, "I hate you, you bitch." This expression is used only after visits with his biological father.

4. *Bruises.* When Thomas was first received in foster care, his foot was badly traumatized. Medical opinion was divided as to whether the injury was from a burn or from a pressure sore. On other occasions, Thomas has returned from visits with bruises, a broken tooth, scratches, and a bump on his head.

5. *Anxiety.* Thomas always resists going to see his father. His fears have generalized to cars that resemble his father's car, men who resemble his father, going to his father's hometown, and strangers who arrive at his foster placement. He avoids strangers until he is assured they are not there to take him to see his father.

Clinical Interview

Thomas and I played with puppets. He treated each of the puppets very gently, obviously getting pleasure out of holding and manipulating them. One puppet has a sad face and a happy face. He quickly learned to use that puppet to express his feelings. He turned a happy face while discussing his foster placement and a sad face at the mention of biological father, stepmother, and stepmother's siblings.

During this play, I asked Thomas, "What does the puppet do if your stepbrother is outside? What does the puppet do if Mom is outside? What does the puppet do if your sister is outside? What does the puppet do if Dad is outside?" To each, but the last question, Thomas responded by turning the happy face toward me and asking, "Are they really there?" When I suggested that his father might be outside (in my waiting room), Thomas's affect changed dramatically. He rushed over to his foster mother. He cried and begged not to be given to his father. He screamed, "I can't want my Dad!" over and over again. He was agitated for several minutes. We brought him to the waiting room to reassure him that his father was not in the office. When he was calmer, I resumed puppet play with him. At this point, Thomas's play became very aggressive. He attacked all the puppets, roaring at them and threatening to bite them.

Obviously, this young child displayed both classic signs of sexual abuse and very atypical behavior for a four year old. The school psychologist was successful in having the child's visits to the biological father's home monitored by a caseworker, and eventually was instrumental in placing the child with his biological mother.

CHALLENGES

School psychologists, like counseling and clinical psychologists, have skills that make them valuable in many diverse settings. They are especially well-suited to family practice in community settings because of their skills and the particular mission of community care. School psychologists have a special challenge to meet, however, when choosing to work outside of school buildings.

The National Association of School Psychologists (NASP) has been so successful in identifying school psychologists with schools and at a nondoctoral entry, that doctoral school psychologists must often prove they are as knowledgeable as members of the other health provider specialities concerning the broad range of clients and client difficulties. Analogously, nondoctoral school psychologists who are trained at the educational specialist level (Ed.S.; at least 66 graduate hours in contrast to the typical 36 hour masters degree) are sometimes not recognized as having skills useful to CMHCs, child guidance centers, and social service agencies. Their Ed.S. degrees may have no niche in the state hiring system for psychologists in exempt agencies.

Perhaps, school psychology's success at becoming a visible profession somewhat separate (at least at the nondoctoral level) from generic psychology creates some career barriers to overcome. Both NASP and the Division of School Psychology of the American Psychological Association are faced with a need to educate employers of psychologists as to the unique contributions of school psychologists *and* the overlap between school psychology training and training in professional psychology.

Individual school psychologists must balance, their professional activities between speciality and generic psychology. At the state level this would imply that school psychologists would be members of both the psychological and the school psychology associations. Most psychologists hold memberships in speciality areas (e.g., behavior therapy, neuropsychology) while maintaining a clear connection with "mainstream" psychology. School psychologists have not consistently maintained this connection, creating the mistaken perception they are "not quite psychologists," but some vague hybrid between education and psychology.

Although school psychology is a definite hybrid, so is neuropsychology, behavioral medicine, pediatric rehabilitation, family psychology, and forensic psychology. These latter hybrids do not face the same obstacles that school psychologists sometimes encounter when seeking licensure and special health service provided certifications.

Vigorous joint action to educate employers and state regulating boards by NASP and Division 16 has been slow to develop because of their longstanding dispute regarding entry level. The inability or unwillingness of the two groups to solve the entry-level issue is a major problem influencing the career flexibility of all school psychologists (Conoley, 1987c).

Solutions are difficult to create in a complex arena of regulating boards, national standards, third party payments, trainee goals, trainer realities, and client needs. The facts of a massive shortage of professional workers and an overwhelming clinical press are not sufficient to promote career opportunities for school psychologists in our heavily regulated society. Some common activity between NASP and Division 16 is critical. The genius available among the 15,000 to 20,000 school psychologists in the United States must turn itself toward propelling the field into parity with all other branches of psychology. When such parity occurs, school psychologists will not consider any sub-speciality of psychology, for which they are ethically prepared, to be nontraditional. They will, rather, enjoy a profession as diverse as humankind itself.

REFERENCES

Abidin, R. R. (1980). *Parent education and intervention handbook.* Springfield, IL: Charles C. Thomas.

Achenbach, T. M., & Edelbrock, C. (1983). *Revised child behavior profile.* Burlington, VT: University Associates in Psychiatry.

Anderson, C. (1981, April). *Family-oriented assessment techniques for school psychologists.* Paper presented at the annual meeting of the National Association of School Psychologists, Detroit, MI.

Anderson, C. (1983). An ecological developmental model for a family orientation in school psychology. *Journal of School Psychology, 21,* 179–189.

Andolfi, M. (1980). Prescribing the families' own dysfunctional rules as a therapeutic strategy. *Journal of Marital and Family Therapy, 6,* 29–36.

Aponte, H. J. (1976). The family-school interview: An eco-structural approach. *Family Process, 15,* 303–311.

Apter, S. J. (1982). *Troubled children/troubled systems.* Elmsford, NY: Pergamon Press.

Apter, S. J., & Conoley, J. C. (1984). *Childhood behavior disorder and emotional disturbance.* Englewood Cliffs, NJ: Prentice–Hall.

Atkenson, B. M., & Forehand, R. (1978). Parent behavioral training: An examination of studies using multiple outcome measures. *Journal of Abnormal Child Psychology, 6,* 449–460.

Atkenson, D. M., & Forehand, R. (1979). Home based reinforcement programs designed to modify classroom behavior: review and methodological evaluation. *Psychological Bulletin, 86,* 1298–1308.

Ayllon, T., Garber, S., & Pisor, K. (1975). The elimination of discipline problems through a combined school–home motivation system. *Behavior Therapy, 6,* 616–626.

Bandura, A. (1978). The self system in reciprocal determinism. *American Psychologist, 33,* 344–358.

Bene, E., & Anthony, J. (1978). *Family Relations Test.* London, England: NFER Publishing.

Boszormenyy–Nagy, I, & Sparks, G. (1973). *Invisible loyalties.* New York: Harper and Row.

Bowen, M. (1978). *Family therapy in clinical practice.* New York: Jason Aronson.

Bronfenbrenner, U. (1984). The changing family in a changing world: America first? *Peabody Journal of Education, 61,* 52–70.

Brown, L. L., & Hammill, D. D. (1978). *Behavior Rating Profile.* Austin, TX: Pro-Ed Publishing

Carlson, C. (1988). Family assessment. In T. Kratochwill (Ed.), *Advances in school psychology, Vol. VI* (pp. 81–129). Hillsdale, NJ: Lawrence Erlbaum Associates.

Children's Defense Fund. (1982). *A children's defense budget: An analysis of the President's budget and children.* Washington, D.C.: Author.

Committee on Employment and Human Resources. (1985). *The changing of American Psychology.* Washington, DC: American Psychological Association.

Conoley, J. C. (1987a). Families and schools: Theoretical and practical bridges. *Professional School Psychology. 2,* 191–203.

Conoley, J. C. (1987b). Strategic family therapy: Three cases of school aged children. *School Psychology Review, 16,* 469–486.

Conoley, J. C. (1987c). "Dr. Future, we presume," said school psychology. *Professional School Psychology, 2,* 173–180.

DeLeon, F., VandenBos, G. R., & Kraut, A. G. (1984). Federal legislation recognizing psychology. *American Psychologist, 39,* 933–946.

deShazer, S. (1985). *Keys to solution in brief therapy.* New York: W. W. Norton.

Dinkmeyer, D., & McKay, G. (1976). *Systematic training for effective parenting.* Circle Pine, MN: American Guidance Services.

Downer, A. (1984). *Evaluation of talking about touching: Personal safety curriculum.* Summary Report. Seattle, WA: Committee for Children.

Dreikurs, R., & Stolz, V. (1964). *Children: The challenge.* Des Moines: Meredith.

Duncker, K. (1945). On problem solving. *Psychological Monographs, 58.*

Edelman, M. W. (1981). Who is for children? *American Psychologist, 36,* 109–116.

Emery, R. E. (1982). Interparental conflict and the children of discord and divorce. *Psychological Bulletin, 92,* 310–330.

Erickson, M. H. (1954a). Special techniques of brief hypnotherapy. *Journal of Clinical and Experimental Hypnosis, 2,* 109–129.

Erickson, M. H. (1954b). Pseudo-orientation in time as a hypnotherapeutic procedure. *Journal of Clinical and Experimental Hypnosis, 2,* 261–283.

Erickson, M. H. (1964). The confusion technique in hypnosis. *American Journal of Clinical Hypnosis, 6*, 183–207.

Farrah, G. A., Milehus, N. J., & Reitz, W. (1977). *The Self-Concept and Motivation Inventory: What Face Would You Wear?* Dearborn Heights, MI: Person-O-Metrics, Inc.

Felner, R. D., Farber, S., & Primavera, J. (1983). Transitions and stressful life events: A model for primary prevention. In R. D. Felner, L. A. Jason, J. N. Moritsugu, & S. S. Farber (Eds.), *Preventive psychology: Theory, research, and practice* (pp. 11–25). New York: Pergamon.

Fine, M. J. (ed.) (1980). *Handbook on parent education.* New York: Academic Press.

Fine, M. J., & Holt, P. (1983). Intervening with school problems: A family systems perspective. *Psychology in the Schools, 20*, 59–66.

Finkelhor, D. (1986). *A sourcebook on child sexual abuse.* Beverly Hills, CA: Sage.

Friedman, R. (1969). A structured family interview in the assessment of school learning disorders. *Psychology in the Schools, 6*, 162–171.

Forehand, R. L., & McMahon, R. J., (1981). *Helping the noncompliant child.* New York: Guilford Press.

Furstenberg, F., & Spanier, G. (1984). *Recycling the family.* Beverly Hills, CA: Sage.

Garfield, S. (1971). Research on client variables in psychotherapy. In S. Garfield & A. Bergin, (Eds.), *Handbook of psychotherapy and behavior change: An empirical analysis* (pp. 271–298). New York: Wiley.

Garrigan, J. J., & Bambrick, A. F. (1977). Introducing novice therapists to "go-between" techniques of family therapy. *Family Process, 16*, 237–246.

Gelman, D., Greenberg, M. F., Coppola, V., Burgower, B., Doherty, S., Anderson, M., & Williams, E. (1985, July 15). Playing both mother and father; The single parent family albums. *Newsweek*, 42–50.

Goh, D., Teslow, C. J., & Fuller, G. B. (1981). The practice of psychological assessment among school psychologists. *Professional Psychology, 12*, 696–706.

Guidubaldi, J., Cleminshaw, H. K., Perry, J. D., & McLoughlin, C. S. (1983). The impact of parental divorce on children: Report of the nationwide NASP study. *School Psychology Review, 12*, 300–323.

Guili, C. A., & Hudson, W. W. (1977). Child's attitude toward mother and father. *Journal of Social Service Research, 1*, 77–92.

Haley, J. (Ed.) (1967). *Advanced techniques of hypnosis and therapy: Selected papers of Milton H. Erickson, M.D.* New York: Grune & Stratton.

Haley, J. (1973). *Uncommon therapy: The psychiatric techniques of Milton H. Erickson, M.D.* New York: Norton.

Haley, J. (1976). *Problem solving therapy.* San Francisco: Gossey-Bass.

Haley, J. (1980). *Leaving home: The therapy of disturbed young people.* New York: McGraw-Hill

Hare–Mustin, R. (1975). Treatment of temper tantrums by a paradoxical intervention. *Family Process, 14*, 481–485.

Hartmen, A. (1979). *Finding families: An ecological approach to family assessment in adoption.* Beverly Hills, CA: Sage.

Hazzard, A., & Angert, L. (1986, August). *Child sexual abuse prevention: Previous resrarch and future directions.* Paper presented at the annual meeting of the American Psychological Association, Washington, DC.

Hetherington, E. M. (1979). Divorce: A child's perspective. *American Psychologist, 34*, 851–858.

Hobbs, N. (1975). *The futures of children.* San Francisco: Jossey–Bass.

Hobbs, N. (1982). *The troubled and troubling child.* San Francisco: Jossey–Bass.

Hoffman, L. (1981). *Foundations of family therapy.* New York: Basic Books.
Holman, A. M. (1983). *Family assessment: Tools for understanding and intervention.* Beverly Hill, CA: Sage
Koss, M. (1979). Length of psychotherapy for clients seen in private practice. *Journal of Consulting and Clinical Psychology, 47,* 210–212.
Kurdek, L. A. (1981). An integrative perspective on children's divorce adjustment. *American Psychologist, 36,* 856–866.
Levitan, S., & Belous, R. (1981). *What's happening to the American family?* Baltimore, MD: Johns Hopkins University Press.
Lightfoot, S. L. (1978). *Worlds apart: Relationships between Families and schools.* New York: Basic Books.
Lindblad–Goldberg, M., & Dukes, J. (1985). Social support in black, low-income single-parent families: Normative and dysfunctional patterns. *American Journal of Orthopsychiatry, 55,* 42–58.
Lusterman, D–D. (1984, June). *School and family as ecosystem: An application of Olson, Sprenkle and Russell's Circumplex Model.* Paper presented at the annual meeting of the American Family Therapy Association.
Lusterman, D–D. (1985). An ecosystemic approach to family school problems. *The American Journal of Family Therapy, 13,* 22–30.
Madanes, C. (1980). Protection, paradox and pretending. *Family Process, 19,* 73–85.
Madanes, C. (1981). *Strategic family therapy.* San Francisco: Jossey–Bass.
Martin, R. P. (1978). Expert and referent power: A framework for understanding and maximizing consultation effectiveness. *Journal of School Psychology, 16,* 49–55.
Mayer, R. E. (1983). *Thinking, problem solving, cognition.* New York: Freeman.
Miller, G. (1983). Children and the congress: A time to speak out. *American Psychologist, 38,* 70–76.
Miller, J. G. (1972). Living systems: The organization. *Behavioral Science, 17,* 19–29.
Minuchin, S. (1974). *Families & family therapy: A family model.* Cambridge, Mass: Harvard University Press.
Minuchin, S. (1970). The use of an ecological framework in the treatment of a child. In E. J. Anthony & C. Koupernik (eds.), *The child and his family (The international yearbook for child psychiatry and allied disciplines, Vol. 1* (pp. 41-57). New York: Wiley.
Mooney, R. L., & Gordon, L. V. (1953). *Mooney problem checklist.* Cleveland, OH: Psychological Corporation.
Moos, R. H. (1974). *Family Environment Scale.* Palo Alto, CA: Consulting Psychologists Press, Inc.
Moynihan, D. (1986). *Family and nation.* San Diego, CA: Harcourt Brace Jovanovich.
National Center on Child Abuse and Neglect. (1982). *Profile of child sexual abuse.* Rockville, MD: Clearinghouse on Child Abuse and Neglect Information.
Newbrough, J. R., Walker, L., & Abril, S. (1978, April). *Workshop on ecological assessment.* National Association of School Psychologists, New York.
Offer, P. (1979). *The psychological world of the teenager: A study of normal adolescent boys.* New York: Basic Books.
Olson, D. H., Bell, R., & Portner, J. (1978). *Family Adaptability and Cohesion Evaluation Scales.* University of Minnesota.
Olson, D. H., & Killarin, E. (1985). *Clinical Rating Scale for the Circumplex Model.* St. Paul, MN: Family Social Sciences, University of Minnesota.
Olson, D. H., McCubbin, H. I., Barnes, H., Larsen, A., Muxen, M., & Wilson, M. (1983). *Families: What makes them work.* Los Angeles: Sage.
Olson, D. H., Russel, C. S., & Sprenkle, D. H. (1983). Circumplex model, VI: Theoretical update. *Family Process, 22,* 169–183.

Olson, H. D., Sprenkle, D. H., & Russell, C. S. (1979). Circumplex model of marital and family systems: I. Cohesion and adaptability dimensions, family types, and clinical applications. *Family Process, 18,* 3–28.

Papp, P. (1980). The Greek chorus and other techniques of paradoxical therapy. *Family Process, 19,* 45–57.

Patterson, G. R., Reid, J. B., Jones, R. R., & Conger, R. E. (1975). *A social learning approach to family intervention, Volume 1: Families with aggressive children.* Eugene, OR: Castalia Publishing Co.

Pedro-Carroll, J. (1986, August). *Preventive interventions for children of divorce: Implementation and evaluation of a time limited group approach.* Paper presented at the annual meeting of the American Psychological Association, Washington, DC.

Pedro–Carroll, J. L., & Cowen, E. L. (1985). The children of divorce intervention program. *Journal of Consulting and Clinical Psychology, 53,* 603–611.

Pfeiffer, S., & Tittler, B. (1983). Utilizing the multidisciplinary team to facilitate a school family systems orientation. *School Psychology Review, 12,* 168–173.

Plas, J. M. (1986). *Systems psychology in the schools.* New York: Pergamon Press.

Poche, C., Brouwer, R., & Swearingen, M. (1981). Teaching self-protection to young children. *Journal of Applied Behavior Analysis, 14,* 169–176.

Quay, H. C., & Peterson, D. R. (1967). *Behavior Problem Checklist.* Champaign, IL: University of Illinois Child Research Center, University of Miami.

Raskin, D. E., & Klein, Z. E. (1976). Losing a symptom through keeping it: A review of paradoxical treatment techniques and rationale. *Archives of General Psychiatry, 33,* 548–555.

Reid, J. B. (Ed.) (1978). *A social learning approach to family intervention, Volume 2: Observation in home settings.* Eugene, OR: Castalia Publishing Co.

Report of the Select Committee on Children, Youth, and Families, 98th Congress. (1983). *U. S. Children and their families: Current conditions and recent trends.* Washington, DC: Foundation for Child Development.

Schaefer, E. S. (1965). Child report of parent behavior. *Child Development, 36,* 413–423.

Selvini–Palazzoli, M. Boscolo, C., Cecchin, G., & Prata, G. (1974). The treatment of children through brief therapy with their parents. *Family Process, 13,* 429–442.

Selvini–Palazzoli, M. Boscolo, C., Cecchin, G., & Prata, G. (1978). *Paradox and Counterparadox.* New York: Aronson.

Soper, P. H., & L'Abate, L. (1977). Paradox as a therapeutic technique. A review. *International Journal of Family Counseling, 5,* 10–21.

Spiegel, H. & Linn, L. (1969). The "ripple effect" following adjunct hypnosis in analytic psychotherapy. *American Journal of Psychiatry, 126,* 53–56.

Stolberg, A. L., & Cullen, P. M. (1983). Preventing psychopathology in children of divorce: The divorce adjustment project. In L. Kurdek (Ed.), *New direction for child development: Children and divorce.* (pp 161–203). San Francisco: Jossey-Bass.

Stolberg, A. L., Cullen, P. M., & Garrison, K. M. (1982). The divorce adjustment project: Preventive programming for children of divorce. *Journal of Preventive Psychiatry, 1,* 365–368.

Stolberg, A. L., & Garrison, K. M. (1985). Evaluating a primary prevention program for children of divorce: The Divorce Adjustment Project. *American Journal of Community Psychology, 13,* 111–124.

Stuart, R. B., & Stuart, F. (1975) *Family Pre-Counseling Inventory.* Champaign, IL: Research Press.

Thorpe, P., Clark, W. W., & Tiegs, E. W. (1953). *California Test of Personality.* New York: CTB/McGraw–Hill.

Toal, S. D. (1985). *Children's safety and protection training project: Three interrelated analysis.* Stockton, CA: Toal Consultation Services.

Treffinger, D., & Fine, M. (1979, November/December) When there's a problem in school. *Gifted/Creative/Talented Magazine,* 3–6.
U.S. Bureau of the Census (1982). *Marriage and marriage rates, by age and previous marital status of women and men: 1981 and 1982.* (Monthly Vital Statistics, Volume 34, Table 5). Washington, DC: U.S. Government Printing Office.
U.S. Bureau of the Census. (1985). *Characteristics of the population below the poverty level: 1983.* (Current population Reports, Series P-60, No. 134). Washington, D.C.: U.S. Government Printing Office.
von Bertalanffy, L. (1981). *A systems view of man.* Boulder, CO: Westview Press.
von Glasersfeld, E. (1984a). An introduction to radical constructivism. In P. Watzlawick, (Ed.). *The invented reality* (pp. 17–35). New York: Norton.
van Glasersfeld, E. (1984b, June). *Steps in the construction of "others" and "reality": A study in self-regulation.* Paper delivered at the 7th European Meeting on Cybernetics and Systems Research, Vienna.
Wallerstein, J. S. (1983). Children of divorce: Stress and developmental tasks. In N. Garmely & M. Rutter (Eds.), *Stress, coping, and development in children* (pp. 265–302). New York: McGraw–Hill.
Wallerstein, J. S., & Kelly, J. B. (1979). Children and divorce: A review. *Social Work, 24,* 468–475.
Watzlawick, P., Beavin, J., & Jackson, D. D. (1967). *Pragmatics of human communication.* New York: Norton.
Watzlawick, P., Weakland, J., & Fisch, R. (1974). *Change.* New York: W. W. Norton.
Weeks, G. R., & L'Abate, L. A. (1979). A compilation of paradoxical methods. *American Journal of Family Therapy, 7,* 61–76.
Wendt, R., & Zake, J. (1984). Family systems theory and school psychology: Implications for training and practice. *Psychology in the Schools, 21,* 204–210.
Wise, P., & Ginther, D. (1981). Parent conferences: A brief commentary and an annotated bibliography. *School Psychology Review, 10,* 100–103.
Yogman, M. W., & Brazelton, T. B. (Eds.). (1986). *In support of families.* Cambridge, MA: Harvard University Press.

3

Private Practice as an Alternative Setting for School Psychologists

WALTER B. PRYZWANSKY
University of North Carolina at Chapel Hill

There was a time in school psychology's not-too-distant past that the mention of private practice drew suspicions of *back-door clinical psychology*. In fact, colleagues often questioned if school psychologists in private practice were "burn-outs" who simply could not cope with the complexities of the school setting. Evidence of those reactions are less likely today, or at least they are held in abeyance until some further diagnostic work can be planned.

When graduate students voiced the goal of entering private practice, this aspiration seemed in direct conflict with the training program's mission of preparing psychologists to work in the schools. In particular, if training programs existed in a university's School of Education, the prospect of substantial numbers of graduates seeking a full-time private practice was a questionable goal to reinforce, especially when considerations of program "fit" were involved. Indeed, a graduate employment pattern that reflects a large percentage of graduates in private practice would seem to raise legitimate questions regarding the program's contribution to the mission of the Education Department, if that mission held the public schools to be the primary target of its efforts. Overall, some of our psychology colleagues also voiced concern about the adequacy of training in school psychology as a *health service specialty* at the time of licensure application. Not as many of our psychological colleagues were as upset about that prospect as might have been thought, although some of their concerns were appropriate. Simply put, the training of some school psychologists to provide *health services* is questionable, particularly when private practice is defined in that way. The use of the term *health service provider* is based on the definition from the National Register of Health Service Providers in Psychology (Council of National Register, 1987). This psychology specialist is described as "a professional who is certified/licensed at the independent practice level in his/her state, who is duly trained and experienced in the delivery of direct, preventive, assessment and therapeutic intervention services to individuals whose growth, adjustment, or functioning is actually impaired or is demonstrably at high risk of impairment (Council, 1987, p. xv).

These introductory comments represent some of the anxieties, concerns, and issues that typically surround any discussion of school psychology private practice. The intent of this chapter is to examine this alternative role, beginning with a conceptual perspective. Likewise, the type of services involved in private practice is briefly explored, as well as the place of this alternative role within the total scheme of school psychological practice. Other aspects of private practice, such as the issues involving credentialing and training, are addressed. An examination of the prevalence of private practice in psychology, generally, and in school psychology, specifically, precede the first section's main objective of sharing reflections on the nature of school psychology practice in the independent practice sector.

BACKGROUND

Recent data suggest that only a small percentage of school psychologists engage in private practice. Based on 1980/1981 employment data for school psychology doctorates, 2.8% reported independent practice as their initial employment setting (Stapp, Fulcher, & Wicherski, 1984). Five years later, a survey of 1985 school psychology doctorate recipients found 5% who reported full-time positions in independent practice settings (Pion, Bramblett, & Wicherski, 1987). In fact, 74% reported employment in educational settings (e.g., schools, universities, other academic sites). In another survey sponsored by the American Psychological Association's (APA) Division of School Psychology, slightly less than half of the school psychologists in the sample had applied for licensure through their state psychology boards (Wendt & Tucker, 1983). Although more than 96% of those surveyed felt there was a role for school psychologists in private practice, only one third indicated that their training program presented private practice as an option. Of the national sample of psychologists who indicated they engaged in private practice, 51% reported working only 0–9 hours per week. So too, while some 33% of Ohio practitioners were involved in private practice, 69% of this private practice group worked 1–9 hours per week (Wendt & Tucker, 1983). In both the national and Ohio samples, the desire to supplement income was given as the primary purpose to engage in private practice. Another interesting finding of the Wendt and Tucker survey was the fact that licensed school psychologists working on a private basis still engaged in assessment activities as their major function. Similarly, studies of psychologists in general independent practice indicated a bimodal distribution with psychologists practicing either on a limited basis or a full-time basis (Norcross, Nash, & Prochaska, 1985). Furthermore, approximately one half of these psychologists involved in private practice were committed to such service for 10 hours or less per week.

The overall interpretation of both sets of data seems obvious. Private practice for a significant proportion of all psychologists is part-time, and the consequences of such a level of commitment needs to be studied in terms of its impact on the nature of service, as well as perceptions of the public concerning such part-time services. It is important to note that since these studies were reported, the cost of malpractice insurance has risen dramatically and has become harder to obtain. As such, these issues may have or will become a factor for those psychologists and, in particular, school psychologists continuing with small practices.

Given the small numbers of school psychologists engaged in private practice, it should not be surprising that little has been written about the independent practice of school psychology. As a result, conditions have been ripe for the development of myths regarding the description of practice. However, even more surprising is the fact that little has been written about private practice in general. As these data indicate, this type of employment is not widespread for psychologists regardless of specialty areas. In 1977, it was reported that 7% of all psychologists were engaged in full-time practice (Dörken, 1977), whereas almost 19% of 17,733 respondents to the American Psychological Association's Human Resources Survey, completed in 1978, reported such employment (VanderBos, Stapp and Kilburg, 1981). Finally, to round out the available data on percentages of psychologists in independent practice, 6.1% of 1979 and 1980 doctoral recipients in all of the applied specialties indicated they had gone into private practice (Stapp et al., 1984) as their first employment setting.

Descriptions of Service Systems and Models of Private Practice Service

Several articles have been written recently addressing proposals of new models for the private practice of psychology. For the most part, this literature deals with applied specialties other than school psychology and consists of two types. In one type, a particular orientation or content area is seen as enhancing private practice. Meltzer's (1986) discussion of the concepts of prevention, crisis intervention, and family, work, health-related consultation are examples of the specialty emphasis approach. In this model, consultation in the private setting deals with providing information on training in such areas as parenting or life-coping skills, such as living with a chronic illness or mental disorder. Crisis interventions are relevant in preparation for or after separation or loss type experiences, in work setting experiences, or in dealing with medical or physical disorders. Prevention involves services such as psychological check-ups for families or individuals, career-related assessments, as well as activities consistent with the holistic medicine movement. Meltzer's notions are based on the premise that there has been a move from the medical model to the community model in terms of treatment objectives. Similarly, Griswold (1980) proposed a *family practice* model which "provides a method of service delivery that not only would emphasize the maintenance of mental health and the prevention of mental illness, but would allow for interventions in the lives of patients that would be conducive to the maintenance of physical health as well" (p. 635). The result is that the practitioner can achieve greater autonomy while offering services to larger segments of the population.

At another descriptive level, several authors have begun to address the conceptual component of the service delivery (i.e., the empirical data base, theoretical notions and basic assumptions), as indicated by Rappaport and Chinsky (1974). Recently, Cummings (1986) presented a model of group private practice similar to the medical-preferred providers organizations (PPOs) in which psychologists with particular content specialties are able to offer a greater range of assistance to an individual client or organization. This model views the psychologist's specializations as that which distinguishes one psychologist from the other. Thus, service opportunities are enhanced as a result of the capabilities of the psychologists in the office. Similarly, Griswold (1980) reasoned that the counseling and school psychology specialties could be integrated in this proposed model of practice. This trend toward a metamorphosis of the traditional applied psychology specialties into one profession has been further developed by Levy (1984). He reasoned that a major realignment and reconceptualization of the specialties within the profession may be called for at this time. He recommended a generic applied profession identified as "human services psychology." This reconfigured professional aspiration would "include all professional psychology specialties concerned with the promotion of human well-being through the acquisition and application of psychological knowledge concerned with the treatment and prevention of psychological and physical disorders" (p. 490). Human services psychology would include, then, clinical psychology, counseling psychology, community psychology, health psychology, and school psychology.

Although Levy's (1984) proposal reflects the changes taking place in clinical psychology, it also contributes to a rather uncertain identity among some members of that specialty, as well as the pluralistic characteristic of the psychology profession as a whole. Levy's notion echoes a direction for all of professional psychology that is similar to what has been implied by those writing about private practice and involved with the APA specialty guidelines for providers of psychology service (APA, 1981a). The boundaries among the psychology specialties belong in this sector of practice as it is experienced today, and even more so as practice in the public area is envisioned for the future. For those school psychologists who embrace a health service provider identity, such a change may be welcomed; this integration of health oriented specialties certainly would result in less dissonance when the psychologist moves among employment settings. However, for those school psychologists who see themselves in the applied educational psychologist role presented by Bardon (1983), the description of private practice would be quite different.

PRIVATE PRACTICE IN SCHOOL PSYCHOLOGY

Within the school psychology literature, very little has been written about private practice. Perhaps psychologists with training in this specialty feel they must shift their content and organizational identity to another area to be creditable and keep up-to-date as private practitioners. Or, some of the earlier points that were made regarding this service emphasis may explain this meager literature. Wenger (1982) suggested three additional reasons for this lack of attention. First, school psychology is a young specialty, still in its developmental stages, and only now beginning to look toward expanding employment opportunities. Also, there may be a "setting-bound" perception in that the specialty is seen as only practical in public schools. However, the very emergence of this book suggests that school psychology may be ready to enlarge past the schools. Finally, private practice may be synonymous with the practice of psychotherapy for some, and given the minimal attention directed toward this type of training in school psychology programs, a competence issue may be involved.

On the other hand, as the private practice option becomes realized, a host of writings may be ushered into the literature. Recently, then, Harries' (1982) chapter deals more with the practical day-to-day details of running a private practice than the nature and type of services that could be delivered. By contrast, Patrick, Sandargas, and Wiberley (1980) described their private practice with a developmental optometrist in which the assessment role is emphasized. In addition, they coordinated a program with the parents and the school, were involved in consultation, and offered mental-health services in conjunction with vision related interventions. Roosa (1982) contrasts the glamour of private practice, which can be imagined from the perspective of the psychologist in the school, with the realities of developing and maintaining independent practice.

In more of a conceptual piece, Wenger (1982) gave examples of the private practice of school psychology as extrapolated from the six major school psychological functions presented in the APA Specialty Guidelines for the Delivery of Services by School Psychologists (APA, 1981b). Those functions and the perceived private practice role for the school psychologist are briefly summarized. The first function is "psychological and psychoeducational evaluation and assessment of the school functioning of children and young persons" (p. 504). Wenger notes that this could be a major component in a private practice through private evaluations for parents and contracted arrangements with schools. Secondly, "interventions to facilitate the functioning of individuals and groups with concern for how schooling influences and is influenced by their cognitive, conative, affective, and social development" (p. 504). In private practice, he sees this function taking the form of psychological counseling, psychoeducational therapy, or coping skills training of moderate duration. A contractual arrangement with schools to enhance their school psychological unit services is one mode of private practice delivery. Thirdly, "interventions to facilitate the educational services and child-care functions of school personnel, parents and community agencies" (p. 505) are seen as having significant prevention potential. Parent counseling and education along with in-service training for school personnel would be examples in this area. The next function, "consultation and collaboration with school personnel and/or parents concerning specific school-related problems of students and the professional problems of staff" (p. 505) could also serve as a major service component in the practice. School psychology training emphasizes this skill and the advantages of the external locus of the service could be maximized. It is argued that the content is "limitless" and could focus on specific cases or entire programs. Next, "program development services and evaluations" (p. 505) provide an opportunity to apply the skills of some school psychologists in private practice. Their training in the evaluation as well as implementation of programs would make them uniquely qualified to provide such services. Finally, "supervision of school psychological services" (p. 505) could be provided through contractual arrangements with one or more systems and would facilitate the application of the school practitioner for licensure in some states. As can be seen from this model, the base of the services remains the prime difference between school practice and private practice, with educational and child care agencies remaining the largest consumers of the service.

In summary, then, while the full-time private practice of psychology is growing, the percentage of psychologists who are committed to this type of employment on a full-time basis is relatively small for psychology as a whole and negligible for school psychology. Furthermore, Taylor (1978) concluded, "fairytale conceptualizations concerning the private practice of psychology are widespread among peers working in other settings, clients, and the general public" (p. 68). In order to obtain information about full-time practitioners in psychology, Tyron (1983) surveyed 165 systematically selected psychologists listed in the 1980 *National Register of Health Service Providers in Psychology* who indicated they were exclusively in private practice. The results were interesting, and some of the findings are germaine to this discussion. The majority of these psychologists (56%) were eclectic in orientation, with 63% of the psychologists accepting children, and 83% accepting adolescents as patients. Among their referral sources, the schools ranked next to last in a list of nine sources and, consequently, such referrals made up only a small percentage of their practice. Ninety-seven percent of the survey respondents held the doctorate. Their comments about the adequacy of their graduate training were somewhat mixed when rated in relation to the objective of preparation for private practice, and particularly weak where the operation/business aspect of a private practice was concerned.

Those who see a continued rise in the number of private practitioners base their projections on several developments, such as (a) the current federal government's inclination to cut back on spending in the public sector, as well as (b) the rapid growth in professional psychology training programs (Psy.D.), (c) the higher income (Stapp & Fulcher, 1981) one can expect in private practice, and (d) the prospect of professional independence. One recent significant development that negates this prospect of growth is the rise of the Health Maintenance Organizations (HMOs) and their influence on patients' use of specialized health care, particularly as it relates to mental-health services. In fact, Cummings (1986) envisioned a future where an individual private practice would be the exception rather than the rule. Instead, he advocates a group practice for psychologists where they would form a Preferred Provider Organization (PPO) in order to compete within this future marketplace. However, rather than the group practice simply serving as a collection of individual psychologists doing their own thing, so to speak, psychologists' PPOs would concentrate on providing brief therapy on an intermittant basis over a significant period of a person's life span. In other words, each psychologist in this practice would have developed a proficiency in certain content and/or skill areas which would distinguish the contribution to the PPO services.

THE NATURE OF SCHOOL PSYCHOLOGY PRIVATE PRACTICE

Well, what does this all mean for school psychology? Should we advocate a private practice role for school psychologists? Is there a contradiction for a specialty, which seems married to a setting by its title, to even consider alternative settings, or an apparently different mode for delivery of its services such as independent practice? Is there an aspect to all of this that borders on a violation of the American Psychological Association's ethical principle regarding competence, which states that the professional should only function within the domains in which they are clearly trained?

Conceptual Issues

Conceptually, when we attempt to describe the private practice of school psychologists, we are faced with an inescapable dilemma inherent in the professional's title. School psychology is psychology *applied to* and *practiced in* the schools. It is setting-specific, then, in the sense that what is unique in the training of these psychologists, in large measure, is their understanding of the schooling process and the institutions in which schooling takes place. Specific knowledge about schooling and the skills for working in the setting may be said to set the school psychologist apart from other psychologists. In reviewing a recent job analysis of applied psychologists' work by the *Educational Test Service,* Bardon (1986) observed that although there were skills and knowledge held in common by the four psychology specialties (i.e., school, clinical, counseling and industrial-organization), there were important differences. He noted that "these were probably differences in orientation, intentions, sensitivity, and attraction to different settings, and special proficiencies that derive from these attitudinal and educational background differences leading each group to differentially perceive and direct its attention and efforts to different problems in different ways" (p. 32). However, he went on to observe that "these are areas of subtle difference about which we know precious little" (p. 32). When one moves to another setting, then, it is hard to envision how the school psychologist could practice school psychology if you accept the premise just articulated. It has been argued that, in the private practice realm, the provision of psychological service from a school, clinical, or counseling psychologist became more alike than different; those aspects of training in each of the specialties became more important than the training that had established them as specialties. But for some of us, school psychology is not setting-specific, and the above argument is rejected. Although that position has yet to be fully articulated, it is relevant, obviously, to the extent that it deals with the *role* of the school psychologist. That role recently has been described as one either of a *health service provider* or an *applied educational psychologist*. When one applies for licensure as a psychologist, and if licensure is independent private-practice-oriented in the State, the health service provider role is consistent with that type of credential. In those instances, hard choices will need to be made by most school psychologists in terms of training emphases and identity. Nonetheless, a helpful exercise may be to speculate as to the private practice of two school psychologists trained within one of these two approaches or service models.

Probably, we can dispense of the extrapolation of the *health service provider* type school psychologist to the private practice setting rather quickly. In this instance, their practice is likely to be child and/or adolescent-oriented and deal with content that parents and referral agencies are most likely to seek out when utilizing private services. These school psychologists' practice is indeed like psychologists from other applied psychology areas espousing a health service identity, except perhaps in areas of specialization. They are likely, but not necessarily, to have training and experience in delivering direct services (assessment and intervention), which would seem to be axiomatic whenever the private practice notion is discussed. To the extent their training experience was toward an indirect service model (e.g., consultation), the shift to a direct service private practice will be difficult. However, the direct-indirect service continuum as a factor in private practice will be addressed later. For now, however, the health service provider role seems to be more compatible with traditional practice in the private sector. It includes, usually, a more traditional diagnostic approach and intervention which is, in most part, provided to the client directly.

In the *applied educational psychologist* approach, both the content and delivery of the service are removed from traditional private practice functions. The psychologist focuses on the instructional process, wherein the cognitive domain receives most of the attention, and the behavioral/emotional domains are considered as they begin to either support or interfere with the learning process. For the most part, the school psychologist in the schools would help the instructional staff in finding the right match between the child's pattern of strengths and weaknesses as a learner and the schooling approaches that would facilitate learning.

What, then, is the nature of the private practice of this school psychologist? A recent request involving the author provides one illustration of that practice. A parent called about his adolescent son who had been diagnosed as Learning Disabled, and was now attending a private high school. There were no school psychologists employed by this private school. Apparently, the teachers were in need of assistance in planning ways to help the young man in the classroom. The father was seeking a psychologist who could evaluate his son and provide such information to the staff. In essence, then, private practice in this sense involves basically doing what might be done in an instructional consultation model. However, the individual parent was paying for the "expert" help which was not available as part of the school services. With little imagination, we could see a role for this applied school psychologist in private practice to become an "agent" and/or "advocate" for the student on behalf of the parents. Not only would parents be assisted in coping with such a formidable responsibility, but the psychologist could continue to represent the parents at Individual Educational Plan (IEP) and/or team meetings or individual conferences with teachers over a planned period of time. The analogy would be arranging for braces for your child. For example, even though some orthodontics patients began as junior high-school students and have long since had their braces removed, their "Crest" smiles would be monitored as part of the original commitment and contracted fee, sometimes well into their college years. In fact, that period can continue through the wisdom tooth stage (which may turn out to be a critical dental period), but yet those consultations would be part of the original fee. The applied school psychologist could provide services following such a service model. Parents would no longer need to feel they had to shoulder all the advocacy responsibilities, have to insure collaborations among all professionals working with their child, and learn to be an expert. To be sure, the school psychologist in private practice would do just that.

In addition to the purpose of the specialty and role influences, two more observations about private practice of school psychology need to be made. First, school psychologists must recognize that a different *orientation* will be involved in this type of service. When working as a member of the school staff the school psychologist is able to take a more wholistic perspective and consider many options for helping the student; in other words, knowing the system on an intimate level facilitates such a scanning process. With this systems information comes the potential to have more leverage in getting things done. The constraint, which is associated with this advantage, is that the professional can also be expected to know what the system is capable of delivering and work out some accomodations that reflect the system's resources and values in any planning efforts.

In private practice the target is the child/student and his/her needs. The practitioner can clearly advocate for the child with no inhibition that the system's constraints need to be a concern in planning for the client. The practitioner is also more likely to deal with issues related to the child's total experience and as such to have more potential to impact on the home environment. However, that leverage with the parents comes at some expense. If part of the problem involves interactional issues at school rather than being child focused (e.g., teacher–student relationships or student–school matches), then the private practitioner is going to face the same constraints anyone external to a system confronts and will be left to rely on exerting expert power. Similarly, the nature of the consultation that is conducted from a private practice office will be influenced by monetary as well as obligatory commitments.

Oakland (1986) recently wrote that an "expansion of independent practice by school psychologists jeopardizes its practice in institutions and increases the likelihood of confrontation with other specialities" (p. 25). *In some respects,* the influence on school practice can be dramatic. For example, the HMO and PPO developments in the medical field are trends that need to be reckoned with already. They have had a significant impact on the independent practice of individual psychologists and, to some degree, group practices. The response has been for psychologists to come together and form mental health PPOs. Such PPOs may include only psychologists, but they could involve other mental health providers such as social workers, psychiatric nurses, and even psychiatrists. The PPOs, in turn, would offer services to employers and some state agencies and, in doing so, compete with other "vendors" of health services. As a result, they would serve as their own "gatekeepers" and reduce the influence of the HMO. It seems very likely that doctoral school psychologists would become involved in such PPOs. With the passing of time, as members of the PPO, or through using this concept form their own School Psychology PPO, contracts would be developed with school systems for school psychological services. In one Division 16 Presidential Message, Pryzwansky (1986) wrote that Cummings' (1986) private practice model offers many intriguing ideas for developing alternative school psychological models of service to what we now find in many school based units. However, the same idea could be applied to a PPO, which then contracts with a school board to provide psychological services. Such contractual services would be much more sophisticated and potentially more professionally viable than the 94–142 contractual services currently offered. Although the benefits of such a PPO model are best realized by school psychologists in schools, it would not be surprising to see it offered to private schools, as well as becoming integrated as part of services offered by larger school systems.

IMPLICATIONS

In the previous section, some background, which needs attention when private practice is considered as an alternative setting for school psychologists, was presented. It is also important that school psychologists, both practitioners and trainers, recognize some important conceptual points related to both (a) the definition of this specialty, like the influence of the primary setting for these psychologists and the role for which they were trained in the setting, and the (b) characteristics of private practice, such as the current expectation for direct service and the orientation of the independent practitioner, when private practice is considered. Finally, there are several external factors that are influencing the private practice of all psychologists such as skyrocketing malpractice insurance rates, the growth of the HMO movement, and credential issues. These factors will have a dramatic influence on private practice and the opportunities for psychologists trained as school psychologists. Ironically, these influences on private practice have the potential to impact practice in the schools as much as any other developments in the specialty.

Additionally, two major considerations remain regarding the independent practice of school psychology. First, developments of the past decade regarding the regulation of all professions can affect the growth of school psychology as a specialty. Also, the fact that two credentials exist for school psychologists complicates the discussion of private practice options. Secondly, the implications of preparing graduates for this alternative role, not only suggest specific skill training, but present interesting questions related to the mission and objectives of training school psychologists.

Credentialing Influences

The two main credentials for school psychologists also dramatize the complexity of the private practice option. Certification of school psychologists by State Departments of Public Instruction (SDPI) represents a state issued educational credential which was legislated to regulate practice *in the schools*. This credential often reflects the degree options available from training programs in the respective states. For school psychology, that characteristic means that any combination of master's degree, specialist training, or doctoral degree may serve as the educational criteria for awarding the credential. Some of these certified personnel, then, have argued that they should be eligible for licensure to offer these same services independently to the public. However, it is important to recognize that the SDPI certification statute is, most likely, not necessarily written to imply competence at an independent level. Rather, it is intended to govern practice in an employment setting with built-in supervisory and/or accountability expectations. Thus, the argument that one should be able to do in the private sector independently what one has been certified to do in the public sector, fails to recognize this important premise of a credential that is setting-specific.

In 1985, the National Association of School Psychologists published its *Standards for the Credentialing of School Psychologists* (NASP, 1985) to "provide guidance to state credentialing bodies for upgrading their school psychology-related certification and licensure practices" (p. 25). The recommended minimum entry-level educational criterion listed in these standards requires the completion of a 60 graduate semester-hour program that includes an internship. Up to 400 hours of the internship can be waived or given credit for previous psychological or educational professional experience. Subsequently, three years of successful supervised experience is also recommended for the independent practice level. Finally, it is suggested that the independent practice credential be renewed every five years subject to acceptance of continuing education activities. NASP *Standards* are intended to authorize "the exclusive use of the title School Psychologist in all settings, public and private" (p. 27).

By contrast, licensure is a statutory credential administered by a board of professionals along with some public members. In the instance of school psychology, where it is considered a specialty of psychology, licensure as a psychologist is most relevant. Licensure may be of two major types (Pryzwansky & Wendt, 1987). In instances where the credential strictly regulated use of a professional title (e.g., psychologist and/or its derivatives), it may be referred to as *certification*. However, in this instance, certification is a psychology credential, as opposed to the credential offered by SDPI. A second type, *licensing*, regulates not only the title, but professional practice as well, in the sense that it delimits the practice to be offered to only those professionals licensed, and protects the right of the professional to offer those services. As with SDPI certification, psychology licensure laws vary, to a certain extent, from state to state, and may recognize levels of degree and various training emphases among their eligibility criteria (American Association of State Psychology Boards, 1986; Pryzwansky & Wendt, 1987). Because a mechanism often does not exist for credentialing the private practice of school psychology,

psychology licensure becomes the available route to private practice. Consequently, the standards of the psychology profession become salient.

As of February 1987, the American Psychological Association adopted a revised Model Licensing Bill (APA, 1987). As a result, they are suggesting to state psychological groups that they strive to duplicate the standards of entry into private practice of psychology as recommended in that Bill. The Bill, then, is an aspirational target, a professional goal in the credentialing area. Several important features of the Bill relate to the practice of school psychology. First, school psychologists "certified by the state education agency are permitted to use the terms 'school psychologist' or 'certified school psychologist' as long as they are practicing in the public schools" (p. 21). This exemption for use of the title "psychologist" also calls for such individuals certified after 1995 to have graduated from a program accredited by an appropriate body. Secondly, in terms of licensure, the doctorate was set as the minimum educational requirement for entry into professional practice. Also by 1995, the applicants' doctorate is to be based on work in a program accredited by the American Psychological Association. It is obvious then, in contrasting this Bill (and the APA *Specialty Guidelines* [APA, 1981] content which it reflects) with the NASP *Standards* (NASP, 1985) that entry level to independent private practice is defined differently by each organization.

Currently, not all states' psychology licensing laws reflect the features of this Bill. For example, at least four states allow for school psychologists to be licensed at a subdoctoral level in psychology (Pryzwansky, 1982). Similarly, Block (1987) reported five additional states in which subdoctoral licensure for private practice by school psychologists is available through another type of regulatory board than psychology. She also reported that additional states may permit the independent practice of school psychologists only in a restrictive manner, and usually that practice is limited to education-related problems. A national certification examination for school psychologists, which would be adopted by SDPIs, has been proposed as another way to ensure the best practice of school psychology and promote the private practice alternative (Lazarus, 1982). In fact, there is a current effort underway that makes the realization of such an exam a viable target for the near future. However, this alternative, as well as the options that have evolved under licensure, have the potential for long-term negative consequences if not carefully pursued. As we can see from the licensure discussion, doctoral-level school psychologists, if they choose to continue their identity within the psychology licensure arena in some states, they could have their practice restricted. Licensure at the doctoral level then might require a shift in their identity if, in fact, any such options would remain open to them. Given the fact that the specialty seems to be approaching its long sought-after status as a doctoral specialty (Fagan, 1986), it would be ironic that school psychology licensure efforts outside the mainstream of psychology would be detrimental to doctoral-level school psychologists. Similarly, SDPI certification usually does not recognize the doctoral degree either by title or other credentialing provision. Even more distressing is the fact that a hallmark of psychology credentials, *Diplomate in School Psychology* from the *American Board of Professional Psychology,* is currently not recognized in the certification process. Yet, it could serve as School Psychology's top ring in the SDPI career ladder framework. Those individuals interested in continuing the strides made toward achieving a comprehensive professional training standard for school psychology in the future will need to address such certification circumstances.

Training Issues

The question of the changes and/or additions to the current training of school psychologists, which may be required when private practice is targeted as an employment objective, is intriguing to say the least. On the one hand, it implies that such practice will be sufficiently different from what is expected in the schools, and that some training changes are involved. Interestingly, in a study of members from the APA Division of Psychologists in Independent Practice who were engaged in part-time independent practice, high percentages of them routinely excluded certain types of clients, such as the physically violent, psychotic, and organically impaired; most of this professional group possessed the doctorate and were employed full-time in clinics or non-university institutions (Norcross, Nash, & Prochaska, 1985). Indeed, this group of part-time practitioners expressed dissatisfaction with their graduate training preparation for independent practice. There is little data regarding school psychologists' experiences in private practice, although Roosa (1982) noted an increase in therapist-related functions but, in general, found himself performing many of the same functions as when employed as a school psychologist. Wendt and Tucker (1983) found "striking similarities" between school practice and practice in the private domain with psychological assessments as the major activity. Some consultation and individual psychotherapy, as well as marital and family therapy were also reported.

It seems reasonable to assume that school psychologists can be expected to engage in similar activities, regardless of employment setting. In fact, Hill and Block (1987) maintain that the independent private practice of school psychology is virtually a mirror image of how it is practiced in the public sector, and the most commonly allowed model is assessment/placement. However, their conceptualization of the school psychologist's role, as discussed earlier in this chapter, may dictate how relevant the preparation of this professional is to the demands and needs reflected by the population seeking private services. In this sense, then, the skills obtained in training are "transportable" among settings, as Hughes (1987) has argued. At the same time, the private practitioner can expect that a proficiency will need to be developed also (e.g., child abuse, eating disorders, family therapy, divorce) to sustain a practice, particularly as the individual practitioner moves beyond a limited private practice commitment. In this latter instance, additional course(s) and supervised field-based training may be required. Indeed, in some instances, post-doctoral training may be appropriate to consider. If the model of group practice discussed earlier was to become standard for the field, then the enhanced training model being described here would seem appropriate.

Although an expanded model of training at the predoctoral level seems reasonable for those who intend a full-time independent practice, training in marketing, office management, and business operation-related skills will be necessary. Similarly, knowledge regarding developments affecting health service providers (e.g., HMO's, hospital privileges, liability insurance) will need to be incorporated into the training. However, given the low percentage of students entering private practice, and the focus of Schools of Education, there is a likelihood that such content covered in great depth will need to be obtained in departments and professional contexts other than those targeted for school psychologists. The task of obtaining such knowledge and orientation is exacerbated for the individual with the specialist's degree, in that such programs are usually at their stretching point in terms of required courses. A more radical option, of course, is for a reduction in the *schooling* emphases in the specialist and doctoral programs and thereby, eliminating this "add to" option. Needless to say, such a shift may have serious implications for the future survival of the specialty in the schools.

Rather than as a full-time employment alternative, larger numbers of school psychologists are likely to continue to become involved with private practice for its supplementary economic benefits and, to a lesser degree, as a way to expand their skills (Wendt & Tucker, 1983). The role of private practice for school psychologists needs an increasing level of attention in the literature because of its status as well as economic implications for school psychologists trained at the specialist's level. In a recent survey of practicing school psychologists (Smith, 1984), a conflict of sorts may be suggested. Although school psychologists wanted to spend less time in assessments (which a move to private practice might not affect), the desire to deal with a general school population would be consistent with the calls for a new direction in psychological practice. Also, school psychologists, like most other psychologists, work in a setting that is not primarily psychological. The schools generally are neither administered by psychologists, nor are psychologists primarily employed in the setting. This absence of a psychological perspective, as Griswold (1980) explained, makes private practice very attractive because it provides the most freedom to function "without the administrative or philosophical encumbrances of other professions" (p. 629). Given that reality, plus the calls for promoting subdoctoral independent practice (Hill & Block, 1987; Lazarus, 1983), some formal preservice training cannot be overlooked by programs. For example, in addition to the usual ethic and standards training, attention should be directed toward those issues not normally addressed (e.g., conflicts of interest with the full-time employment setting responsibilities, intensive continuing education requirements, unethical practices, setting priorities regarding psychological investments in two settings, etc.). Similarly, exposure to experiential accounts of school psychologists who were/are engaged in private practice should be reviewed. For example, Roosa (1982) provided a sobering and balanced review of five assumptions which often prompt the consideration of private practice. They include (a) the assumptions that the private practitioner is the "real" psychologist, (b) the expectation that private practitioners earn more money, (c) therapy will be a meaningful part of the workday, (d) the psychologists in private practice lack control over their work and time, and (e) it is easy to start a private practice. Taylor's (1978) point that private practice is not a "bed of roses" helps to set the stage for a realistic view of training needs. Finally, Harries' (1982) chapter deals with the mechanics of establishing and maintaining a private practice in school psychology in a most comprehensive manner.

Ultimately, training for the independent practice of school psychology should be held to the professional model of practice which is conceptualized. For example, in Griswold's (1980) family practice model, he suggests *generalist* training that seems to embrace the *scientist-practitioner* training model with psychological content in assessment, normal psychological processes, human development, learning and interpersonal relations, not at all unlike school psychology training. Levy (1984) proposed a *human services psychology matrix* of training along a content level and modes of treatment dimensions for his amalgamated professional. He advocates the uncoupling of professional/occupational titles from training program titles so that graduates will be eventually called by the titles for which their training qualifies them. With this in mind, school psychology training programs should make clear the goals of their training and professionals must ultimately consider their competency to offer services independently when considering this alternative role. Taking into account the whole set of complex issues which were introduced in this chapter, simple answers to the questions posed earlier regarding the viability of this role should not be expected. However, it is time they be addressed by trainers and practitioners as we turn the corner in our development toward a mature specialty vis-a-vis psychology and educationally related settings. Some school psychologists will, no doubt, continue to offer services in the private domain and for good reason. It is a viable alternative service opportunity; however, we need to be clear what the practice is about. The future of applied psychology is changing, and we should be an active partner in the direction it takes and the influence it has on the school psychology specialty.

REFERENCES

American Association of State Psychology Boards (1986). *Handbook of licensing and certification requirements for psychologists in North America.* Washington, DC: Author.

American Psychological Association (1981a). Specialty guidelines for the delivery of services. *American Psychologist, 36,* 639–681.

American Psychological Association (1981b). Specialty guidelines for the delivery of services by school psychologists. *American Psychologist, 36,* 670–681.

American Psychological Association (1987). *Model act for state licensure of psychologists.* Washington, DC: Author.

Bardon, J. I. (1983). Psychology applied to education. *American Psychologist, 38,* 185–196.

Bardon, J. I. (1986). The path to professionalism is uneven but traversable. *Professional School Psychology, 1,* 29–33.

Block, N. (1987). NASP independent practice task force summary of December, 1984 survey. In D. Hall & N. Block (Eds.), *Independent practice of school psychology* (Rev.) (pp. 14–25). Washington, DC: National Association of School Psychologists.

Council for the National Register of Health Service Providers in Psychology (1987). *National register of health service providers in psychology.* Washington, DC: Author.

Cummings, N. A. (1986). The dismantling of our health system. *American Psychologist, 41,* 426–431.

Dörken, H. (1977). The practicing psychologist: A growing force in private sector health core delivery. *Professional Psychology, 8,* 269–274.

Fagan, T. K. (1986). School psychology's dilemma. *American Psychologist, 8,* 851–861.

Griswold, P. M. (1980). A family practice model for clinical psychology. *Professional Psychology, 11,* 628–636.

Harries, J. T. (1982). Perspectives on the private practice of school psychology. In C. R. Reynolds & T. B. Gutkin (Eds.), *The handbook of school psychology* (pp. 688–720). NY: John Wiley & Sons.

Hill, D., & Block, N. (Eds.). (1987). *Independent practice of school psychology* (Rev.). Washington, DC: National Association of School Psychologists.

Hughes, J. L. (1987, March). *The school psychologist as a community service provider.* In R. C. D'Amato (Chair), *Nontraditional activities for school psychologists.* Symposium conducted at the convention of the National Association of School Psychologists, New Orleans.

Lazarus, P. J. (1982). Training concerns regarding the independent practice of school psychology: Some fundamental questions. *Trainer's Forum, 2,* 1–2.

Lazarus, P. J. (1983). The private practice of school psychology by specialist level practitioners—Are we ready, willing and able? *Trainer's Forum, 3*(1), 3–4.

Levy, L. H. (1984). The metamorphosis of clinical psychology. *American Psychologist, 39,* 486–494.

Meltzer, M. L. (1986). Community psychology as a model for the new private practice of psychology. *Journal of Clinical Psychology, 42,* 392–407.

National Association of School Psychologists (1985). *Standards.* Washington, DC: Author.

Norcross, J. C., Nash, J. M., & Prochaska, J. O. (1985). Psychologists in part-time independent practice: Description and comparison. *Professional Psychology: Research and Practice, 16,* 565–575.

Oakland, T. D. (1986). Professionalism within school psychology. *Professional School Psychology, 1,* 9–27.

Patrick, G. L., Saudargas, R. A., & Wiberley, J. A. (1980). The role of the school psychologists in the private practice of the developmental optometrist. *Psychology in the Schools, 17,* 87–89.

Pion, G. M., Bramblett, J. P., & Wicherski, M. (1987). *Preliminary report: 1985 Doctorate Employment Survey.* Washington, DC: American Psychological Association.

Pryzwansky, W. B. (1982). Licensure practices affecting the school psychology specialty. *Professional Practice of Psychology, 3,* 13–16.

Pryzwansky, W. B. (1986). Credentialing: Some new challenges. *The School Psychologist, 41,* 1–2.

Pryzwansky, W. B., & Wendt, R. N. (1987). *Psychology as a profession: Foundations of practice.* New York: Pergamon Press.

Rappaport, J., & Chinsky, J. M. (1974). Models for delivery of service from a historical and conceptual perspective. *Professional Psychology, 5,* 42–50.

Roosa, L. W. (1982). The prodigal school psychologist: One psychologist's journey into the world of private practice and back. *School Psychology Review, 11,* 442–446.

Smith, D. K. (1984). Practicing school psychologists: Their characteristics, activities, and populations served. *Professional Psychology: Research and Practice, 15,* 789–810.

Stapp, J., & Fulcher, R. (1981). *Salaries in psychology: 1981.* Washington, DC: American Psychological Association.

Stapp, J., Fulcher, R., & Wicherski, M. (1984). The employment of 1981 and 1982 doctoral recipients in psychology. *American Psychologist, 39,* 1408–1423.

Taylor, R. E. (1978). Demythologizing private practice. *Professional Psychology, 9,* 68–70.

Tryon, G. S. (1983). Full-time private practice in the United States: Results of a national survey. *Professional Psychology: Research and Practice, 14,* 685–696.

VanderBos, G. R., Stapp, J., & Kilburg, R. R. (1981). Health service providers in psychology: Results of the 1978 APA Human Resources Survey. *American Psychologist, 36,* 1395–1418.

Wendt, R. N., & Tucker, R. L. (1983). Licensure and school psychology: An emerging alternative. *Professional Practice of Psychology, 4*(1), 59–66.

Wenger, R. D. (1982). Private practice of school psychology: Implications from the APA Specialty Guidelines. *Psychology in the Schools, 19,* 503–507.

4
School Psychology in Medical Settings

DAVID L. WODRICH
Phoenix Children's Hospital

STEVEN I. PFEIFFER
Ochsner Clinic and Ochsner Medical Foundation

Questions about school psychologists' acceptability probably occur more frequently in medical settings than in any other location. After all, a school psychologist in a medical setting is something of a logical contradiction. *School* modifies *psychologist* and specifies the location in which he/she practices. If the psychologist is not practicing in a school, he/she is not a *school* psychologist. At least that is how it appears on the surface.

Superficial logic of this type sometimes confronts the school psychologist in medical settings and often takes one of two forms. The first possible contention is that school psychologists should confine their practice exclusively to educational facilities. Regardless of what they might know or what skills they might possess, schools are the only place in which school psychologists should function. A second, more mild, suggestion is that if a school-trained psychologist serves in any arena other than a school (e.g., a hospital), he/she should refrain from being identified as a school psychologist. Neither of these positions has much merit, as we hope this chapter will demonstrate. Specifically, in this chapter we intend to show that the practice of school psychology in health care facilities is completely appropriate, especially when services are rendered to children. In fact, school psychologists' skills match the requirements of many medically-related tasks so well that this type of psychologist is often seen as especially valuable and competent. In addition to presenting a rationale for this position, this chapter contains illustrative instances of practices in a medical setting that highlight the potential contribution that school psychology can make in this non-traditional setting.

That psychologists as a professional group frequently practice in medical settings is widely recognized. Some school psychologists are readily accepted into medical settings and practice occurs freely and easily. In other instances, the school psychologist finds that professional colleagues—from both medicine and psychology—are unclear about what capacity will be filled if the school psychologist is accepted. Mistaken beliefs over what the *school* in school psychology means seem contributory when problems arise.

Unfortunately for school psychologists, the other two applied branches of psychology in medical settings—clinical and counseling psychology—have an apparent advantage in that their titles seem to better fit this setting. Part of the problem occurs because the terms *clinical* and *counseling* are adjectives that possess general meaning in English. They denote emphasis on pathology and the case study model, and on a particular technique (i.e., the counseling process), respectively. As such, clinical and counseling psychology seem to say nothing about location of practice; hence the title is seen completely at home in a hospital as well as in many other possible locations. Had the early history of these other specialties been described with nouns—identifying typical locations of practice—as school psychology did, clinical psychology might have been entitled "VA psychology," and counseling psychology might have been entitled "counseling center psychology" (Reynolds, Gutkin, Elliott, & Witt, 1984).

School is a noun, of course, that denotes a specific location. When *school* is placed as an adjective modifying *psychology,* a quite specific meaning is produced that implies practice located in one setting only—the school. Implicitly, the school psychologist must be confined to school settings, whereas clinical and counseling psychology can occur anywhere. Explicitly, however, school psychologists, like clinical and counseling psychologists, possess skills and competencies, and it is these considerations that need to be carefully examined when determining who can best practice where. More will be said about this point later in the chapter as the skills and characteristics of school psychologists are examined.

The term *clinical* also is sometimes confusing because it possesses two distinct meanings that often go unappreciated by the speaker. In the eyes of the American Psychological Association (APA), a clinical psychologist is one who has received a certain training sequence and who is consequently one of three (with counseling psychology and school psychology) recognized "professional psychology" specialties. To the general public and to many in allied health professions, however, "clinical" psychology and professional psychology are often used interchangeably, which is inaccurate and inappropriate (Fox, Barclay, & Rodgers, 1982). Considering these points, it is easy to see why some individuals whom one may encounter in medical settings insist only clinical psychologists may practice there. These individuals are inaccurately phrasing a reasonable request that "professional psychologists" (i.e., those with applied skills) practice in this milieu.

The foregoing argument notwithstanding, is it appropriate for school psychologists to venture outside educational facilities into hospitals and clinics? If they choose to do so, how will the school-trained psychologist fit in? Answers to these questions call for examining two issues: a brief discussion of the statutory and administrative considerations bearing on school psychologists' ability to practice, followed by a review of school psychologists' skills and competencies as they relate to the tasks confronting psychologists in medical settings.

ADMINISTRATIVE ISSUES RELATED TO MEDICAL SETTING PRACTICE

Generally, a minimum requirement for psychology practice in medical settings is a state license or certification for independent practice. Certification allows the use of the title "psychologist," whereas licensure regulates the practice of psychology. With one or two exceptions, all 50 states provide for either psychology licensure or certification, the possession of which allows the recipient to be recognized as a professional service provider and facilitates third-party reimbursement—the historic method of funding professionals in medical settings. Most states recognize doctoral-level school psychology training as an acceptable element for licensure for independent practice. Typically proficiency in general psychology by earning an acceptable score on the Examination for Practice in Professional Psychology must also be demonstrated. Many states require internship and/or post-doctoral supervised experience, for which a school psychology internship may be wholly or in part sufficient (see Lahman, 1980, for each state's standards).

Bardon (1982) pointed out that four states (California, Florida, Connecticut, and Illinois) have come to recognize school psychology as a profession distinct from psychology and consequently grant licenses for independent practice. According to Bardon, three additional states (Ohio, Virginia, and Wisconsin) had by 1982 allowed separate licensure for school psychologists within the existing state licensing laws for psychology. The trend among these seven states has been to create standards that allow non-doctoral practitioners to receive school psychology licenses, whereas licensure for psychologists has remained at the doctoral level. How these licensed school psychologists are treated differently from licensed psychologists with school psychology training is unclear. It is likely that hinderances to practice by way of categorical exclusion from certain facilities or because of lack of access to third-party pay differentially disadvantage the school psychologist compared to the psychologist. This chapter is concerned exclusively with doctoral-level psychologists with school psychology specialization who are certified/licensed by their Board of Psychologist Examiners.

Meeting state laws and regulations for independent practice, of course, does not guarantee that the psychologist will be welcomed in all medical settings. In many instances, he/she may practice in clinics, physicians' offices or multi-disiplinary group practices if licensed, but often must meet additional criteria to practice in hospitals—generally regarded as the most exclusive medical setting. Among the numerous criteria that hospitals may impose in addition to licensure are evidence of appropriate experience (often prior supervised experience in a health-care setting and sometimes an approved internship in a hospital) and evidence of professional malpractice insurance. Those psychologists who meet the criteria may be granted some form of hospital "privileges." In most states, privileges allow the psychologists to provide consultative duties, but do not give them principal responsibility for patient care or writing hospital orders (e.g., for consultation, discharge, etc.).

The extent to which hospitals nationwide allow professional psychologists with school psychology training to acquire staff privileges has not, to our knowledge, ever been clearly elucidated. We personally know school-trained psychologists who render services at general (medical/surgical) hospitals, teaching and university hospitals, private physicians' offices, and large health maintenance organizations. And each of us is a school-trained psychologist who holds "affiliate" membership in hospitals that allow school psychologists privileges so long as they—like all other psychologists—demonstrate appropriate training and experience. Although hospital membership criteria vary greatly, the criteria for affiliate privileges at Phoenix Children's Hospital, as an example and as a basis for discussion, are listed in Table 4-1.

School psychologists meet each of the criteria listed for hospital membership. First, the Arizona Board of Psychologists Examiners awards certificates based on a credentials check, which approved graduates of school psychology training programs typically pass, and on satisfactory scores on the Professional Psychology Certification Examination. Second, the program criterion is met by graduates of APA-approved professional psychology training programs (clinical, counseling, or school). Many doctoral-level school psychologists from programs lacking APA accreditation may still meet this second criterion provided their program meets rather minimal standards for a "psychology" training program.

TABLE 4.1
Psychologist Privileges at Phoenix Children's Hospital

Granting of Privileges

To qualify for Affiliate Staff membership, a Psychologist shall meet the following criteria:

I. Current valid certificate awarded by the Arizona Board of Psychology Examiners.

II. Doctoral degree from a professional psychologist training program approved by the American Psychological Association or a program that shall meet the following criteria:

  A. Is located in a regionally accredited institution of higher learning.
  B. The program, wherever it is administratively housed, must be clearly identified and labeled as a psychology program. Such program must specify in pertinent instructional catalogs and brochures its intent to educate and train professional psychologists.
  C. The psychology program must stand as a recognizable coherent organizational entity within the institution, which has an integrated organized sequence of study.
  D. The program must have an identifiable body of students who are matriculated in that program for a degree, and the program must include an identifiable psychology faculty and a psychologist responsible for the program.

III. A psychology internship or residency that demonstrates appropriate course work and experience with children as listed below:

  A. Consists of a minimum of 1800 hours of supervised experience.
  B. Includes face to face supervision by psychologist in a health care setting or organized setting employing psychologists.

*Delineation of Privileges**

Specific privileges for Affiliate Staff in Psychology shall be granted in the following categories: 1) Child consultation and evaluation (inpatient and outpatient); 2) Child therapy and treatment (inpatient and outpatient).
Psychologists must meet the minimum criteria for granting of privileges in each of these categories:

I. *Child consultation and evaluation:*

  A. Ten semester hours or equivalent in course work primarily dealing with child psychology, developmental psychology, abnormal or handicapped children, or diagnostic techniques applied to children.
  B. One thousand hours of supervised experience in the provision of service in children under 12 years of age.

II. *Child therapy and treatment:*

  A. Demonstration of appropriate training and experience in child psychotherapy and psychological treatment as determined by the Psychology Sub-committee.
  B. Ten semester hours or equivalent in course work primarily dealing with child psychology, developmental psychology, abnormal or handicapped children, or diagnostic techniques applied to children.
  C. One thousand hours supervised experience in the provision of service in children under 12 years of age.

*Unpublished and undated document; Department of Psychiatry, Phoenix Children's Hospital.

Third, a full-time internship including appropriate supervision and experience with children is called for and is seldom problematic for school psychologists. Finally, specific privileges for consultation and evaluation or treatment require course work related to children and at least 1000 hours of supervised experience with children. This last criterion is typically met far more easily by school psychology graduates than by psychologists from adult-oriented clinical or counseling programs that may provide minimal child course work or experience. Again, however, the school psychologist interested in hospital privileges must remember that there are no uniform standards and that some hospitals, especially those that serve general medical/surgical patients, may have different or more restrictive criteria than those of Phoenix Children's Hospital.

Besides hospital credentialing guidelines, which are sometimes determined by quite local considerations, state laws and psychology's own internal standards also control where and how psychologists practice. In Arizona, as a case in point, the regulation for psychology practice specifies that "a psychologist's certificate may be suspended, revoked, or placed on probationary status for . . . engaging or offering to engage as a psychologist in activities *not congruent with the psychologist's professional education, training, or experience*" A.R.S. statute § 32-2081 (italics added). These regulations avoid differentiating among the various types of professional psychologists. Nor do they specify the nature of services that any particular psychologist may render or the location in which they may be rendered. Instead, all psychologists must perform services consistent with their preparation. Later in the chapter, we discuss school psychologists' training and experience and how these bear on practice in medical settings.

Apparently motivated by lack of clarity about the scope of practice and the use of titles, psychologists themselves stepped into an arena traditionally controlled by legislation and by state regulatory bodies. A group of psychologists in the 1970s attempted to establish a set of national guidelines defining applied "health services" in psychology and delineating those qualified to render services in this area. A definition was arrived at by the National Register of Health Service Providers in Psychology:

> A health service provider in psychology is defined as a psychologist, certified/licensed at the independent practice level in his/her state, who is duly trained and experienced in the delivery of direct, preventative, assessment and therapeutic intervention services to individuals whose growth, adjustment, or functioning is actually impaired or demonstrably at high risk of impairment. (Council for the National Register of Health Service Providers in Psychology, 1985)

This is a broad definition of health services. Prevention, assessment, and therapeutic intervention occur in the daily practice of school psychologists regardless of whether services are provided in a public school or, for instance, in consultation to a hospital-based medical and behavioral diagnostic team. Similarly, the vast majority of individuals for whom school psychologists provide services are already identified as handicapped (e.g., learning disabled, mentally retarded, seriously emotionally handicapped) or at risk for such handicaps. School psychologists who wish to be viewed as health service providers should embrace this definition.

A set of training and experience criteria were also established for qualification as a health service provider in psychology. There are three criteria:

1. Current licensure or certification by the State Board of Examiners of Psychology at the independent practice level of psychology.
2. A doctoral degree in psychology from a regionally accredited educational institution.
3. Two years of supervised experience in health service in psychology, of which at least one year is in an organized health service training program, and one year is post-doctoral. (Council for National Register of Health Service Providers in Psychology, 1985).

School psychologists licensed for independent practice may be accepted for listing by the National Register. The principal stumbling block, provided that the school psychologist's degree is from a regionally accredited program, is the third criterion—experience in an organized health service program. At present, the National Register recognizes school psychology internships as sufficient to meet the one-year criterion as an organized health service program, provided that certain criteria such as an organized sequence, sufficient number of students, and sufficient contact with the supervisor are met. With cooperation from the National Register, the Council of Directors of School Psychology Programs (1983, 1987) produced two documents designed to enhance the quality of internship experiences for school psychologists and to help ensure conformity with the requirements of the National Register. (School psychology internship sites that meet the Director's guidelines may also be listed in the Directory of Internship Programs in Professional Psychology Internship Centers; APIC, 1986, an association traditionally concerned principally with clinical psychology internships.) The key point is that many school psychologists are recognized as health services providers by a national body. Indeed, at present many school-trained psychologists are listed among those in the National Register (A. Wellner, personal communication, June 2, 1987).

In summary, although little uniformity exists, professional psychologists with school psychology preparation may be certified for independent practice, may practice in varied medical arenas, and may be granted formal status as health care providers including hospital privileges and listing in the National Register. In the same light, even though our designation as "school" psychologists suggests to some that we can be defined by the location in which we have traditionally practiced, it is our contention (and we are supported by some state regulations) that all psychologists can provide services wherever they choose so long as they practice in a manner which is consistent with their training. Administratively and legally, school psychologists can practice in medical settings.

SCHOOL PSYCHOLOGISTS' TRAINING AND MEDICAL PRACTICE

Beyond the administrative and legal considerations for practice, the real bottom line ought to be competency—the capability to render services professionally, effectively, and ethically in medical settings. The very basics of applicant selection from industrial/organizational psychology indicate that suitability to function in any job is best determined by examining the skills and characteristics of the potential worker (in this case a professional psychologist) and the demands of the job (in this case practice in medical settings) (Cronbach, 1970). Of course, few generalizations can be made about the demands for psychology services in medical settings. Medical settings encompass facilitites ranging from medical schools to outpatient clinics, from physicians' offices to hospitals. Patients range from very young to very old, from gravely ill to perfectly healthy. Contained within the rubric of the medically related are diagnostic and treatment services, purely educative services, and purely behavioral science programs. Still, this approach to assessing the psychologist's ability to function in various settings has advantages because it goes beyond generalizations about perceived competencies (e.g., only psychologists with medical setting internships may practice in hospitals). Instead, it moves toward identifying specific demands (e.g., in this medical setting, the psychologist must be able to serve as consultant without case ownership, he/she must know applied behavior management skills with children, etc.), and then determines which type of training and background best prepare a psychologist to practice in a particular setting. A priori assumptions regarding the uniform suitability of any branch of psychology for any setting are minimized, while capability to perform necessary tasks is maximized. Titles such as *clinical, counseling,* and *school psychology* have diminished relevance when this approach is used because they are insufficiently precise to predict preparedness to perform the expected tasks.

An examination of school psychologists' training and experience is in order, followed by descriptions of the demands in various medical settings where school psychologists might work. The match between skills and demands can then be assessed.

A reasonable place to begin evaluating school psychologists' background and training is with the most recent Specialty Guidelines for the Delivery of Services by School Psychologists (APA, 1981). The guidelines for school psychologists, as well as clinical, counseling, and industrial/organizational psychologists, begin with APA's position that licensing be generic. The holder of a general license to practice is not prohibited from providing any services, so long as those services are within the scope of that person's training. This is an important point because it suggests that training in psychology is not sufficiently homogeneous within any speciality to predict precisely what training experiences are provided nor to guarantee which skills are possessed by program graduates. Appreciable demands for judgment reside with the individual practitioner to determine to what extent his/her skills and training are sufficient to meet any particular service demand. The guidelines then go on to highlight the common core of all specialty training by stating that school psychologists will receive instruction in "the basic area of psychology," as well as training in "assessment, intervention, consultation, program development, and supervision" (APA, 1981).

Skills peculiar to school psychology are identified to include: Psychological assessment of school functioning of children and young persons including intellectual assessment, affective behavior, neuropsychologic status, and so forth; interventions including counseling, affective education, and parents' counseling; consultation with parents regarding school-related problems and assistance to parents so that they can contribute to their child's development. Tremendous exposure to cognitive development and the myriad of instruments available to assess it over the developmental span extending through the school years are one important component of school psychology training. In addition, scrupulous training in psychometric theory, training in practical interventions that must work promptly and must be understandable and usable by both parents and teachers, plus the unique understanding of how schools operate and the effect that the education process—including its special education offerings—has on the child, among other things, make APA's proposed training for school psychologists powerful and in some ways unique.

Surveys of training trends in school psychology have shown recently that the areas actually emphasized in curricula are consistent with APA's guidelines. Surveys by Bardon and Wenger (1976), Goh (1977) and Pfeiffer and Marmo (1981) have shown emphasis on psychological and psychoeducational assessment (of school-age children). Other areas receiving emphasis include consultation, behavior modification, child development, as well as learning disability and educational remediation. This is a truly substantial array of services—all related to some aspect of education, but none so specific as to prevent application outside of public schools.

Before concluding the discussion of school psychologists' training there is an additional point to mention. We must admit to dealing in generalizations as we characterize school psychologists' training and skills. APA's Education and Training Board Task Force on Review of the Scope and Criteria for Accreditation, for instance, in its review of specialty training, has noted much overlap in predoctoral curriculum and practica; its recent job analyses have shown "there are common bodies of knowledge and skills, as well as professional responsibilities, across entry level jobs of different specialties" (APA, 1987, p. 6). The background and training among the three "professional" psychology specialties—clinical, counseling, and school psychology—show overlap, and so do many of the initial job demands encountered by graduates of these programs as they enter the work force. Nonetheless, there are discernable differences in the focus of training among the specialties and, we suggest, in the skills each brings to various job situations.

Some overlap of training no doubt exists among the professional psychology specialties. Even so, school psychology training is arguably unique because of its emphasis on understanding the child as he/she relates to school, the nature and diagnosis of learning and developmental problems, hands-on experience with behavior modification in children, as well as in-depth understanding of child development. The school psychologists' in-depth training in the aforementioned areas results in substantial skills that can be appraised for their match with medical setting job expectations.

SCHOOL PSYCHOLOGISTS' SKILLS APPLIED IN MEDICAL SETTINGS

Now that it is clear that licensed, doctoral-level school psychologists' may legitimately practice in medical settings, are often permitted recognition as health care providers, and have knowledge and skills that overlap to some extent but are in some ways distinct from other professional psychologists, let us turn to an examination of how these skills might fit in various medical settings. A case approach followed by rationale and explanation of school psychologists' skills is used.

Pediatric Neurology: A Case Study

Junior is a 7-year-old Caucasian male who was seen by a pediatric neurologist who worked at a children's hospital. Records show that the child was born four weeks prematurely, had slight neonatal jaundice, but was released from the hospital to return home within normal time intervals. Development seemed to proceed reasonably well, and Junior acquired most developmental milestones within normal times, except that he had a slight speech articulation problem as a preschooler.

At age 2½ years, Junior experienced a single, generalized tonic-clonic seizure. Following a complete neurologic workup, he was prescribed an anticonvulsant (Tegretol) that prevented subsequent seizures. He was then followed in a pediatric neurology practice with regular office visits.

At age 7 years, his mother reported to the pediatric neurologist during a regularly scheduled follow-up visit that Junior's teacher suggested he be retained in the first grade. The mother reported that during the past year he had experienced difficulty completing his classwork and that his marks had been consistently low. She commented that he was extremely inconsistent in class, often failing to retain skills one day that seemed completely mastered the previous day. Uncertain about the benefits of repeating first grade, Junior's mother turned to the pediatric neurologist. With similar concerns about class placement and more focused questions about the cause of Junior's school failure, the pediatric neurologist requested a psychological evaluation and follow-up educational planning assistance.

The school psychologist is the ideal professional to address these issues by conducting a thorough psychoeducational assessment and by conferring with the local school. His/her training has led to the ability to perform just such services, and, indeed, school psychologists at innumerable educational facilities across the country effectively perform these tasks daily. That the school psychologist was located geographically in a medical setting in this particular instance had no bearing on the quality or competence of services rendered. The match between the psychologist's competencies and the job demands was maximal.

Is this an atypical or contrived case example? The answer is absolutely not. Data suggest that approximately 4.4 to 6.6 children per thousand suffer from epilepsy (Epilepsy Foundation of America, 1975). Frequently occurring questions about developmental status and the need for educational guidance are typically handled initially by the child's neurologist or pediatrician, but often ultimately require more specialized consultation. When psychological assistance is called for, as is often the case with children such as these, the practitioner with school psychology training is in the best position to be of assistance. When one adds other neurologic conditions to the count, such as Tourette's syndrome, genetic disorders, degenerative disorders, sequelae of perinatal complications, and children who are at risk because of closed head injuries, it becomes clear that there are enormous numbers of youngsters who require ongoing assessment, guidance, advocacy for educational intervention, and parental support. These kinds of tasks are virtually identical to the services performed by school psychologists on a daily basis with handicapped learners in the public school.

Sometimes more specialized psychological assessment, i.e., neuropsychological assessment, is called for in pediatric neurology. The purpose of this testing is to help the neurologist determine the presence, location, and extent of brain dysfunction or injury. Though both clinical and school psychology guidelines mention assessing "neuropsychological status," neither training program should be assumed to uniformally train its graduates to perform detailed neuropsychological evaluations of general patients, let alone pediatric patients. It can be argued, however, that school psychology programs place their graduates in ideal positions to acquire specialized skills in this area whether by focused doctoral course work and experience or by post-doctoral training. With pediatric populations in particular, this position seems true because school psychology training, more than other specialties, emphasizes assessment of cognitive and information processing skills, while simultaneously emphasizing child development. The close link between child neuropsychology and school psychology is evident merely by examing the published neuropsychology textbooks and articles of recent Lighter Witmer Award winners, an honor bestowed upon the outstanding young school psychologists by Division 16 of APA each year (e.g., Hartlage & Telzrow, 1986; Hynd & Cohen, 1983; Hynd & Obrzut, 1981, 1986).[1]

Child Psychiatry: Starting a Day Hospital Program

Variations on child psychiatry inpatient programs that have recently gained popularity include partial hospitalization or day hospital programs. These programs offer medical involvement (e.g., there is a treating physician, and care is at least partially provided by nursing staff) together

[1]Lighter Witmer Award winners are George Hynd, Cathy Telzrow, Cecil Reynolds, and Raymond Dean.

with educational, behavioral, and social services, but the child returns home each evening to rejoin his/her family. Such programs afford the opportunity for in-depth diagnosis and treatment of conduct, emotional, behavioral, developmental, and combined medical/behavioral problems such as psychosomatic disorders. Partial hospitalization programs represent a less restrictive variant of traditional inpatient psychiatric programs.

To what extent do school psychology skills aid in the establishment and maintenance of hospital-based programs such as these? The school psychologists' abilities in program development and consultation prove invaluable here, as does first-hand familiarity with self-contained special education programs for seriously emotionally-handicapped children. For instance, hospital programs often operate surrounding a structured environment, use incentive systems or token economies, incorporate behavioral contracts, and use level systems with varying degrees of privileges. These programs often use educational/therapeutic activities that are targeted on the mastery of specific behavioral objectives.

Often programs such as these include a special education classroom to diagnose the youngster's emotional and educational needs and to promote educational growth during the stay. These hospital-based programs are similar to though more intense than school-based programs for emotionally-handicapped youngsters.

While enrolled in these programs, children frequently receive one or more detailed professional evaluations or consultations to assess their status. Among the consultations that may be accomplished are psychoeducational, speech/language, occupational therapy, and/or a variety of medical consultations including psychiatry, neurology, developmental pediatrics, or audiology (Wodrich & Joy, 1986). The information derived from these consultations should be organized and integrated so that it can be presented to the local school in an understandable and useful form.

Much like the school programs for seriously emotionally-handicapped children, these programs often involve parent training. School-trained psychologists may offer didactic instruction on topics such as children's emotional needs, characteristics, and considerations of living with attention deficit-disordered children, or the learning and educational requirements of children with emotional handicaps. Besides these supplemental offerings, direct instruction in behavior management is often provided. Familiarity with both the psychology of instruction and the treatment needs of emotionally-handicapped children make the school psychologist a particularly qualified team member.

The discerning reader has by now observed considerable similarity between the demands of this particular hospital-based work situation and the skills possessed by many psychologists with school psychology specialization. It is clear that although the program may be located within a hospital, many of the expectations and responsibilities of the professional staff are akin to those encountered in structured educational setting such as an emotionally-handicapped, school-based program. School psychologists, of course, have considerable experience in this realm and are thus well prepared to help create programs, work as consultants after programs have been started, act as continuing aides to integrate complex multi-disciplinary data, and interface with public schools.

Outpatient Pediatrics

Six-year-old Sara has been followed medically by her pediatrician since birth. She has suffered many respiratory infections and has recently been diagnosed as having reactive airway disease or asthma. Her mother and father have always been responsive to their child's needs and are now scrupulous about administering Sara's medication. Shortly after beginning medication, the girl has a temper outburst, begins wheezing, and finds that parents are not only attentive to her every move but are willing to modify their previously-enforced limits. If she shows signs of respiratory difficulty, for example, she may remain up past normal bedtime to be held and soothed by mother.

Sara's pediatrician recognizes that although her parents did not cause her asthma, their present methods of managing her probably have perpetuated or exaggerated her symptoms. Moreover, the parents have begun to argue between themselves about the best procedure for disciplining their daughter in general and about how to treat her asthma symptoms in particular. The contemporary pediatrician who works with a psychologist in her office quickly turns to her behavioral colleague in situations like this to provide parental guidance. Most psychologists with school psychology speciality training have acquired behavior management experience with children, and they suspect that Sara is learning new operant behaviors. Some school-trained psychologists have family systems training, and they may begin speculating about family interaction patterns. Regardless of orientation, the psychologist can be of assistance in innumerable cases such as this where suspected physical and psychological dysfunctions occur simultaneously.

The professional psychologist with school psychology specialization, who has acquired training and experiences in health care settings, can be of assistance. The school psychologist lacking prior exposure to children with medical problems or lacking experience with families would, of course, require supervision and/or supplemental training in cases such as this. Keith-Spiegel and Koocher (1985), for example, suggested that professionals should proceed cautiously when no formal practice standards exist—as is the case for family therapy or for treating children's psychosomatic disorders. In such instances, consulting colleagues widely regarded as experts in a particular area for guidance about training suggestions and practice standards is advised, as is acquiring direct supervision from a practitioner deemed competent in that area. These procedures permit the professional to better gauge his/her own competence. The same caveats exist for all psychologists, of course. Of interest, Keith-Spiegel and Koocher make specific comment about the inappropriateness of those trained exclusively in adult clinical psychology providing services to children.

Although children with combined physical and psychological dysfunction represent a substantial portion of outpatient visits to pediatricians' offices (Duff, Rowe, & Anderson [1972] estimated 52%), pediatricians encounter numerous other problems that provide opportunities for psychologists' involvement, especially those with school psychology skills. Because of their position as the primary health-care contact for children and families, pediatricians are confronted with problems such as: early diagnosis and triage of handicapped children, diagnosis and guidance about school learning problems, input and decisions about beginning school and grade retention, guidance on discipline and child management, decisions on day care, assistance in overcoming enuresis and encopresis, suggestions about sibling rivalry and peer problems, and direction during times of divorce including suggestions about visitation. Reviewing demands such as these, Pfeiffer, Dean, and Shellenberger (1986) contended that school-trained psychologists are in an ideal position to contribute because their orientation and training matches the demands of the busy pediatric practice on several dimensions. Among these are:

1. an emphasis on education and preventative orientation
2. familiarity with normal child rearing problems, including situational and developmental conflicts
3. the ability to interface with community resources, especially local schools
4. a treatment orientation that is short-term in nature
5. experience in working in a high-volume, cost-efficient manner
6. an assessment orientation that emphasizes cognitive, developmental, and psychoeducational competencies
7. a philosophy comfortable with sharing "joint" case ownership and responsibility with the pediatrician.

Just as the school psychologist lends expertise to the primary care pediatrician when collaborating in problems like these, so too can he/she serve effectively as a teacher. As pediatricians increasingly recognize the demand for developmental and behavioral expertise, school psychologists will find increasingly important roles in residency and medical school training.

POSSIBLE FUTURE DIRECTIONS

Many hospitals and health care facilities already benefit from the services of psychologists trained to apply their skills to educational problems. These same facilities benefit from psychologists with other training as well. Still, the potential for all of psychology to contribute to health care is as of yet barely tapped. It is to our collective advantage if each of psychology's specialties in the future examine their course curricula and applied pre-internship and internship experiences so as to maximize their contribution in health settings. Our discipline as a whole must decide what formal post-internship training options are appropriate (and perhaps necessary) to perform various tasks. Psychology must also decide if more specialties are needed as ever-increasing knowledge, skills, realms of practice, and locations in which to apply these skills develop. We contend that the school-trained psychologist has much to offer in medical settings and that an ever-expanding proliferation of specialties is not productive. Several suggestions are proposed, which we believe will strengthen the ability of school psychologists to function effectively in medical settings.

First, all school psychologists should receive increased exposure to the biological bases of behavior in general and to their role in learning and developmental handicaps in particular as part of their training. For instance, excellent, highly readable texts on the biological aspects of handicapped children are now available (e.g., Batshaw & Perret, 1986) and could be easily incorporated into the school psychology curriculum. Similarly, sources created with the school psychologist in mind now exist that provide basic information about the various medical subspecialties that typically diagnose children and under what circumstances it might be appropriate to access these practitioners when performing evaluations of learning disabled or mentally retarded children (Wodrich & Joy, 1986). Knowledge of this sort will benefit all school psychologists, regardless of whether they ever practice in a medical setting.

Second, school psychologists with particular interest in medical settings would benefit from specialized course work and experiences. Although presumably the basic course work and experiences of doctoral-level school psychology training create many skills applicable in medical settings, additional special proficiencies and competencies are sometimes required. For instance, school psychology training provides much information about skill acquisition, behavioral assessment, psychometrics, and consultation with parents. Thus, the professional psychologist with school psychology training working in a hospital-based rehabilitation unit, for instance, would possess a general basis to perform, but might require particular information about cognitive retraining or guidance about working with a multidisciplinary team led by a physician. Like psychologists of all specialties, the school psychologist would find it helpful to receive focused predoctoral course work (e.g., an applied course on pediatric rehabilitation) and/or direct experience (e.g., a one-semester externship in a rehabilitation setting).

Third, some school psychologists may choose to develop considerable special proficiencies and competencies to expand beyond traditional school psychology. Examples are the school-trained psychologist who chooses to focus on pediatric neurology or pediatric psychology. Although the school psychologist's general knowledge of psychology and his/her "traditional" skills are a basis, varying degrees of extra training *may* be required beyond the basic course work and field experiences. Opportunities for internships that focus entirely on these areas, or are offered as significant "rotations," are advocated for school psychology trainees. A full-time, one- or two-year post-doctoral experience is sometimes appropriate, and ought to be available to school psychologists who possess appropriate credentials and training.

Unfortunately, school psychologists-in-training sometimes find the doors of internships in health care settings closed to them. A cursory review of the 1986-87 APIC directory found only approximately 25% of those internship sites that offered a major rotation with child patients accepted applicants from school psychology programs. Somewhat more positive was the finding that approximately 22 of 38 sites listed with "children," "pediatric," or "youth" in the title accepted school psychology graduates as interns in their programs. Interestingly, some large and prestigious facilities do welcome school psychology applicants including Columbia Presbyterian Medical Center, Massachusetts General Hospital, and Harvard Medical School's Affiliated Hospital (McClean Hospital), Children's Hospital of Michigan, Johns Hopkins Medical Center, and Primary Children's Medical Center in Utah, among others. Exclusion of school psychology-trained applicants makes little sense on purely rational grounds when one examines preparatory course work for its match to the on-site demands of the trainee. Nor does the first-hand experience of those of us who have trained students in both school psychology and clinical psychology in pediatric settings bear out this position. Broader training opportunities for school psychologists are both appropriate and warranted.

Finally, as school-trained psychologists apply their skills in increasingly diverse settings, the issue of our specialty title must be examined. Is *school* really the appropriate title, or is such a title too restrictive? If *school* is too restrictive, are there alternatives that are better, such as *applied education psychology,* as explored by Bardon (1982)? Our specialty has diverse skills of tremendous importance that are presently applied by competent practitioners in many educational and non-educational settings. It is important that something as trivial as a title used to describe our specialty at its inception not hinder it in the present nor impede its progress in the future.

As school psychologists expand into increasingly diverse employment settings, their unique background and training, in our opinion, will become even better appreciated. The future bodes well for nontraditional applications of school psychology in general and for its application in medical settings in particular.

REFERENCES

American Psychological Association (1981). *Specialty guidelines for the delivery of services.* Washington, DC: Author.

American Psychological Association (1987). *Memorandum from APA Education and Training Board Task Force on review of the scope and criteria for accreditation.* Washington, DC: Author.

Arizona Revised Statutes § 32–2081.

Association of Psychology Internship Centers (APIC) (1986–1987). *Internship programs in professional psychology.* Washington, DC: Author.

Bardon, J. I. (1982). Introduction: The future of school psychology. *Professional Psychology, 13,* 954–968.

Bardon, J. I., & Wenger, R. D. (1976). School psychology training trends in the early 1970s. *Professional Psychology, 7,* 31–36.

Batshaw, M. L., & Perret, Y. M. (1986). *Children with handicaps: A medical primer* (2nd ed.). Baltimore: Brookes Publishing Co.

Council for the National Register of Health Service Providers in Psychology (1985). *National register of health service providers in psychology.* Washington, DC: Author.

Council of Directors of School Psychology Programs (1983). *Guidelines for meeting internship criteria in school psychology.* Washington, DC: Author.

Council of Directors of School Psychology Programs and the Division of School Psychology, American Psychological Association (1987). *Economically effective, professionally sound internships for doctoral students in schools.* Washington, DC: Author.

Cronbach, L. J. (1970). *Essentials of psychological testing* (3rd ed). New York: Harper and Row.

Duff, R. S., Rowe D. S., & Anderson F. P. (1972). Patient care and student learning in a pediatric clinic. *Pediatrics, 50,* 839–846.

Epilepsy Foundation of America (1975). *Basic statistics on the epilepsies.* Philadelphia: F. A. Davis Co.

Fox, R. E., Barclay, A. G., & Rodgers, D. A. (1982). The foundations of professional psychology. *American Psychologist, 37*, 306–312.

Goh, D. S. (1977). Graduate training in school psychology. *Journal of School Psychology, 15*, 207–218.

Hartlage, L. C., & Telzrow, C. F. (1986). *Neuropsychological assessment and intervention with children and adolescents.* Sarasota, FL: Professional Resource Exchange.

Hynd, G. W., & Cohen, M. (1983). *Dyslexia: Neuropsychological theory, research, and clinical differentiation.* New York: Grune and Stratton.

Hynd, G. W., & Obrzut, J. E. (Eds.) (1981). *Neuropsychological assessment and the school-age child.* New York: Grune and Stratton.

Keith-Speigel, P., & Koocher, G. P. (1985). *Ethics in psychology: Professional standards and cures.* New York: Random House.

Lahman, F. G. (1980). *Licensure requirements for psychologists, USA and Canada* (2nd ed.). Evansville, IN: University of Evansville Press.

Pfeiffer, S. I., Dean, R. S., & Shellenberger, S. (1986). The school psychologist in medical settings. In Kratochwill, T. R. (Ed.). *Advances in school psychology, Vol. V* (pp. 177–202). Hillsdale, NJ: Lawrence Erlbaum Associates.

Pfeiffer, S. I. & Marmo, P. (1981). The status of training in school psychology and trends towards the future.*Journal of School Psychology, 19*, 211–216.

Reynolds, C. R., Gutkin, T. B., Elliott, S. N., & Witt, J. C. (1984). *School psychology: Essentials of theory and practice.* New York: John Wiley & Sons.

Wodrich, D. L., & Joy, J. E. (Eds.) (1986). *Multidisciplinary assessment of children with learning disabilities and mental retardation.* Baltimore: Brookes Publishing Co.

5
School Psychology Applied to Business

PATTI L. HARRISON
The University of Alabama

GEORGE MCCLOSKEY
American Guidance Service

The idea of a school psychologist in a business setting may form an unlikely image. The picture of a school psychologist managing a restaurant or clothing store might immediately come to mind after reading the title of this chapter. Although school psychologists have managed very successful restaurants and clothing stores, the purpose of this chapter is not to give guidelines to school psychologists for opening their own businesses! Instead, we wish to provide a rationale for the need of school psychology services in business and a description of how the skills and training of school psychologists are applicable in a business setting. In doing so, the authors intend to present a new career option for school psychologists and an expansion of the field of school psychology.

RATIONALE FOR SCHOOL PSYCHOLOGY IN A BUSINESS SETTING

School psychology in a business setting requires a reconceptualization of the traditional clients and settings of school psychologists. According to Reynolds, Gutkin, Elliott, and Witt (1984), the major goal of school psychology has been to provide psychological services, both direct and indirect, to children and youth to improve their educational development and mental health. The goal of school psychology should be revised to include individuals across the life span, educational development beyond elementary and secondary school, and education in settings other than public schools. With this revision, the goal of school psychology becomes responsive to the changing needs and trends of society (Levinson & Hohenshil, 1983; Levinson & Shepard, 1986).

It is well documented that a major age shift is occurring in this country and that greater numbers of people in the population are progressing into older ages (Levinson & Hohenshil, 1983; Levinson & Shepard, 1986). Psychologists, counselors, and educators are finding it necessary to develop new techniques and skills to address the needs of the older people in our society as the numbers of older people increase. Hohenshil (1979) reported that the changing nature of the adult population is forcing professionals to direct an increased amount of attention to issues such as the rights of women and minorities, the effects of technological advances on adult development, mid-life career changes, and the elimination of forced retirement.

The need for continuing education is implicit in our older society. Education is a lifelong process and educational development of individuals is not limited to the ages of 3 to 18 (Bardon, 1982; Hohenshil, 1979, 1984; Tractman, 1981). In recent years, many avenues have been developed to foster continuing education across the life span, such as workshops, classes, seminars, hospices for the elderly, and lowered college tuition for older individuals. According to Hohenshil (1979), continuing education can be categorized into two types. Leisure education involves recreation and mental health activities, whereas occupational training and retraining involves job-related skills. Education is, of course, not limited to public school settings. While leisure education and occupational training and retraining for adults are often offered by public school districts, increasing numbers of communities, colleges, and business are developing programs for continuing education.

Is there a role for school psychologists in working with the adults in our country and providing services for their continued educational development in settings outside of school? This question must be answered with a resounding "Yes!". School psychology is not defined by the type of client served or the setting in which the activities take place; it is defined by the nature of the services provided. Tractman (1981) broadened the definition of school psychology to include education, regardless of setting. Bardon (1982) stated:

> . . . the professional school psychologist is not defined by whether employment is with the schools. Definition is by speciality or expertise. The persons identified as school psychologists may be employed by a school system as pupil personnel service workers, or as supervisors, or as administrators, depending on what other credentials they hold acceptable to the education establishment. However, school psychologists may also be em-

> ployed in areas not commonly associated with the direct delivery of school services. In this conception, school psychologists are no longer identified because of tasks performed or job function but because of broad knowledge and skills related to application of psychology to problems of schooling. School psychologists might practice anywhere where such knowledge and skills are applicable. What matters are not the tasks to be performed but what training, education, and experience in school psychology have led the school psychologist to be . . . What is important here is that these persons *are* school psychologists. That is their professional specialty. They are school psychologists because of what they know and how they think about problems. (pp. 12–13)

Thus, a needed expansion of the field of school psychology requires a change in the emphasis from public school services only to include post-secondary services, and from educational concerns only to broader mental health and vocational concerns, including societal adjustment and employment (Fagan, 1981). In this chapter, we discuss the *post-secondary school psychologist.* Post-secondary school psychologists may be found in a variety of nontraditional settings, including colleges and universities (Anderson, 1982; Bardon, 1979; Sandoval & Love, 1977) or community agencies (Hughes, 1987), but in this chapter we will focus on the role of post-secondary school psychologists in a business setting.

At the present time, some school psychologists have extended their services to business settings. For example, Levinson and Shepard (1986) described the positive experiences of one school psychologist with vocational appraisal and counseling of a large group of soon-to-be-displaced workers. The authors of this chapter have both applied their skills and training in school psychology to employment with a test publisher. These cases, however, appear to be more the exception than the rule. A survey of 250 school psychology training programs was recently conducted to try to obtain an estimate of the number of school psychologists who are currently employed in business settings. Thirty-five program directors responded to the survey. Of these respondents, only 3 indicated having knowledge of school psychologists who are currently employed in business settings. The total number of school psychologists identified by these directors was 3. Although response to the survey was much less than overwhelming, input was received from what could be considered a nationally representative sample of training programs. We believe that the results are an accurate reflection of the current employment status of school psychologists in general; there are very few school psychologists employed in business settings at the present time.

Although there are relatively few school psychologists employed in businesses, there are substantial numbers of psychologists working in business settings. Individuals who wish to apply their skills as psychologists in businesses often complete their graduate training in the industrial/organizational specialty area. To assume, however, that all psychologists who work in business settings have been trained as industrial/organizational psychologists would not be accurate. Rosenfeld, Shimberg, and Thornton (1984) conducted a survey of licensed psychologists as part of a comprehensive job analysis for the American Association of State Psychology Boards. Out of approximately 1,500 licensed psychologists who responded to the survey, 11.3% reported industrial/organizational psychology as the area in which they received their highest graduate training degree. In contrast, 16.3% of the respondents indicated industrial/organizational psychology as their current employment specialization.

In terms of employment settings, 7.5% of the respondents reported at least part-time employment in businesses, and 21.7% reported at least part-time employment with consulting organizations that could provide services to businesses. In terms of activities performed by psychologists in the various settings, 22.8% reported at least part-time involvement with personnel activities (e.g., employee selection and training, organizational development, etc.) and 4% indicated at least part-time work relating to human factors research and applications.

The results of the Rosenfeld et al. survey are quite informative. They indicate that more psychologists work in organizations and businesses and claim industrial/organizational psychology as their specialty than report being trained in that specialty area. Apparently, psychologists from specialty areas other than industrial/organizational are finding substantial employment performing activities that benefit businesses.

If there are so many opportunities for the employment of psychologists in business settings, why are there so few reports from training programs of school psychologists working in business settings? Is there some basic deficiency in the training or abilities of school psychologists that makes them less functional in business settings than psychologists from other specialty areas? We think not, and in the remainder of this chapter we will present our reasons for believing that the particular skills of the school psychologist are a needed service in business settings. First, we will discuss the types of training experiences to which school psychologists are exposed, and compare these with the skills required for effective functioning in business settings. We then discuss some of the activities that can be performed by school psychologists in business settings and provide some examples of the types of businesses in which these activities can be performed. We then present a discussion of future directions for training in school psychology and conclude with general suggestions for school psychologists who wish to seek employment in business settings.

TRADITIONAL TRAINING AND SKILLS OF THE SCHOOL PSYCHOLOGIST

Training and expertise in both psychology and education differentiates school psychologists from human service professionals in other specialty areas. As indicated by Bardon (1982), "Their education and experience have given them a unique perspective about how education operates and what psychology can offer to the solution of education-related problems. They move in vastly different directions and acquire and promote a multitude of different skills" (p. 13). In this section of the chapter we describe the traditional training and skills to illustrate their diversity and their application to settings other than public schools and clients other than children and youth.

The National Association of School Psychologists (NASP) *Standards for Training and Field Placement Programs in School Psychology* (1984) and the American Psychological Association (APA) *Accreditation Handbook* (1983) require a sound graduate education in general psychology and education for school psychologists. Courses in many areas of psychology and education are listed as essential in the NASP and APA standards for training: biological bases of behavior, normal and abnormal human learning and development, social bases of behavior, history and systems of psychology and education, instruction, assessment, direct and indirect intervention, research and statistics, measurement, and ethics and standards. Practical experiences and an internship of one year are also required. School psychologists, therefore, complete their training with a wide variety of skills and experiences. Traditionally, many of the courses and activities of school psychology students have been geared to children and youth in public schools, but the general education in psychology and education also encompasses the life span.

Phillips (1982) and the publication *School Psychology: A Blueprint for Training and Practice* (National School Psychology Network, 1984) listed training components of school psychology programs, many of which have direct application to adult clients outside a school setting. These include assessment of learning difficulties and behavior and social problems, psychodiagnostics, intervention and consultation techniques, learning, personality assessment, preventive mental health, basic academic, social, and life skills, research, human relations and communication skills, program development and evaluation, personnel development, quantitative skills, community agency relations, individual and group counseling, system analysis and evaluation, organizational change, and administrative skills. As indicated by Levinson and Hohenshil (1983), many of the components in school psychology training are similar to those of organizational psychology because both schools and industries are organizations and many of the activities in the two settings operate under the same theoretical principles.

The training of school psychologists results in five general types of services offered by practicing school psychologists (Reynolds et al., 1984). Assessment is defined as the "comprehensive process of deriving meaning from data, achieving a broad but detailed description and understanding of individuals, behaviors, environments, and reciprocal interactions among each of these elements" (Reynolds et al., 1984, p. 115). Thus, assessment in school psychology is much broader than testing and mere focus on internal characteristics of individuals. The second type of service provided by school psychologists is consultation, or a collaborative approach to problem solving in which a specialist provides assistance to one or more persons. School psychologists provide intervention services, which include instruction, counseling, therapy, behavior management, and ecological management. The fourth type of school psychology service is research, or the collection of data to resolve problems and elaborate theories. Finally, school psychologists provide inservice training and education.

Brown (1982) summarized many models that have been adopted during the history of school psychology: clinical/medical, psychoeducational, educational programming, data-oriented problem solving, social facilitation, preventative mental health, multidisciplinary team training, professional child psychology, consultation, and program evaluation. As with training and types of services provided by school psychologists, many of the models are directly applicable to clients other than children and youth and settings other than schools.

PSYCHOLOGY SKILLS REQUIRED IN BUSINESS SETTINGS

Psychologists in business settings practice a wide variety of skills in the service of their clients. Although this section describes the activities typically performed by psychologists in business settings, readers should note a high degree of similarity between these descriptions and our earlier discussions of the training and practice of school psychology. As argued by some (Levinson & Hohenshil, 1983; Levinson & Shepard, 1986), school psychologists often receive as much training, if not more than psychologists in other specialty areas, in the use of those skills necessary for competent practice of psychology in business.

Similar to Reynolds et al. (1984) discussion of the types of services provided by school psychologists, McCormick and Tiffin (1974) identified four major areas of focus for psychologists in business settings:

research, program development, individual evaluation, and consultation. Research includes areas such as understanding consumer behavior, identifying the effects of advertising on consumers, measuring organizational climate factors such as employee attitudes, morale, and job satisfaction, performing job and task analyses, and understanding factors that effect job performance, job satisfaction, and productivity. Program development often involves designing and implementing training and educational programs for both labor and management levels. Individual evaluation can involve the construction or selection and use of measurement instruments to recruit and select employees, and to evaluate job performance or organizational climate factors. Typical consultation activities might involve working with management staff to improve the organizational climate and interpersonal relationships, solve conflicts between management and labor groups, or plan new research or program development activities.

Landy and Trumbo (1980) discussed three major subareas of industrial/organizational psychology: testing, human relations, and experimental/industrial engineering. Psychologists involved with testing programs make use of prediction and measurement systems or develop new tests for the purpose of employee selection and performance appraisals, or determine equitable pay plans for employees through job analysis and evaluation. Psychologists providing human relations services investigate intraindividual variables such as job satisfaction and work motivation, develop motivation programs for managers, conduct seminars on leadership for executives, and evaluate training programs. Experimental/industrial engineering activities deal primarily with human-machine interactions, and may involve using information processing theory and research to design effective information displays, researching the effects of environmental conditions on job performance, or determining the characteristics of a new set of machines that will fit best with the capabilities and limitations of the organization's employees.

Dunnette's *Handbook of Industrial and Organizational Psychology* (1976) presented an extensive list of topics that serve as a guide to the varied work activities of psychologists in business settings. Each chapter in the handbook is designed to provide psychologists with knowledge about a specific job function. Dunnette's handbook includes the following topics: motivation theory and applications; human learning theory and applications; measurement theory and applications; design and conduct of research in field settings; measurement of aptitudes, abilities, skills, and vocational preferences; assessment of personality; background data collection techniques; job and task analysis procedures; engineering psychology; organizational effectiveness; personnel recruitment, selection, and job placement; personnel training; design and implementation of managerial assessment centers; conflict resolution techniques; organizational development theory and applications; consumer research techniques; nature and sources of job satisfaction; stress management; decision making and problem solving techniques; group influences on individual behavior; leadership; communication skills in organizations; organizational change processes; and cross-cultural issues.

Levinson and Hohenshil (1983) and Toomer (1982) noted an increase in the human relations functions of psychologists in business settings with the introduction of new services such as employee assistance and wellness programs and career development programs. More psychologists in business settings are becoming attuned to the personal needs of the work force emphasizing counseling, job satisfaction, career development, and job training activities. Klatzky, Alluisi, Cook, Forehand, and Howell (1985) discussed many applications of psychology to industry and business, such as human factors research and applications (understanding human-machine interactions and how they affect the design and manufacture of products and systems) and applied cognitive psychology (the applications of cognitive theory to the problems of users of tools and systems).

Toomer (1982) elaborated on the role of psychologists in business settings, citing personnel functions such as manpower planning; ongoing career development for employees; matching employees with available positions throughout the company; providing counseling and career planning assistance during outplacement or termination; developing and implementing Employee Assistance Programs that deal with individual counseling for a number of problem areas such as alcoholism/chemical dependency, legal, financial, and chronic physical problems, and interpersonal conflicts with other employees or family members. Toomer (1982) noted that psychologists may also be involved with health professionals in conducting preventative measure clinics for smoking withdrawal, weight loss, stress reduction, or work safety programs. According to Toomer (1982), psychologists can also apply assessment skills in the selection of appropriate procedures for use with minority groups and protected classes of individuals, and to test the validity of the selected procedures in terms of job-relatedness; can function in assessment centers evaluating difficult-to-measure skills such as leadership, decision making, and planning; and can assess employee suitability for transfer, including the suitability and adaptability of both the employee and his/her family; measuring the attitudes of employees towards benefit plan programs. In the area of organization development, psychologists can perform training functions such as teaching negotiations teams ways to use listening skills, conflict resolution, and confrontation and assertiveness techniques and can design and implement training programs for the updating of employee skills.

A job analysis study performed by Rosenfeld et al. (1984) for the American Association of State Psychology Boards found that out of a list of 111 job functions, 49 of these functions were performed by psychologists in all specialty areas; the common core of activities for all psychologists was much greater than the separate strands of activities that uniquely characterize the different specialty areas. In many respects, the job functions of the psychologist are the same, regardless of the area of specialization or the work setting. School psychologists interested in the transition from a school to a business setting will find it helpful to focus on activities that are routinely performed by psychologists in both school and business settings, such as the assessment of personality, aptitudes, abilities and skills, the collection of detailed background information, the application of knowledge of learning theory, the ability to design educational programs that are suited to the characteristics of the learner, the ability to evaluate existing programs, and the ability to design and implement research in field settings. We cannot overemphasize the important fact that school psychologists, with their broad training in both education and psychology, are often provided with a better background in the particular skills needed in business settings than psychologists from other specialty areas, including industrial/organizational psychology. With a slight shift in perspective (e.g., viewing school psychology services as a part of the educational process across the life span and outside of the school setting) and some additional informational resources, school psychologists can transfer their skills directly from the school setting to the business setting.

There are some business setting functions described earlier that, at first glance, might appear foreign to the work of school psychologists. On closer inspection, it can be seen that many of these functions are often part of the school psychologist's role when dealing with the school as an organization. Areas and topics such as job satisfaction, job performance, communication skills, conflict resolution, stress management, decision making and problem solving may all be dealt with in the provision of services to school staff. With additional training in the form of coursework and practica, school psychologists may find it easy to transfer their knowledge of schools-as-organizations to the setting of businesses-as-organizations.

Human factors research and the understanding of human-machine interactions may seem to be the business skill area most unlike the daily practice of school psychology. In reality, the school psychologist's unique ability to closely observe children as they perform mental and physical tasks provides them with a solid basis for developing skills in this area. Children often come into contact with machines and other products of industry, such as computers, vending machines, personal hygiene and home care appliances and so forth. Who could better advise on the development of products specifically developed for children than a professional who carefully observes children's abilities on a daily basis? In addition, applying observational skills to the study of adult-machine interactions would pose little difficulty for the competent school psychologist.

ACTIVITIES OF SCHOOL PSYCHOLOGISTS IN BUSINESS SETTINGS

Now that we've summarized the traditional training and expertise of school psychologists and the needs of business for the types of services that school psychologists provide, we can focus more closely on the specific activities of school psychologists in business settings. We feel that these activities are potentially numerous, but we have selected only a few general activities to discuss. We begin with one of the traditional activities of school psychologists: working with handicapped individuals. As in the schools, however, school psychology services should not be limited to handicapped individuals, so we describe the personnel assessment and training, counseling, and organizational interventions that can be conducted with the general business client. Finally, we discuss activities in research and publishing.

Services for Handicapped Employees

One of the major roles of school psychologists throughout the history of the field has been to serve handicapped individuals. Logically, service to handicapped employees must be included in the role of post-secondary school psychologists. Hohenshil and his colleagues (e.g., Hohenshil, 1979, 1982, 1984; Levinson & Hohenshil, 1983; Hohenshil & Warden, 1977) introduced and developed the speciality area of vocational school psychology to focus on the needs of handicapped youth and adults. Hohenshil (1982) defined vocational school psychology as a field of study, practice, and research which combines vocational education and rehabilitation and career planning for the handicapped with the traditional field of school psychology. The need for vocational school psychologists was supported by federal legislation and funding to serve the needs of the disadvantaged and handicapped, including the Rehabilitation Act of 1973, Career Education Implementation Incentive Act of 1977, the 1978 Comprehensive Education and Training Act Amendment, and the Job Training Partnership Act (Hohenshil, 1984).

The NASP *Standards for the Provision of School Psychological Services* (1985) indicated that vocationally oriented services should be included as a routine part of the practice of school psychology. However, a survey of school psychologists conducted by Shepard and Hohenshil (1983) indicated that most school psychologists were not significantly involved in many vocational services and felt unprepared to provide these services. Vocational school psychology has gained some momentum since that time, as seen by several university training programs in vocational school psychology and an increasing amount of research on the subject.

Hohenshil (1982) suggested that the vocational aspects of school psychology serve a particularly important role in secondary schools as more handicapped adolescents continue their formal schooling in the secondary levels. One of the dominant goals for these students is the acquisition of vocational skills, rather than academic skills only, which will prepare students for independent living upon leaving school. The vocational needs of handicapped individuals do not diminish when they leave school, however. School psychology services are needed as the individuals seek employment and enter the work place and the needs continue throughout their careers. Fagan (1981) pointed out that handicapped individuals leave one system (school) to go into another system (work) that is less responsive and defines its responsibilities differently. School psychologists are needed to bridge the gap between school and society for handicapped individuals.

According to Levinson and Hohenshil (1983) many of the businesses in the United States are required to take affirmative action to employ the handicapped and to make available to handicapped individuals opportunities such as job assignments, promotions, and transfer. Businesses must also make accommodations in jobs and working conditions. Furthermore, older employees are protected from discrimination in employment practices. Businesses have an increasing need for professionals who have training and experience with handicapped individuals in order to insure that requirements are met.

Four of the services provided by vocational school psychologists are assessment, counseling, training, and consultation. For all four services, school psychologists must have thorough knowledge of the physical and mental requirements of the various occupations that handicapped employees pursue. During assessment, vocational school psychologists are required to determine how specific aptitudes and interests of the handicapped individuals relate to various occupations and to make predictions about the probability of success in an occupation (Hohenshil, 1979). Assessment of handicapped employees includes the administration of traditional tests used by school psychologists as well as vocational instruments. Capps, Levinson, Hohenshil (1985) summarized different aspects of vocational assessment. Overall intellectual functioning is assessed to determine the level to which a handicapped person might progress in an occupation and specific intellectual strengths and weaknesses are evaluated to determine the potential to meet various demands of a job (e.g., visual-spatial skills, verbal skills, memory). Evaluation of motor skills determines a person's capability for physical tasks, such as operating machinery. Academic achievement is assessed to determine if a person has the minimum reading, writing, and arithmetic skills required of most jobs or the higher-level academic skills required for specific jobs. Adaptive behavior and personality are evaluated to determine general self-help, socialization, and communication skills, job related behaviors such as attendance and punctuality, and personality characteristics relevant to vocational interest and choice, such as need for structure, compulsivity, distractibility, and self-concept. Finally, vocational instruments are administered to evaluate general vocational aptitude and interest and specific skills related to particular occupations.

Vocational counseling of handicapped employees includes job-interviewing procedures and work adjustment counseling (Hohenshil & Warden, 1977). Hershenson (1984) described vocational counseling with learning disabled adults, but his ideas are also applicable to adults with other handicaps. Three domains of work characteristics must be considered: work personality (e.g. self-concept, motivation), work competencies (e.g. work habits, physical and mental skills, interpersonal skills relevant to work settings), and crystallized work goals. Hershenson (1984) pointed out that these domains may present more problems for handicapped than nonhandicapped individuals. For example, a history of failure in school may adversely affect a handicapped person's work personality. Work competencies may be affected by deficits such as perceptual problems, clumsiness and accident proneness, difficulties in sequencing tasks, problems with time sense and meeting deadlines, problems with focusing attention on tasks, and inadequate social skills. Handicapped individuals may have work goals that are inappropriate, unrealistic, or unformulated.

Hershenson (1984) identified several special issues that may present themselves during vocational counseling with handicapped employees. The first issue is that vocational counseling incorporates a large amount of printed occupation information that handicapped employees may be unable to read and much of the printed information may not address the special considerations of handicapped employees. Another issue involves planning and implementing a course of action with a client. Many handicapped individuals may experience difficulty conceptualizing a plan that requires a series of steps or may be weak in the organization or time skills necessary for following through with a plan. Counselors may find it necessary to structure a plan so that one step at a time is presented and implemented. A third issue is that many handicapped individuals may have poor interpersonal perception and the counselor must make sure that the client is "reading" communications correctly. Finally, counselors may have to deal with maladaptive behavior patterns that impede the counseling situation, such as low self-esteem, unrealistic expectations, anger, passivity, or denial of limitations.

Occupational training is an important activity for vocational school psychologists. Handicapped individuals are characterized by their learning difficulties and these difficulties are exhibited when learning job skills, just as they are when learning academic skills in a school environment. In many cases, adaptation of training materials and activities is required for the handicapped employee. Vocational school psychologists can also provide a valuable consultative service to businesses which employ handicapped workers. For instance, they can supply employers with information about the characteristics and limitations of various handicaps, the types of jobs for which handicapped workers are best suited, and the working conditions that are necessary. These services may be provided by school psychologists to almost any large business or industry.

School psychologists typically provide services for mentally retarded, learning disabled, and emotionally/behaviorally disturbed children in school settings. These handicaps are also present in the work place. Livingston, Korn, and McAlees (1982) listed additional handicapping conditions that may receive the services of vocational school psychologists: cardiovascular disorders, orthopedic disabilities, amputation, paraplegia and quadriplegia, arthritides, diabetes mellitus, and hearing and visual impairments.

Vocational school psychologists may be employed by most businesses that employ handicapped workers. In addition, they can serve handicapped workers in private and public rehabilitation agencies, sheltered workshops, universities and colleges, employment agencies, and consulting firms.

General Business Services

Although school psychologists have traditionally worked with handicapped students in schools, their services are not limited to the handicapped population. Work with handicapped employees is a logical extension of school psychology services to business settings, but as in schools, school psychologists in business settings serve non-handicapped business clients as well. In this section of the chapter, we discuss four types of services provided to general business clients: personnel assessment, education and training, organizational interventions, and counseling.

The services that school psychologists provide in business settings often assume the label of consultation. Consulting, however, is not discussed in this section of the chapter as a type of service per se. There has been a great deal of discussion in the professional literature about the widespread confusion over defining what constitutes consultation, and the concern over the proliferation of the use of the term in so many different contexts (Reynolds, et al., 1984). Professionals from many different specialty areas still debate whether consultation is a process used within various content areas or a content area per se (Gallessich, 1985; Kurpius, 1985). Some professionals have suggested that psychologists refer to all psychological services provided to business clients as consulting because this term has less negative connotations than labels such as counseling or personnel assessment (Ridley & Hellervik, 1982). We believe that trying to unravel the complexities of these issues in order to discuss consultation as a separate area of service provided by school psychologists in business settings is beyond the scope of this chapter. We therefore chose to concentrate our efforts on well-defined areas of service, keeping in mind that these services may be offered to business clients under the label of consultation, or that there may be a unique set of consultation activities, offered by school psychologists to business clients, that we have not specifically addressed in this chapter.

Personnel Assessment. Psychologists in the schools often perform student assessment functions. Psychologists is business settings are often responsible for personnel assessment functions. To ascertain the difference between student assessment and the personnel assessment functions, the following list of activities should be considered:

- assessing the current status of aptitudes and abilities;
- assessing individual personality characteristics, and how they mesh with the personality characteristics of others;
- identifying an individual's strengths and weaknesses and directions/strategies for continued personal growth;
- evaluating assessment instruments for their technical and clinical adequacy and selecting the most appropriate techniques for individualized assessment situations;
- developing questionnaires and conducting interviews to obtain background information and to supplement test findings;
- developing new assessment techniques specifically tailored for unique assessment situations;
- observing individuals as they perform daily routines;
- using background information and assessment results to develop recommendations tailored to the individuals specific needs;

- identifying the "most appropriate placement" for an individual;
- evaluating the suitability of an individual for a change of placement;
- providing verbal and written summaries of assessment results to examinees and others with a need to know.

We have little doubt that these activities are extremely familiar to psychologists practicing in the schools. This is not, however, a list of the student assessment functions of the school psychologist. This list actually represents a synthesis of the personnel assessment activities performed by psychologists in business settings as described by Toomer (1982), Landy and Trumbo (1980), McCormick and Tiffin (1974), Dunnette (1976), Gough (1976), Owens (1976), and Guion (1976). Like their counterparts of assessment responsibilities in the schools, personnel assessment duties frequently involve identifying and selecting or developing test instruments and data collection techniques that are well-suited to situational needs, conducting assessments or supervising the collection of assessment information, summarizing and reporting on assessment results, and developing recommendations based on these results. In the case of the psychologist in a school setting, the examinee is a child or young adult, and the results of the assessment will effect the examinee primarily in the context of the organizational environment known as the school. In the case of the psychologist in a business setting, the examinee is an adult, and the results of the assessment will effect the examinee in the context of the organizational environment known as the workplace or business setting.

The purposes for which these assessment activities are conducted are also very similar in school and business settings. Psychologists in school settings use assessment instruments to identify strengths and weaknesses in order to determine the most effective instructional approaches or behavioral management strategies, to ensure the most appropriate placement or change of placement for students with special needs, and to develop individualized education programs. In similar fashion, psychologists in business settings use instruments such as the General Aptitude Test Battery, the Flannigan Aptitude Classification Tests, the Wonderlic Personnel Test, and the Myers-Briggs Type Indicator, to identify strengths and weaknesses in order to assist employees with self-awareness and personal growth and to find the "most appropriate placement or change of placement" for new and experienced employees.

Many school psychologist will find they have great potential for transferring their knowledge of assessment activities to the business setting and providing valuable services to the business community. Because of the prominence of the assessment activities in the schools, school psychologists have the greatest opportunity to develop an intimate knowledge and understanding of the individual assessment process. School psychologists often continue to interact with the individuals they assess, and can develop a deep sensitivity to the effects of the assessment process on the examinee and on the organizational environment in which they must function (i.e., the school). Because of the somewhat ambiguous and publicly controversial nature of the constructs that they attempt to assess, such as intelligence, adaptive behavior, and social maladjustment, school psychologists have been sensitized to the need to evaluate carefully and critically the assessment instruments they use. For the same reasons mentioned above, school psychologists quickly learn the importance of being very adept at the interpretation, summary, and presentation of assessment results and recommendations based on these results. The school psychologist's experienced approach to the assessment process can prove to be a valuable skill with which to make the transition to business settings.

Personnel Education and Training. Businesses are becoming increasingly more aware of the need for and profitability of continued educational opportunities and specific, job-related training experiences for employees (Toomer, 1982). Technology continues to progress at a rapid rate constantly changing the way people approach work tasks and molding the environments in which they work. As work environments change, new patterns of employee interaction and communication emerge and new methods of managing employees come into play. Successful employees are those who have the ability to adapt to rather than resist change, and who continue to pursue learning as a career long after graduation from high school or college. Businesses are also beginning to see the value in wellness programs that provide education promoting healthy living on and off the job (Toomer, 1982).

Psychologists are being called on more frequently to assist with the development and implementation of programs to address the growing education and training needs of businesses. Some of the topics psychologists may be asked to address are effective listening, group problem solving and decision making, team effectiveness, conducting effective meetings, time management, teaching technicians how to train others (teaching the teachers), interviewer and interviewee skills, telephone and public relations skills, and stress management. Psychologists may find themselves responsible for all aspects of education and training programs in a business setting, including identifying areas where training is needed, developing specific objectives, and curriculum materials for the training program, developing specific strategies for presenting information during training, and conducting and evaluating the training.

As Toomer (1982) pointed out, psychologists must frequently address the training process rather than the specific content of the program, especially when dealing with technical areas. In such cases, "credibility must be established through the effective consulting steps of entry, needs assessment, "problem" definition, objective clarification, implementation, and evaluation rather than as the process of relating as one engineer to another" (p. 15). Toomer supported the contention that the key to a successful education program is being able to communicate on a common sense level with individuals of diverse educations and backgrounds.

With the possible exception of educational psychologists, school psychologists typically receive more training in human learning theory and applications than any other specialty area of psychology. In terms of practical applications in field settings, (i.e., applying and testing learning theory in actual classroom situations on a daily basis), the opportunities provided the school psychologist surpass those afforded psychologists in other specialty areas. It is not uncommon to find school psychologists who obtained training and experience as classroom teachers before receiving graduate training in psychology. School psychologists with strong backgrounds in theory and applications of human learning and the fundamentals of classroom teaching are especially well-suited to make the transition to business settings.

Toomer (1982) noted that it is a knowledge of the process and an ability to communicate with persons of diverse background that makes one an effective educator and trainer in business settings. School psychologists have extensive experience in communication processes. In their daily routine, school psychologists often must communicate with administrators, counselors, social workers, teachers, teacher aides, special service providers, and parents from the most diverse set of backgrounds imaginable. Administrators, counselors, and teachers, realizing the school psychologists abilities to communicate effectively, frequently call on them to assist with teacher, parent, or student conferences that involve delicate matters where communication must be especially clear. These difficult communication situations provide school psychologists with opportunities to sharpen their presentation skills with diverse groups of students and adults. School psychologists often are called on to share their knowledge and expertise in the form of staff presentations, in-service programs for various school employee groups, and presentations to colleagues at professional meetings.

School psychologists are often called on to help classroom teachers find specific instructional approaches that will work best with individual students. Good observational skills and knowledge of learner characteristics and learning environments help to make the school psychologist effective at matching the students abilities with appropriate methods of presenting information. The skills school psychologists develop in matching learners with instructional methods can be effectively applied in any situation, whether the learner is a child in a school or an adult in a factory or office.

Organizational Interventions. Activities classified as organizational interventions focus on issues relating to the functioning of groups, organizations, and systems rather than individuals. Although the emphasis in school psychology is frequently on the individual case study, several authors and trainers of school psychologists (Reynolds, et al., 1984; Sarason, 1971; Schmuck, 1982) have recognized the need for school psychologists to conceive of schools as organizations or systems that can be the source of problems such as poor academic performance, high levels of disruptive behavior, ineffective teaching, and poor parental support and cooperation.

School psychologists are often faced with a wide range of system-related problems that may best be dealt with using an organizational intervention approach (Reynolds, et al., 1984). In situations where special education service systems have become overloaded or ineffective, rather than attempting to process an unrealistic number of individual referrals, school psychologists may find themselves helping administrators and teachers examine the methods by which special education students are identified, referred, diagnosed, and treated, and/or assisting multidisciplinary teams to examine their structure and group interactions in order to become more effective problem solving units. A school psychologist taking an organizational intervention approach may help a school deal with teacher burnout by examining support systems available to teachers, administrative and community pressures and expectations placed on the teaching staff, community awareness of school problems, and community involvement in helping to solve school problems.

School psychologists faced with large numbers of referrals for a single type of problem may choose an organizational intervention approach rather than a case-by-case treatment of each individual referral. These types of large scale referral problems may be approached on a school-wide basis, dealing with administrators, teachers, counselors and various school committees, or on a classroom basis, dealing with a particular teacher and various support services staff. Effective communication is an important part of all successful organizations. The school psychologist's training and skill in effective communication can be put to use to help various subgroups of an organization improve communication among themselves and to clarify job priorities and organizational goals. The ability of school personnel to conduct organized, effective meetings can have a great impact on children's educational programs. School psychologists may find themselves examining various elements of the meeting processes of a particular school (e.g., group leadership, agenda and goal setting, member participation, group problem-solving and conflict resolution, and verbal and written summary techniques) and designing in-service programs to help the staff conduct more effective meetings.

School psychologists employ the familiar techniques of interviewing and observing when gathering information to identify and generate solutions to organizational problems. In addition, school psychologists sometimes make use of survey data collection techniques and organizational climate assessment instruments. School psychologists may employ a wide variety of techniques to effect organizational interventions. Games and simulation exercises, such as the *Lake St. Clair Incident* (Canfield & Starr, 1978), can be used to improve group processes. Problem-solving groups, survey feedback processes, and in-service training programs may all be used to increase skill knowledge and application and to improve early recognition and treatment of problem situations.

School psychologists who have developed a high level of competency in effecting organizational interventions will find that applying their skill in a business setting often requires little or no additional training because of the similarities in purpose, structure, and climate of the two types of organizations. Schools and businesses are both organizations with specific purposes and goals, they both employ staffs to serve the purposes of the organization, and they both hire executives and managers to refine organizational goals and to supervise staff members as they work toward the accomplishment of these goals. The organizational stresses, conflicts, and problems that effect groups working in the schools are found just as readily in the business environment. Businesses must deal with staff burnout, overloaded work systems, poor problem-solving by work teams, ineffective meetings, poor communication between individuals and departments, and conflicts between administration and staff.

Schools and businesses are so similar that the organizational problems encountered by psychologists in schools and business are nearly identical in scope and nature. Just like the psychologists in schools, psychologists in businesses may find themselves dealing with organizational problems by examining support systems and expectations of management, helping a company examine its relationships and image with its customers or the community in which it is located, assisting staff members to improve communication between subgroups and individuals, improving effectiveness of meetings and problem solving and conflict resolution processes, or helping a manager to deal with more general personnel problems rather than dealing on an individual basis with each staff member.

The techniques used to explore organizational problems and the types of interventions employed are also similar in school and business settings. Personnel interviews, on-site observations, survey data collection, and organizational climate assessment instruments are all employed to identify and clarify organizational problems. Games and simulation exercises, problem-solving groups, survey feedback processes, and in-service training programs are all intervention strategies that are used as often in businesses as in schools.

Counseling. Counseling is considered one of the standard activities in the repertoire of school psychologists (NASP, 1984; National School Psychology Training Network, 1984). As Reynolds et al. (1984) noted, school psychologists typically utilize short-term counseling techniques with children that are considered to be relatively normal. Given the typical school psychologist's work situation, short-term counseling approaches can be considered the most effective use of the school psychologist's limited time. The amount and breadth of counseling activities practiced routinely varies from one school psychologist to another. Some school psychologists choose to focus their counseling efforts on specific types of problems, such as adjustment to divorce situations, school phobia, drug abuse, disruptive behavior, poor study skills, or self-exploration. Others prefer providing more general, crisis intervention or short-term counseling services.

In high school settings, school psychologists often find themselves assisting students in the exploration of career and vocational choice issues. Developmental theorists (Crites, 1976; Havighurst, 1953; Herr & Cramer, 1979; Tiedeman, 1961) have noted that thoughts about career plans and activities are an integral part of the psychological environment of the adolescent and young adult. Dealing with these types of issues is a logical extension of the school psychologist's psychoeducation assessment activities at the junior and senior high school levels. A school psychologist's interpretation of test results and other information in a student's cumulative record folder can often assist a student in more realistic career exploration and planning. Discussions relating to work/study habits, personality characteristics, and personal likes and dislikes can also be of assistance to students who are struggling to understand how these factors relate to education and career choices and job satisfaction. As mentioned earlier, the area of vocational school psychology is beginning to draw more attention and will play a greater part in the future of psychological service provision in the schools.

Students experiencing difficulties with family or peer relationships often need help in dealing with these types of problems. The school psychologist can assist by utilizing any of a variety of short-term counseling approaches, especially those that emphasize techniques such as modeling effective problem-solving behaviors, providing constructive feedback, and helping students evaluate the effectiveness of their actions. School psychologists can also help students explore the emotional benefits of conflict resolution, and provide support when solutions to difficult problems produce hostile or otherwise negative reactions from peers. Sometimes, school psychologists find it necessary to provide short-term counseling services to other school staff members, such as school counselors, administrators, teachers, and resources aides, or to the parents of a student who has been referred for psychological services.

School psychologists interested in using their counseling skills in business settings may find locating suitable clients to be a more difficult task than in other areas of service provision. Of all the psychological services offered to businesses today, direct counseling interventions are the least well established. Ridley & Hellervik (1982) have noted among businesses a strongly ingrained bias against counseling service provision. Despite evidence to the contrary, these businesses hold the belief that employee counseling services do not provide a substantial return on investment, and are therefore not cost effective. Osipow (1982) has presented an optimistic outlook for the future:

> As industry begins to make certain assumptions about its employees, counseling can become an acceptable function. Schools have tended to assume that students are there to learn and develop personally; thus, counseling has played an important role in that process. Students are to be nurtured and their growth facilitated, and thus counseling easily fits. Industry exists for different reasons (products or services) but always for profit. Thus, industry has tended to take a different view of employees. It sees employees as serving the institution rather than the other way around. However, as industry comes to see employees as important resources and assets needing periodic "maintenance, repair and improvement" (analogous to maintenance needed by machinery and physical plants), then counseling will be accepted not on an abstract philosophical, humanitarian basis, but rather in terms of profit statements and productivity. (p. 19)

Business and industry counseling programs that have been successful have been able to demonstrate tangible benefits to the companies that institute them, such as decreased alcoholism, drug abuse, and absenteeism resulting in a reduction in lost person-hours, and improved health habits resulting in reductions in the amount of medical care funds used by employees (Toomer, 1982; Osipow, 1982). Although some companies are beginning to see the advantages of providing counseling services to employees (Ridley & Hellervik, 1982; Osipow, 1982; Toomer, 1982), the most accepting businesses are still not likely to view as profitable the employment of a psychologist to do long-term counseling with a limited number of workers. As a result, counseling activities provided in business settings are typically short-term in nature. Full-time employment of psychologists for counseling purposes is also not well-established and psychologists functioning in this capacity often maintain an itinerant or consulting role.

The successes of some business counseling service programs has led to a dramatic increase in Employee Assistance Programs (EAPs) over the past decade (Toomer, 1982). These programs focus on worker health issues and other areas of assistance such as counseling for marital and family problems, supervisor/subordinate and other interpersonal conflicts, and career and retirement counseling. As an extension of the personnel function of assessing employees for suitability of transfer to another location or position, psychologists can counsel employees and family members to help relieve the strain of the move. Equal Employment Opportunity (EEO) complaints filed by employees (e.g., non-promotion, harassment) often involve elements of psychological trauma. Psychologists can intervene with direct counseling to help alleviate the employees distress and to help both parties involved in a complaint achieve a rational solution. Both employers and employees are beginning to recognize the stress components of daily work activities. Through individual counseling, psychologists can help workers implement effective self maintenance programs to reduce the negative effects of stressful activities or to change stress producing routines.

Many businesses are beginning to understand the realtionship between profitability and employee career development (Toomer, 1982; Osipow, 1982). Professional employees often accomplish major job goals shortly after joining a company, and consequently find themselves reaching a plateau early in their careers. These employees often need assistance to avoid stagnation and to continue to grow professionally by finding new areas to explore or new ways to use their abilities. Managers in most companies must continue to develop their skills and advance or be subject to demotion or movement away from the mainstream of the organization's vital activities. A skilled psychologist can assist managers in dealing with questions of continuing patterns of work achievement that capitalize on the managers personal knowledge and ability strengths, and help to achieve the company's long-term goals. Employees nearing the end of their work careers often need assistance to plan for retirement. Issues such as economics, personal values, self-esteem, family relations, time management, and health all must be addressed in a constructive way in order to maintain the quality of life of retiring employees and their family members (Osipow, 1982). Employees who leave a company earlier in their career for personal or work-related reasons need assistance in finding new employment and establishing themselves in a new work environment or geographical location. Realizing that satisfied former employees are good ambassadors for their company, more businesses are beginning to provide outplacement or termination counseling services (Morin, 1981; Toomer, 1982).

School psychologists who effectively use counseling techniques in their daily work would not find employment in the business arena much different from the school setting. School psychologists typically serve as itinerant school staff members and, like their counterparts in the business setting, must usually form only short-term counseling relationships. School psychologists often find both students and school staff to be among their clients, and may be required to intervene in administrator-teacher or teacher-student conflicts—situations that are not unlike the employee or supervisor-subordinate relationship problems that are dealt with by psychologists in the business setting. Like their counterparts in business settings, school psychologists frequently deal with issues such as peer and family relations, work/study habits, and career exploration and planning, and often conduct their counseling activities in the service of skeptical employers (school administrations).

Research

Research is a basic activity in most businesses. Research in business may include marketing research with consumers or potential consumers of products, productivity and efficiency research with employees, research concerning the effects of working conditions or training programs on employee behavior, or surveys of employee attitudes or attitudes of community members about the business. Research about human characteristics and behavior, especially as they relate to learning and development, is one of the major types of services provided by school psychologists and a large portion of the training of school psychologists includes courses in research design, statistics, and measurement. Reynolds et al. (1984) stated that the principle goal of research in school psychology is to provide an empirical basis for action and this goal is easily transferred to business settings.

Reynolds et al. (1984) discussed four research approaches in school psychology, all applicable to research in business: descriptive research, case studies and $N = 1$ studies, experimental designs, and quasi-experimental designs. Descriptive research includes the gathering of facts and the identification and clarification of relationships. Much of the research in social science, as well as in business, is descriptive in nature. The researcher does not attempt to manipulate variables and is more concerned with the natural state of affairs. Examples of descriptive research in business settings are the determination of the numbers and characteristics of consumers who prefer a company's product to another product, the average scores of different groups of employees on personnel tests, and the relationship between test scores and later job performance.

The second approach to research in school psychology is case studies and $N = 1$ studies. These studies involve a comprehensive analysis of one individual. Case studies and $N = 1$ studies may involve no experimental controls or simple experimentation. For example, a school psychologist in a business setting may work with a handicapped employee who is having difficulties meeting productivity quotas. The psychologist might then analyze the characteristics of the employee and the work environment to develop hypotheses about the cause of the difficulties. A study might be implemented to test the effects of various manipulations of the environment on the employees' behavior.

In an experimental design, the researcher manipulates a set of variables to observe their effects on other variables and uses random selection of subjects and random assignment of subjects to conditions. The researcher exercises complete control over the pertinent variables, and as a result of this control, is able to infer relationships of cause and effect between variables. For example, the executives of a company may want to determine the effect of a training program on employee productivity before allocating the funds necessary to provide all employees with the specialized training. In an experimental design, the researcher randomly selects a group of employees who receives the training and compares their productivity to a randomly selected group of employees who did not receive the training. In quasi-experimental designs, the researcher's control is limited, usually in the random selection of subjects and the random assignment of subjects to groups. Most children are already grouped into classrooms in schools and similar conditions exist in business which often prevent true random selection and assignment.

School psychologists can be employed in a research capacity by almost any type of business. Marketing and advertising agencies and research organizations provide additional employment avenues for school psychologists. School psychologists may also be asked to serve as free-lance consultants for research conducted in business and industry.

Publishing

School psychologists have long been employed in the publishing industry. Some school psychologists are employed by publishers of text books and children's materials and their activities include development, marketing, and sales of the materials. The primary type of publisher to which school psychologists provide an integral service is test publishers, especially those that publish individual psychological and educational tests. Publishers of individual tests are able to draw on the expertise of school psychologists in measurement, statistics, and research design for development and sales of their products. The factor which differentiates school psychologists from measurement specialists in individual test publishing, however, is the clinical skills of school psychologists in administering and interpreting individual tests.

In preparation for this chapter, we surveyed 13 of the leading publishers of individual tests used by school psychologists and received nine responses. Five of the nine companies employ school psychologists as full-time staff members and the other four companies indicated their willingness to do so in the future. Although questions about the use of school psychologists as consultants were not specifically asked in the survey, most of the responses emphasized the role that school psychologists play as consultants in test development or participants in test research programs. Four of the nine companies had served as sites for school psychology internships and an additional four companies expressed their willingness to have school psychology interns in the future.

The school psychologists employed by the test publishers hold a variety of positions; chairman of the board, vice president, research associate/project director, marketing manager, and sales consultant. Most of the positions held by school psychologists are those of research associate/project director and sales consultant. Research associates/project directors perform many types of activities related to the development and use of tests. These activities include managing item development, item tryout, and standardization programs, conducting reliability and validity studies, writing and editing test manuals and technical reports, reviewing new tests being considered for publication, conducting training workshops, and answering questions from test users. Sales consultant also conduct training workshops and answer questions from test users. They make calls on school districts, clinics, and other facilities and manage exhibits at professional conventions.

As indicated earlier, we have both been employed by a publisher of individual tests and educational programs. We began our employment as research associates and were later promoted to senior research associates. At this particular company, research associates serve primarily as project directors who manage all aspects of a test's development and publication. Development typically begins with reviewing and evaluating proposals from prospective test authors and making recommendations for acceptance or rejection. The review process typically includes estimating costs, resource and personnel needs, projected work schedules and timelines for all stages of the test's developmental period. Once a test is accepted for publication, the research associate prepares a detailed master budget and work schedule for the developmental period. As work progresses, the master budget and schedule are revised on a yearly basis.

A research associate works closely with the test authors on the initial writing, formatting, and smaller-scale field testing of potential test items. After field testing, a national item tryout is conducted. The research associate supervises and participates in the production of test materials, the selection of the sample to be tested, and the coordination of the activities of tryout test coordinators and examiners across the country. The data collected in the item tryout are coded and analyzed according to specifications prepared by the research associate. The author and the research associate then select the items to be used in the standardization of the test. The standardization program consists of activities similar to those conducted during the national item tryout, but on a much larger scale. The research associate maintains contact with as many as 50 testing sites located throughout the country, managing the testing activities of 150 to 200 examiners.

To assure that the newly developed test meets the standards set forth by the *Standards for Educational and Psychological Testing* (APA, 1985), reliability and validity studies are also planned and conducted as part of the standardization program. Following standardization, the research associate plans and directs data analyses and the development of norms and other data tables, and writes parts of the test manual. He or she also works with editors on content and copy editing of manuals and other test components, and collaborates with production staff on aspects of design, format, art, typesetting, printing, and packaging of all test materials. During the test development process, the research associate also assists the marketing and sales department with the design and writing of copy for advertising and promotional materials. After 3 to 5 years, the test is ready for publication, and the research associate assumes the role of teacher and information disseminator. Post-publication activities include conducting training workshops for sales consultants and test users, answering letters and telephone calls from test users, and preparing technical updates for the test. The responsibilities of a senior research associate are similar to those of a research associate, but include additional managerial and administrative functions, such as hiring and supervising additional staff members, (e.g., research assistants, editors, resource aides) allocating resources, and filing monthly departmental status reports.

FUTURE DIRECTIONS FOR TRAINING

Although the traditional training of school psychologists provides a strong background in psychology and education, which may be applied to adults and to a business setting, some of the activities of post-secondary school psychologists may require additional training. Many universities now have or will have in the future avenues for obtaining additional training in specialty areas of school psychology. The practicing school psychologist who wishes to seek employment in a business setting or the school psychology student who wants to include adult and business oriented activities in his or her training program may find it necessary to review the requirements of particular activities in a business setting and "fill in the gaps" in his or her current training. As indicated by Levinson and Shepard (1986), a move to a business setting may not require an advanced degree; additional training may be obtained through single courses, seminars, workshops, readings, and post-degree practica and internships. In some cases, additional training may be obtained on the job in a business setting.

For school psychologists who wish to serve handicapped or non-handicapped individuals in a business setting, additional training may be needed in several areas (Hohenshil, 1984; Hohenshil & Warden, 1977). Knowledge and competency in vocational assessment, vocationally oriented education and in-service training, requirement of various occupations, and career planning and counseling are prerequisites for practice in business. School psychologists must also acquire skills in decision making processes, strategic planning, and organizational intervention and evaluation. The vocational aspects of life-span development and legal requirements in employment practices may also represent additional training needs of the post-secondary school psychologist. Work with handicapped workers demands knowledge of special instructional methodologies, unique education and career development needs of special groups, and community resources for handicapped persons.

School psychologists who wish to conduct research in business settings may need to obtain more training in research design, statistics, and measurement than required by some training programs. School psychologists who wish to serve as project directors for test publishers may also need to obtain more training in these areas, and in technical writing, editing, production of written materials, and organizational management. As sales consultants for publishing companies, school psychologists may wish to obtain skills in marketing, communication, and persuasive selling.

The school psychology internship may provide valuable experiences in a business setting. According to the 1984 NASP *Standards for Training and Field Placement Programs in School Psychology,* only one-half of the yearlong internship must be spent in a school setting. Interns may want to consider a business setting for the other half of the internship. Most of the test publishers we surveyed had school psychology interns in the past or were willing to do so in the future. Other types of businesses could also be used as sites for internships.

CONCLUSION

Employment in a business setting is a viable career option for school psychologists. In this chapter, we described our arguments for the conceptualization of post-secondary school psychology and the need for school psychological services in business and industry. We discussed several of the activities in businesses that fit the expertise and experiences of school psychologists: work with handicapped employees; personnel assessment, education, and training; organizational interventions; counseling; research; test publishing.

School psychologists may want to enter a business setting for several reasons. Dissatisfaction with current employment is probably one of the primary reasons. Anderson, Hohenshil, and Brown (1984), for example, found that 14% of a sample of school psychologists expressed dissatisfaction with their work situation. Other school psychologists express general job satisfaction, but are uncertain that schools are the best place for them to use their training and skills. Other school psychologists may simply wish to explore the alternatives offered by a new setting.

School psychologists who feel a need to involve themselves in further career exploration should not restrict themselves from considering a business setting simply because they did not declare this as their lifelong ambition while completing graduate studies. School psychologists who wish to consider employment in a business should do a careful self-assessment and examine areas such as the skills which they perform best and enjoy most, the work situations where their skills lead to the most job satisfaction, the aspects of their job they like most, and the aspects they want to change. They should then compare these areas to the experiences offered by business and industry settings.

School psychologists should assess their attitudes about business, as these attitudes may be incompatible with the general goals of businesses and may seriously hinder attempts at obtaining employment or functioning effectively in a business setting. Ridley and Hellervik (1982) noted that a common implicit assumption of some psychologists is that "business and industry are the enemy of the humanitarian tenets ostensibly espoused" (p. 53) by the profession of psychology. Osipow (1982) shares this view, explaining:

> . . . psychologists have tended to shy away from profit statements. Yet, in order to be accepted and have a function in industry, such a perspective must be at least acceptable and, to some extent, promoted. We must be willing to accept the view that profits, humanely obtained, are an integral part of our society. Outcomes can be measured in terms of savings obtained by reducing turnover and absenteeism, both resulting in improved profits because of reduction in costs of production." (p. 19)

We hope that this chapter has paved the way for more school psychologists to expand their career options and fulfill their potential by entering the business arena. We have found growth and satisfaction in our business activities. Our experiences have given us greater understanding of education and psychology and of profits, budgets, "bottom-lines", and corporate culture. Above all, we have always considered ourselves to be school psychologists, even though we practiced our profession in a business setting.

REFERENCES

American Psychological Association (1983). *Accreditation handbook.* Washington, DC: Author.

American Psychological Association (1985). *Standards for educational and psychological testing.* Washington, DC: Author.

Anderson, W. T. (1982). Roles for school psychologists in community colleges. *Psychology in the Schools, 19,* 221–225.

Anderson, W. T., Hohenshil, T. H., & Brown, D. T. (1984). Job satisfaction among practicing school psychologists: A national study. *School Psychology Review, 13*(2), 225–230.

Bardon, J. I. (1979). Educational development as school psychology. *Professional Psychology, 10,* 224–233.

Bardon, J. I. (1982). The psychology of school psychology. In C. R. Reynolds & T. B. Gutkins (Eds.), *The handbook of school psychology* (pp. 3–14). New York: John Wiley.

Brown, D. T. (1982). Issues in the development of professional school psychology. In C. R. Reynolds, & T. B. Gutkin (Eds.), *The handbook of school psychology* (pp. 3–14). New York: John Wiley.

Canfield, A. A., & Starr, D. D. (1978). *The lake St. Clair incident.* Ann Arbor, MI: Humanics Media.

Capps, C. F., Levinson, E. M. & Hohenshil, T. H. (1985). Vocational aspects of psychological assessment: Part III. *Communique, 13*(5), 5–6.

Crites, J. O. (1976). A comprehensive model of career development in early adulthood. *Journal of Vocational Behavior, 9,* 105–118.

Dunnette, M. D. (Ed.) (1976). *Handbook of industrial and organizational psychology.* Chicago, IL: Rand Mcnally.

Fagan, T. (1981). Role expansion in the eighties: Counseling and vocational school psychology. *Communique, 9*(6), 1–2.

Gallessich, J. (1985). Toward a meta-theory of consultation. *Counseling Psychologist, 13*(3), 336–354.

Gough, H. (1976). Personality and personality assessment. In Dunnette, M. D. (Ed.). *Handbook of industrial and organizational psychology.* Chicago, IL: Rand Mcnally.

Guion, R. M. (1976). Recruiting, selection, and job placement. In Dunnette, M. D. (Ed.). *Handbook of industrial and organizational psychology* (pp. 777–828). Chicago, IL: Rand Mcnally.

Havighurst, R. J. (1953). *Human development and education.* New York: Longmans Green.

Herr, E. L., & Cramer, S. H. (1979). *Career guidance through the life span: Systematic approaches.* Boston, MA: Little, Brown and Company.

Hershenson, D. B. (1984). Vocational counseling with learning disabled adults. *Journal of Rehabilitation, 50*(2), 40–44.
Hohenshil, T. H. (1979). Adulthood: New frontier for school psychology. *School Psychology Digest, 8,* 193–198.
Hohenshil, T. H. (1982). School psychology + vocational counseling = vocational school psychology. *Personnel and Guidance Journal,* 6(1), 11–14.
Hohenshil, T. H. (1984). The vocational aspects of school psychology: 1974–1984. *School Psychology Review,* 13, 503–509.
Hohenshil, T. H., & Warden, P. (1977). The emerging vocational school psychologist: Implications for special needs students. *School Psychology Digest, 7,* 5–17.
Hughes, J. L. (1987, March). The school psychologist as a community service provider. In R. C. D'Amato (Chair), *Nontraditional activities for school psychologists.* Symposium conducted at the meeting of the National Association of School Psychologists, New Orleans, LA.
Klatzky, R. L., Alluisi, E. A., Cook, W. A., Forehand, G. A., & Howell, W. C. (1985). Experimental psychologists in industry: Perspectives of employers, employees, and educators. *American Psychologist, 40*(9), 1031–1037.
Kurpius, D. J. (1985). Consultation interventions: Successes, failures, and proposals. *Counseling Psychologist, 13*(3), 368–389.
Landy, F. J., & Trumbo, D. A. (1980). *Psychology of work behavior.* Homewood, IL: The Dorsey Press.
Levinson, E. M., & Hohenshil, T. H. (1983). The practice of vocational school psychology in business and industry: Possibility or pipe dream? *Psychology in the Schools, 20,* 321–327.
Levinson, E. M., & Shepard, J. W. (1986). School psychology in business and industry: possibility becomes a reality. *Psychology in the Schools, 23,* 152–157.
Livingston, R. H., Korn, T. A., & McAlees, D. C. (1982). Alternative strategies in vocational rehabilitation. In C. R. Reynolds & T. B. Gutkin (Eds.), *The handbook of school psychology* (pp. 3–14). New York: John Wiley.
McCormick, E. J., & Tiffin, J. (1974). *Industrial psychology.* Englewood Cliffs, NJ: Prentice–Hall.
Morin, W. (1981). *Successful termination.* Chicago, IL: Professional Educational Materials.
National Association of School Psychologists (1984). *Standards for training and field placement programs in school psychology.* Stratford, CT: Author.
National Association of School Psychologists (1985). *Standards for the provision of school psychological services.* Stratford, CT: Author.
National School Psychology Training Network (1984). *School Psychology: A blueprint for training and practice.* Minneapolis, MN: Author.
Osipow, S. H. (1982). Counseling psychology: Applications in the world of work. *The Counseling Psychologist, 10*(3), 19–24.
Owens, W. A. (1976). Background data. In Dunnette, M. D. (Ed.). *Handbook of industrial and organizational psychology* (pp. 609–644). Chicago, IL: Rand Mcnally.
Phillips, B. N. (1982). Reading and evaluating research in school psychology. In C. R. Reynolds & T. B. Gutkin (Eds.), *The handbook of school psychology* (pp. 3–14). New York: John Wiley.
Reynolds, C. R., Gutkin, T. B., Elliott, S. N., & Witt, J. C. (1984). *School psychology: Essentials of theory and practice.* New York: John Wiley.
Ridley, C. R., & N. W. Hellervik (1982). Counseling psychology in the corporate environment. *The Counseling Psychologist, 10*(3), 53–54.
Rosenfeld, M., Shimberg, B., & Thornton, R. (1984). Job analysis of licensed psychologists. *Professional Practice of Psychology, 5*(1), 1–20.

Sandoval, J. J., & Love, J. A. (1977). School psychology in higher education: The college psychologist. *Professional Psychology, 8,* 328–339.

Sarason, S. B. (1971). *The culture of the school and the problem of change.* Boston, MA: Allyn & Bacon.

Schmuck, R. A. (1982). Organization development in the schools. In C. R. Reynolds & T. B. Gutkin (Eds.), *The handbook of school psychology* (pp. 3–14). New York: John Wiley.

Shepard, J. W., & Hohenshil, T. H. (1983). National survey of career development functions of practicing school psychologists. *Psychology in the Schools, 20,* 445–449.

Tiedeman, D. V. (1961). Decision and vocational development: A paradigm and its implications. *Personnel and Guidance Journal, 40,* 15–20.

Toomer, J. E. (1982). Counseling psychologists in business and industry. *The Counseling Psychologist, 10*(3), 9–18.

Tractman, G. (1981). On such a full sea. *School Psychology Review, 10,* 138–182.

6
The School Psychologist in Neurologic Settings

BRIAN J. STONE
JEFFREY W. GRAY
Ball State University

RAYMOND S. DEAN
Neuropsychology Laboratory, Ball State University
Indiana University School of Medicine

Neuropsychology is the study of relationships between brain functions and patterns of behavior. Thus, the field involves a partnership between psychology and other neurosciences (Dean, 1985a). Clinical neuropsychology focuses on the assessment of behavioral functions that have implications for the diagnosis, understanding, and treatment of disorders with neurologic underpinnings (Dean, 1985a; Lezak, 1983). Although the field of neuropsychology has evolved in a number of ways, its emphasis on assessment and diagnosis has remained the crucial factor in its development (Lezak, 1983). Unlike other applied specialities in psychology, the foundation of school psychology also rests firmly upon assessment for diagnosis and intervention. As such, the school psychologist is well positioned to offer a unique understanding of children referred for neuropsychological services. Indeed, these same competencies that allow the school psychologist to function in the neurological setting also offer an excellent background from which to profit from special training in clinical neuropsychology. This chapter explores the neurologic setting as an alternative to practice in the schools.

OVERVIEW OF NEUROPSYCHOLOGY

The recent surge of interest in neuropsychology can be largely attributed to the geometric increase in our understanding of the brain (Hynd & Hartlage, 1983). Concomitant with our expanding knowledge of cortical functioning has come the need for psychologists to apply these principles in various settings. A recent study by D'Amato, Dean, and Holloway (1987) demonstrated a significant increase in the number of positions requiring neuropsychological skills over the past 10 years, across clinical settings and geographical regions of the United States. Some 10% of the psychology positions available in 1986 required skills in neuropsychology, demonstrating a marked increase over the less than 1% requiring such skills in 1976. Clearly, there is a growing need for psychologists trained in neuropsychology.

The present level of sophistication in neuropsychology can be attributed, in part, to the availability of patients with localized brain lesions as a result of the second world war (Lezak, 1983). With such a patient population, various psychological measures could be validated as predictors of specific brain damage. Psychology's early success in diagnosing and documenting the effects of neurologic disorders led to the rapid development of neuropsychology in the medical setting (Kolb & Whishaw, 1980).

These efforts to localize brain functions were significant in that cortical damage was often considered a unitary phenomenon. Indeed, Chapman and Wolff (1959) argued the concept of "organicity" in a seminal paper, which portrayed the amount of brain tissue destroyed as the determining factor in predicting cognitive impairment, regardless of the site of the lesion. This rather naive concept of brain function as a unitary phenomenon has continued with us in the search for "tests of organicity" (e.g., the Bender Visual-Motor Gestalt Test) (see Lezak, 1983). Typically, single tests designed to identify brain damaged individuals yield a high rate of false negatives. This is not surprising in light of the fact that cognitive deficits depend on the site and extent of the lesion, as well as many other factors (Jarvis & Barth, 1984). Clearly, conclusions based on a single measure of neuropsychological functioning are tenuous at best (Gray & Dean, in press; Jarvis & Barth, 1984). Traditionally, neuropsychology in North America has centered on a quantitative-experimental approach, as seen in the work of Halstead (1947) and Reitan (1964). This actuarial tradition has involved the administration of standardized test batteries. Data resulting from these tests are compared with normative standards for brain damaged and normal populations. Although a one-to-one correspondence between performance on specific tests and individual structures of the brain has not been supported by research (e.g., Reitan, 1969), a quantitative approach to the localization of dysfunction remains (Dean, 1985a). Indeed, although some simple behaviors are clearly localized in the brain, more complex behaviors involve multiple functions of the cerebral cortex. Specific localization is also often confounded, because areas of the brain may compensate for others in performance of various functions (Kolb & Whishaw, 1980; Luria, 1966; Luria, 1973).

From this actuarial approach to understanding brain functioning comes a need for a multidimensional battery (Gray & Dean, in press). The primary goal of neuropsychological assessment remains to understand brain function from patterns of behavior. The present quantitative practice in North America has produced a method of demonstrating the validity of these procedures. These studies have been important in documenting the behavioral effects of brain damage as well as the utility of differential diagnosis (Gray, Rattan, & Dean, 1986; Rutter, 1982).

The present state of scientific reasoning in neuropsychology favors a broad band comprehensive battery in the assessment of cognitive, sensory-motor, and emotional impairment resulting from a given neurologic condition (Dean, 1985a). The neuropsychological battery attempts to account for the fact that a given lesion may effect multiple functions. With such a wide range of components, the neuropsychological examination can therefore be seen as providing the most comprehensive assessment possible for a given patient.

The comprehensiveness of the neuropsychological examination encourages multiple tiers of interpretation. At the first level, the battery provides information concerning the individual's overall level of functioning. With data regarding the subject's cognitive, intellectual, sensory-motor, and emotional functioning, an interpretation may be offered without consideration of the neurologic implications. The next level of inference considers the neurologic significance of specific levels of performance, left-right hemispheric differences, pathological signs, and complex patterns of performance (Reitan, 1964).

Particularly with children, where our knowledge base is limited (Boll, 1987), interpretations often must remain at the level of a comprehensive psychological assessment. The ability to proceed beyond this tier is inhibited by the complex interaction of premorbid status, age at onset, type of disorder, and the psychologist's training and experience. Clearly, specific training and experience in neuropsychology aids the psychologist in understanding the neurologic relevance of their findings. Hence, the depth of contribution in the neurologic setting is related, at least from an assessment point of view, to both training as a school psychologist, and the ability to make these findings relevant to questions inherent to the setting.

The school psychologist has considerable expertise in psychoeducational assessment, learning theory, cognition, consultation, and intervention. In fact, many measures administered by the school psychologist have evolved as part of the neuropsychological examination (e.g., tests of intellectual functioning such as the Wechsler Intelligence Scale for Children-Revised, sensory-motor tests such as the Bender Visual-Motor Gestalt, achievement tests such as the Wide Range Achievement Test-Revised and Peabody Individual Achievement Test, and receptive language tests such as the Peabody Picture Vocabulary Test-Revised). However, as one would expect, the neuropsychological interpretation of these standard instruments may differ drastically from that traditionally offered by the school psychologist (Dean, 1982).

Often, the major contribution of a neuropsychological examination is the ability to detail a subject's functional strengths and weaknesses as they would interact with known psychotherapeutic, educational, and social interventions (Boll, 1987). The examination also provides the psychologist data useful in predicting independent functioning and general progress. Regardless of the setting, a neuropsychological approach offers a framework useful in the integration of information pertaining to a subject's functioning in their premorbid environment.

Neuropsychology has much data to contribute to the knowledge base of school psychology, particularly in regard to assessment techniques and differential diagnosis procedures (Hynd & Hartlage, 1983). With its emphasis on cognitive-cortical relationships, research in neuropsychology offers valuable information in the understanding of children's individual differences within an educational setting (Gaddes, 1985).

CLINICAL CHILD NEUROPSYCHOLOGY

Given the emphasis on children in the school psychologist's training, child neuropsychology would seem to offer the school psychologist a good match with existing competencies. Indeed, given the difference between neuropsychological functioning of children and adults, and the primitive level of knowledge in child neuropsychology, it has been argued that even the adult neuropsychologist is often unprepared to practice child neuropsychology (Boll, 1987).

The preparation for the practice of clinical child neuropsychology requires training in applied psychology, neurology, clinical psychology, child developmental psychology, and the study of educational systems (Boll, 1987). The school psychologist is in an advantageous position to combine knowledge in these areas. From another point of view, school psychology and child neuropsychology are currently facing many similar issues, such as differential diagnosis, assessment of the learning process, and effective remediation and intervention strategies (Boll, 1987).

The emphasis in child clinical neuropsychology is on comprehensive assessment, and neuropsychological interpretation of results (Boll, 1987). Interpretation concerns level of performance, pattern of functioning, right-left comparisons, and specific pathognomic indicators, such as constructional dyspraxia or aphasic disorders (Jarvis & Barth, 1984; Lezak, 1983). Boll (1987) argues,

> . . . the major contribution of a [child] neuropsychological examination is not in detailing the neurological structures that are likely to be misfiring. It is more likely to be the case that the neuropsychological contribution will be a much more comprehensive and detailed explanation of the child's ability, strengths, and weaknesses, as these interact with his or her ability to respond to psychotherapeutic, educational, and parental interactions. (p. 18).

The school psychologist's competencies, although often lacking in neuropsychology, include assessment and an in depth understanding of children and instructional methods. Clearly these competencies would be beneficial to the practice of clinical child neuropsychology.

Neuropsychology in the Neurologic Setting

Neurology concerns the diagnosis and treatment of disorders arising in the nervous system. Disorders of the brain often affect higher level cognitive and emotional functions. Indeed, deficits in higher order functions are sometimes the first and only symptom of a less pervasive central nervous system disorder (Dean, 1985a). In such cases, the neuropsychological examination, with its demonstrated utility in assessing cognitive and emotional deficits, offers insight in the diagnosis, rehabilitation, and prognosis of central nervous system disorders (Dean, 1985a).

The neurologist typically receives information from the patient's general physical examination, medical history, and routine laboratory tests in conjunction with the neurologic examination. As part of the initial examination the neurologist assesses the patient's overall neurologic status. This is accomplished through a series of short screening procedures, which generally involve the assessment of the cranial and spinal nerves, reflexes, gross and fine motor coordination, and the sensory, cerebellar, and language functioning of the patient. The neurologist often conducts a mental status examination of the patient, which serves as a structured interview involving the patient's orientation, and basic social and cognitive functioning (Jarvis & Barth, 1984). Results from this initial examination may lead to more specific tests, such as measures of brain electrical activity (electroencephalagram), and/or structure (computerized axial tomography scan). Obviously, a working knowledge of these procedures is desireable for the school psychologist working in this setting (Pfeiffer, Dean, & Shellenberger, 1987). Clearly, these neurologic data are capable of providing insights into the patient's neuropsychological functioning.

As advances in brain imagery techniques continue to revolutionize neurology with noninvasive information regarding brain structure, the psychologist's role will continue to shift away from providing diagnostic and localization information, to considering issues of prognosis and rehabilitiation strategies (Dean, 1985a). Thus, the psychologist will be increasingly called upon to determine the patient's abilities and deficits from the neuropsychological examination, and incorporate them into a treatment framework. In this case, the psychologist works to more clearly define and predict the patient's current and future functioning. To this end, the psychologist in this setting works to link neuropsychological, educational, and behavioral assessment to prognosis and rehabilitiation strategies (Dean, 1985a).

In rehabilitation efforts, a multidisciplinary team approach is often employed, wherein the psychologist works with other specialists (e.g., speech pathologist, physical and occupational therapists) as a member of a multidisciplinary team (Pfeiffer, Dean, & Shellenberger, 1987). This approach should be a familiar one to school psychologists, given the similar requirements of P.L. 94-142.

As part of the multidisciplinary team, the psychologist provides a comprehensive overview of the patient's abilities and deficits across cognitive, emotional, and adaptive behavioral domains. The school psychologist in the neurologic setting should be capable of integrating this information into the treatment plan of remedial or special educational programming. Seen as the expert in such matters, the psychologist may be consulted by team members on issues relating to cognitive, emotional, or educational functioning. Ultimately, the primary responsibility for the patient rests with the physician. Therefore, within this framework, a clear definition of each team member's patient care role reduces the potential for miscommunication and overlapping responsibilities.

Differential diagnosis is often the first task in the neurological setting. As part of the team, the psychologist attempts to integrate the patient's test data with known behavioral patterns associated with specific neurological disorders. The school psychologist in this setting may be able to provide unique information that transcends the differential diagnosis and addresses the patient's interaction with the educational system. The school psychologist's knowledge of the educational process, and the manner in which patient's patterns of test performance relate to this process, enables the clinician to offer the team a view of the patient that is not commonly available in the neurological setting. Unlike clinical or counseling psychologists, the school psychologist is in a position to make useful educational placement recommendations for the child following medical treatment.

As mentioned previously, a number of factors complicate the neurologic interpretation of psychological data. The patient's age at onset, severity of pathology, premorbid functioning, and individual differences all interact to increase the difficulty of making neurologic conclusions (Dean, 1985a). Yet, rehabilitation efforts often depend upon precise documentation of behavioral deficits (Lezak, 1983). Under these conditions, the psychologist's role in the neurologic setting often involves the collection of baseline data concerning the patient's functioning as a precursor to rehabilitation efforts (Dean, 1983). This role, which emphasizes cognitive, emotional, and behavioral strengths in treatment planning, is a familiar one to psychologists who function in the schools (Reynolds, 1988). The school psychologist's training and experience in psychodiagnostics and cognitive intervention strategies are clear assets in the neurologic setting.

An often overlooked aspect of treatment is the patient's emotional reaction to their neurological dysfunction (Dean, 1983). The psychologist must be aware of the patient's adjustment to their disorder, and how this adjustment should be considered in prognosis. The school psychologist's background in the assessment of emotional reactions and their educational implications (e.g., distractibility, anxiety, and impulsivity), as well as an awareness of the emotional concomitants of learning disorders (Clarizio & McCoy, 1983) provides an often neglected view of the patient. Emotional reactions may be temporary, but severity of the neurological problem and time since onset must be considered in the prognosis of emotional functioning (Reed & Reitan, 1963). Indeed, the school psychologist's remediation planning, emphasizing strengths, and reducing potential failures, plays an important part in limiting the adverse emotional reactions expected with failure (Dean, 1982; Reynolds, 1988).

As suggested above, many of the school psychologist's activities are similar in both the neurologic and educational settings. These roles involve an emphasis on assessment of functional strengths in remedial planning and/or rehabilitation. So too, the school psychologist's background in case management, and following individual cases during rehabilitation are important skills in the neurologic setting. School psychologists also bring valuable knowledge and skills in conducting and interpreting research in assessment and treatment to the neurologic setting.

The school psychologist intending to practice in a medical setting must be aware of the hospital as a social institution. In the schools, the roles of the principal, the teachers, and the support personnel are often more clearly defined. Whereas in the medical setting, the psychologist must be aware of the hierarchal roles of health care providers, (e.g., the physician, physician's assistant, intern, resident, etc.) within particular specialty areas. The psychologist in the neurologic setting should work to understand the hierarchal roles of other support personnel (e.g., the registered nurse, licensed practical nurse, nurse practitioner, etc.), as well as acknowledge the roles of other health care providers within their areas of expertise (e.g., psychiatric technicians, occupational and physical therapists, etc.).

The psychologist in this setting must endeavor to define his or her role within a medical context, and offer professional expertise accordingly. Indeed, role confusion limits the team's functioning and is at cross purposes with patient care.

NEUROPSYCHOLOGY IN THE PEDIATRIC SETTING

The neuropsychological problems seen in a pediatrics department tend to be less severe and more developmental than those in either neurologic or psychiatric settings. A survey of pediatrics departments showed that the most frequently reported referrals were learning disabilities (32%), conduct disorders (26%), mental retardation (11%), and developmental delays (11%) (Tuma, 1982). Clearly, this patient population tends to mirror the school psychologist's case load within an educational setting. Neuropsychological skills could improve a psychologist's effectiveness with such a population. In fact, in a recent survey, 92% of practicing school psychologists indicated that neuropsychology training would increase their usefulness in working with educationally handicapped children (Leavell & Lewandowski, 1988).

In sum, psychological referrals to a pediatric department tend to involve either behavioral concerns, developmental delays in cognitive/academic abilities, and/or neuropsychological risk areas such as perinatal complications or head injuries (Deysach, 1986). It is in the latter two areas in which neuropsychological training most benefits the school psychologist. Developmental delays are often seen as suggestive of organic disorders (Dean, 1985c). Under these conditions, neuropsychological assessment is often called for in an effort to rule out a hypothesis of cerebral dysfunction. After diagnosis, a treatment plan is developed for improving functional living skills and to further educational rehabilitative efforts to prevent early academic failure (Deysach, 1986).

When there is prior medical evidence of neurologic dysfunction, the neuropsychological assessment provides information concerning higher-level cognitive abilities related to the insult. The systematic assessment of these abilities offers data that are separate from the neurological examination. These data are often of use to the multidisciplinary team in developing a rehabilitative strategy. This approach may also require the school psychologist to employ his or her consultation skills with parents and educators in the implementation of an academic and social treatment plan. The scope of the psychologist's consultation skills does not end here, however. In some instances, the psychologist must provide assessment information and clinical expertise regarding patient prognosis to legal personnel involved in disability litigation (Deysach, 1986).

The neuropsychologically trained school psychologist also offers the pediatrics department expertise in the growing field of early identification of high risk and handicapped children (Deysach, 1986; Gray, Dean, Strom, Wheeler, & Brockley, 1987). Neuropsychological assessment is particularly crucial, given the federal emphasis on early identification (P.L. 99-457, 1987), and the estimated 10% incidence of preschool children at risk of developing minor neurological disorders and related adjustment difficulties (Kalverboer, 1971).

Children in pediatric departments are often required to take medications that have behavioral side effects (Hutchins & Hynd, 1987). School psychologists are capable of employing psychometric expertise in investigating the effects of drugs on higher level cognitive and emotional functioning. Therefore, the psychologist can further assist the physician by providing information on the cognitive and emotional effects of various dosages and administration strategies employed in stabilizing the patient on medication. The school psychologist can also integrate cognitive functioning results of the medicated patient within a rehabilitation program, as well as address the effects of medication within the educational setting.

One role of pediatric departments involves the identification of childhood disturbances, and perinatal risk factors as predictors of future behavioral disturbances. For example, in a 4-year study, Pfeiffer, Heffernan, and Pfeiffer (1985) reported a significantly higher morbidity rate for behavioral disorders in high risk infants. In related research, Gray, Dean, Strom, Wheeler, and Brockley (1987) examined the effects of perinatal complications on school-age children. The results showed developmentally delayed children to be significantly more likely than a normal control group to have had high risk factors occuring in the prenatal and perinatal periods.

Although research opportunities abound in pediatric departments, time is often limited. The high patient load of pediatric departments dictates that the psychologist function efficiently and economically. School psychologists are no strangers to stringent case load demands.

The school psychologist brings many unique skills into any medical setting. However, the school psychologist trained in neuropsychology brings a more in depth understanding of brain behavior relationships and their interaction with the educational process. The school psychologist possesses the skills necessary to respond to the emotional sequelae of neuropsychological disorders (Dean, 1983; Pfeiffer, Dean, & Shellenberger, 1987). Also, the school psychologist is experienced in the consultation skills necessary to relate neuropsychological information to nonpsychologist colleagues, as well as to parents, and the community.

The role of a school psychologist in a pediatrics department bears a close resemblance to the traditional practice of school psychology, in that the psychologist is expected to reconcile, interpret, and evaluate the cognitive and behavioral functioning of impaired children (Pfeiffer, Dean, & Shellenberger, 1987). However, with neuropsychological training, the school psychologist is able to offer more in-depth service to both the pediatrics and neurologic department. What follows is an overview of the areas in which the school psychologist with background and training in neuropsychology may make a unique contribution.

RESEARCH

The vast majority of what is known about brain functioning has come during the last two decades (Dean, 1982). Given our rather primitive knowledge neuropsychology is still in its formative years. Many complex issues in child neuropsychology have yet to be addressed. Clearly, an expanded foundation of research is crucial to the growth of our understanding of brain behavior relationships. The school psychologist's training in research is vital to neuropsychology. In this vein, current research that links neuropsychology and school psychology is examined below.

NEUROPSYCHOLOGY AND LEARNING DIFFICULTIES

As previously mentioned, over one fourth of the patients in departments of pediatric neurology present with learning problems (Dean, 1985a). The assessment and treatment of learning disorders is certainly familiar to the school psychologist. Clearly, the school psychologist's training in assessing such problems, as well as his or her knowledge of the educational system are well served in such cases.

It is established in the literature that children identified as "learning disabled" represent a heterogenous group (Adelman & Taylor, 1986; Algozzine & Ysseldyke, 1986; Gaddes, 1985; McNutt, 1986; Torgeson, 1986). This fact is paid homage in P.L. 94-142, which stresses differential diagnosis and treatment of these disorders (Hynd & Hartlage, 1983). Using neuropsychological methods, a number of researchers have begun to isolate distinct subtypes of learning disabilities (Rattan & Dean, 1987; Rourke & Strang, 1983). These subtyping efforts are important for they have implications for understanding the etiologies and providing common approaches to treatment (Gaddes, 1985; Rattan & Dean, 1987; Torgeson, 1986).

Recent research with learning disabled children has shown neuropsychological assessment data to offer unique information beyond that traditionally gleaned from psychoeducational testing (D'Amato, Gray, & Dean, 1988). Indeed, neuropsychological data have been shown to add incrementally to the school psychologist's ability to predict achievement (Strom, Gray, Dean, & Fischer, 1987). As the purpose of psychoeducational testing is to predict and understand performance, neuropsychological assessment would seem to offer much to our understanding of the school-age child.

NEUROPSYCHOLOGY AND CHILDREN'S HEAD INJURIES

Traumatic head injury is the most common cause of neurological impairment in persons under the age of 42 (Lezak, 1983). With advances in medicine, a greater proportion of brain injured patients survive than in previous years and go on to present with severe behavioral deficits. Given the prevalence of childhood head injuries and the high likelihood that the patient will return to the classroom, a neuropsychological appreciation is important for psychologists in both the medical and school setting (Gray & Dean, in press). Neuropsychological research provides a structured framework to better appreciate the complex relationship between emotional and cognitive disturbance in children with head injuries.

Some 50% of children with severe head injuries develop psychiatric disorders (Brown, Chadwick, Shaffer, Rutter, & Traub, 1981; Chadwick, Rutter, Brown, Shaffer, & Traub, 1981; Rutter, Chadwick, Shaffer, & Brown, 1980). The neuropsychological examination provides information concerning the severity of the head injury as well as the probability of an ensuing psychiatric disorder (Dean, 1986). It is interesting to note that the risk following head injury includes not only psychiatric dysfunction resulting from cerebral damage, but also the child's emotional reaction to these physiological changes, as well as a decrease in the child's ability to cope with premorbid emotional difficulties (Dean, 1986). From this point of view, neuropsychological impairment may be seen to interact with psychosocial stressors as etiologic factors in post traumatic psychiatric disorders (Gray & Dean, in press).

The cognitive rehabilitation of the brain injured child would seem to be best approached by identifying strengths and using these areas to organize a treatment plan (Gray & Dean, in press). This style of remediation is central to the school psychologist's assessment and academic intervention pattern in the schools, in that identified functional strengths are emphasized in remediation to compensate for known weaknesses (Reynolds, 1988). Therefore, the school psychologist is seen as bringing similar training to this area, albeit somewhat narrower in scope.

NEUROPSYCHOLOGY AND CHILDREN'S PSYCHIATRIC DISORDERS

The majority of research in this area concerns the differential diagnosis of psychiatric disorders (Dean, 1985a), particularly schizophrenia, and to a lesser extent, depression. Indeed, most referrals for neuropsychological examination in clinical psychiatric settings seek to discriminate between functional and organic psychiatric disorders. In fact, our present state of knowledge suggests that functional and organic disorders would be better represented as a continuum rather than a nosological dichotomy (Dean, 1985a).

Although much of the research in this area is based on adult subjects, findings do have relevance for the treatment of the school-age child when considering issues of differential diagnosis, screening, and treatment of emotional handicaps. Recent research has shown neuropsychological measures hold utility as diagnostic markers of psychiatric disorders, as well as providing data for treatment and prognosis (Gray, Dean, D'Amato, & Rattan, 1986; Gray, Rattan, & Dean, 1986; Woods & Short, 1985).

Affective disorders have been linked to dysfunction in the temporal-parietal lobes of the brain's right hemisphere through neuropsychological assessment (Dean, Gray, & Seretny, 1987; Gray, Dean, Rattan, & Cramer, 1987; Taylor, Greenspan, & Abrams, 1979). Whereas schizophrenic patients have typically shown diffuse impairment, with relatively greater deficits on neuropsychological tasks seen to measure left frontal-temporal functioning (Dean, Gray, & Seretny, 1987; Taylor & Abrams, 1984). The present state of knowledge in hemispheric lateralization would support language mediated thought as being subserved by the left hemisphere, and mood and affective tone by the right.

Perinatal complications have been linked to schizophrenia in high-risk subjects genetically predisposed towards this illness. Perinatal factors are seen as part of the diathesis stress model, whereby an individual's genotype interacts with the environment to produce a phenotype expressive of the disorder (Parnas, Schulsinger, Teasdale, Schulsinger, Feldman, & Mednick, 1982; Silverton, Finello, Mednick, & Schulsinger, 1985).

NEUROPSYCHOLOGY AND PERINATAL COMPLICATIONS

Children born with perinatal complications are more likely to present with neurologic disorders during childhood (Gray, Dean, Strom, Wheeler, & Brockley, 1987). Perinatal complications have been shown to be directly related to mental retardation, cerebral palsy, and epilepsy (Gray & Dean, in press). In addition, children who suffered perinatal difficulties are more likely to demonstrate less pervasive neuropsychological disorders, such as developmental delays, cognitive and behavioral disorders, learning difficulties, hyperactivity, speech difficulties, and attention deficits (Field, Dempsey, & Shuman, 1979; Field, Dempsey, & Shuman, 1981; Pfeiffer, Heffernan, & Pfeiffer, 1985).

The psychologist in the neuropsychological setting must take perinatal factors into account when evaluating a child, or an active pathology may be assumed from symptoms of a perinatal trauma. Indeed, the link between factors in the perinatal period and the child's later development is just beginning to be understood.

Understanding the effect of perinatal complications on later cognitive, physical, and emotional development has utility in both the school and neuropsychology setting. This is particularly true in the area of early identification of handicapping conditions (e.g., P.L. 99-457). Accurate information concerning the perinatal period of development can lead to early diagnosis, and therefore, early intervention (e.g., infant stimulation programs) (Parmalee, Beckwith, Cohen, & Sigman, 1983).

In fact, early intervention programs are being challenged to demonstrate program impact (Rosenberg, Robinson, Finkler, & Rose, 1987). Given the school psychologist's skills in assessment, intervention, identification, and outcome-based research, the school psychologist is in a position to identify and provide intervention, as well as to quantitatively document changes that have resulted from early interventions with handicapped youth (Keith, 1987; Rosenberg, Robinson, Finkler, & Rose, 1987).

Given the link between perinatal complications and risk for neuropsychological disorders, early intervention has been shown to improve the high-risk child's psychological and educational prognosis (Parmalee, Beckwith, Cohen, & Sigman, 1983). Indeed, early identification through perinatal screening should be a vital first step in an effective intervention program.

TRAINING

Training in school psychology would appear to allow a significant contribution in the understanding of individuals referred for neuropsychological services. However, the school psychologist's contribution would clearly be enhanced with specialized training and experience. Organized study is necessary in the interpretation and integration of neuropsychological results for a given patient. Training in neuropsychology also offers the school psychologist an expanded role within the neurologic setting. The goal of training in school psychology and neuropsychology provides a link between elements of neurology, education, and psychology. The objective of neuropsychology training in school psychology is not one of adulteration nor the formation of a new speciality, but rather to provide for the development of the competencies necessary as an independent practitioner.

The Task Force of the International Neuropsychological Society (INS) and Division 40 of the American Psychological Association (APA) have recommended specific elements in clinical neuropsychology training (Report of the Task Force on Education, Accreditation and Credentialing, 1981). These training components include (a) a basic psychology core, (b) a generic clinical core, (c) specialized training in the neurosciences, (d) specific clinical neuropsychological training, and (e) completion of a doctoral dissertation (Report of the INS—Division 40 Task Force on Education, Accreditation and Credentialing, 1987). In addition, a 1800-hour internship in a neuropsychological setting is recommended (full time for one full year, which may be completed in a 2-year period), preceded by appropriate practicum experience. Postdoctoral experience is often seen as desirable, and is designed to provide opportunity for advanced-level training as an independent practitioner of clinical neuropsychology (Report of the INS—Division 40 Task Force on Education, Accreditation and Credentialing, 1987).

Meier (1981) has argued for distinct models for training in neuropsychology, which have been adopted by INS.

Model I. Neuropsychology is offered as a subspeciality within doctoral level applied psychology programs (i.e., clinical, counseling, or school psychology).

Model II. Neuropsychology is offered as an interdepartmental program (similar to a minor), whereby students earn relevant course credits outside of their major department (assuming distinct psychology, neuropsychology, and neuroscience departments are available).

Model III. An integrated Ph.D. program is offered in clinical neuropsychology, based upon the scientist-practitioner model.

Model IV. An intact graduate neuropsychology curriculum is offered containing separately credentialed Ph.D. and Psy.D. components to reflect either a research or practitioner emphasis.

Neuropsychology as a subspeciality or a minor (Models I and II) predominate as training approaches in the United States (Hynd, 1981). Indeed, there are very few doctoral training programs in clinical neuropsychology per se (Golden & Tupperman, 1980).

In days of declining enrollments and austere academic budgets, it would be surprising to find large numbers of universities willing to commit the resources necessary to establishing a doctoral-level neuropsychology program. A less obvious reason relates to the fact that clinical neuropsychology has yet to be recognized as a speciality by the American Psychological Association. Therefore, graduates of such a program would not fit conveniently within the existing infrastructure of applied psychology. It is also the case that the majority of neuropsychologists have been initially trained within a broad speciality area and hence identify with clinical, counseling, or school psychology. With this as a backdrop, it is understandable to find the majority of training in neuropsychology falling within Meier's (1981) first two models. These training approaches are more readily accomodated within existing general doctoral psychology programs.

Although school psychologists and trainers have begun to recognize the value of a neuropsychological approach (Hynd, 1981; Leavell & Lewandowski, 1988), few school psychology programs offer training which satisfies the INS Division 40 Task Force or the models outlined by Meier (1981). In fact, while most doctoral-level school psychology training programs offer neuropsychology courses or elements into existing training, few have made a major commitment to neuropsychological training.

The Ball State University school psychology program is offered as a model for training neuropsychologists. This model offers the emphasis of neuropsychology within the framework of school psychology. The neuropsychology speciality is offered as a cognate option within an APA approved Ph.D. school psychology program. The primary objective of such training is to prepare school psychologists who are capable of applying neuropsychological principles (Dean, 1985b).

Traditional school psychology training is taken concomitant with neuropsychological coursework. Rigorous child and adult neuropsychology practica requirements are provided in conjunction with interdepartmental training. Didactic coursework in neuropsychology includes medical neuroanatomy, brain physiology, neuropsychological assessment and diagnosis of adults and children, cognitive rehabilitation, and a foundation of statistical and research design. The program aspires to develop student's neuropsychological and research skills.

The internship experience provides the focus for specialization within neuropsychology. Internships are designed to foster advanced-level training in applied and research aspects of neuropsychology, as well as to provide the necessary competencies for independent practitioners of both school psychology and neuropsychology (Dean, 1985b).

As the role of neuropsychology grows within the health services, the demand for neuropsychologists will increase (Boll, 1987; D'Amato, Dean, & Holloway, 1987; Dean, 1985a). Graduate education models will be called upon to meet this demand (Meier, 1981). The growth of neuropsychology as a science and as a profession will be enhanced by practitioners with backgrounds that integrate expertise in many relevant areas. Training models exist to provide this integrated understanding of neurological bases of behavior within different settings. Specific course preparation combined with practicum and internship experiences allow the refinement of the practice of school psychology into the neurological setting (D'Amato & Dean, 1988, Dean, 1982).

REFEPENCES

Adelman, H. S., & Taylor, L. (1986). Summary of the survey of fundamental concerns confronting the LD field. *Journal of Learning Disabilities 19,* 391–393.

Algozzine, B., & Ysseldyke, J. E. (1986). The future of the LD field: Screening and diagnosis. *Journal of Learning Disabilities 19,* 394–398.

Boll, T. J. (1987). The role of neuropsychology in the general practice of child and adolescent psychology. *Journal of Child and Adolescent Psychotherapy, 4,* 13–18.

Brown, G., Chadwick, O., Shaffer, D., Rutter, M., & Traub, M. (1981). A prospective study of children with head injuries: III. Psychiatric sequelae. *Psychological Medicine, 11,* 63–78.

Chadwick, O., Rutter, M., Brown, G., Shaffer, D., & Traub, M. (1981). A prospective study of children with head injuries: II. Cognitive sequelae. *Psychological Medicine, 11,* 49–61.

Chapman, L. F., & Wolff, H. G. (1959). The cerebral hemispheres and the highest integrative functions of man. *Archives of Neurology, 1,* 357–424.

Clarizio, H. F., & McCoy, G. F. (1983). *Behavior disorders in children* (Third Ed.). New York: Harper and Row Publishers.

D'Amato, R. C., & Dean, R. S. (1988). School psychology practice in a department of neurology. *School Psychology Review, 18,* 416–420.

D'Amato, R. C., Dean, R. S., & Holloway, A. F. (1987). A decade of employment trends in neuropsychology. *Professional Psychology: Research and Practice, 18,* 653–655.

D'Amato, R. C., Gray, J. W., & Dean, R. S. (1988). A comparison between intellectual and neuropsychological functioning. *Journal of School Psychology, 26,* 283–292.

Dean, R. S. (1982). Neuropsychological assessment. In T. R. Kratochwill (Ed.), *Advances in school psychology* (Vol. II), (pp. 171–201). Hillsdale, NJ: Lawrence Erlbaum Associates.

Dean, R. S. (1983, August). Integrating neuropsychological and emotional variables in the treatment of children's learning disorders. Presented at the Annual Convention of the American Psychological Association, Anaheim, CA.

Dean, R. S. (1985a). Neuropsychological Assessment. In J. D. Cavenar, R. Michels, H. K. H. Brodie, A. M. Cooper, S. B. Guze, L. L. Judd, G. L. Klerman, & A. J. Solnit (Eds.). *Psychiatry* (pp. 72–88). Philadelphia: J. B. Lippincott Company.

Dean, R. S. (1985b). Neuropsychology Specialization: School Psychology Internship Training Program. Ball State University: Educational Psychology Department.

Dean, R. S. (1985c). Foundation and rationale for neuropsychological bases of individual differences. In L. Hartlage & C. Telzrow (Eds.), *Neuropsychology of individual differences: A developmental perspective* (pp. 7–39). New York: Plenum Press.

Dean, R. S. (1986). Neuropsychological aspects of psychiatric disorders. In J. E. Obrzut & G. Hynd (Eds.), *Child neuropsychology* (Vol. 2) (pp. 83–112). New York: Academic Press, Inc.

Dean, R. S., Gray, J. W., & Seretny, M. L. (1987). Cognitive aspects of schizophrenia and primary affective depression. *International Journal of Clinical Neuropsychology, 9,* 33–36.

Deysach, R. E. (1986). The role of neuropsychological assessment in the comprehensive evaluation of preschool-age children. *School Psychology Review 15,* 233–244.

Field, T., Dempsey, J., & Shuman, H. H. (1979). Developmental assessments of infants surviving the respiratory distress syndrome. In T. Field, A. Sostek, S. Goldberg, & H. H. Shuman (Eds.), *Infants born at risk* (pp. 220–246). New York: Spectrum.

Field, T., Dempsey, J., & Shuman, H. H. (1981). Developmental follow-up of pre- and postterm infants. In S. L. Friedman & M. Sigman (Eds.), *Preterm birth and psychological development* (pp. 299–312). New York: Academic Press.

Gaddes, W. H. (1985). *Learning disabilities and brain function: A neuropsychological approach* (2nd Ed.). New York: Springer-Verlag.

Golden, C. J., & Tupperman, S. K. (1980). Graduate training in clinical neuropsychology. *Professional Psychology, 11,* 55–63.

Gray, J. W., & Dean, R. S. (in press). Implications of neuropsychological research for school psychology. In T. B. Gutkin and C. R. Reynolds (Eds.). *The Handbook of School Psychology* (2nd Ed.). New York: Wiley and Sons.

Gray, J. W., Dean, R. S., D'Amato, R. C., & Rattan, G. (1986). Differential diagnosis of primary affective disorder using the Halstead-Reitan Neuropsychological Test Battery. *International Journal of Neuroscience, 35,* 43–49.

Gray, J. W., Dean, R. S., Rattan, A., & Cramer, K. (1987). Neuropsychological aspects of primary affective depression. *International Journal of Neuroscience 32,* 911–918.

Gray, J. W., Dean, R. S., Strom, D. A., Wheeler, T. E., & Brockley, M. (1987). Perinatal complications as predictors of developmental disabilities. Manuscript submitted for publication.

Gray, J. W., Rattan, A. I., & Dean, R. S. (1986). Differential diagnosis of dementia and depression in the elderly using neuropsychological methods. *Archives of Clinical Neuropsychology, 1,* 341–350.

Halstead, W. C. (1947). *Brain and intelligence: A quantitative study of the frontal lobes.* Chicago: University of Chicago Press.

Hutchins, T. A., & Hynd, G. W. (1987). Medications and the school-age child and adolescent: A review. *School Psychology Review, 16,* 527–542.

Hynd, G. W. (1981). Training the school psychologist in neuropsychology: Perspectives, issues, and models. In G. W. Hynd & J. E. Obrzut (Eds.), *Neuropsychological assessment and the school-age child* (pp. 379–404). New York: Grune & Stratton.

Hynd, G. W., & Hartlage, L. C. (1983). Brain-Behavior Relationships in Children. In G. W. Hynd (Ed.), *The school psychologist: An introduction* (pp. 231–268). Syracuse: Syracuse University Press.

Jarvis, P. E., & Barth, J. T. (1984). *Halstead-Reitan test battery: An interpretive guide.* Odessa, FL: Psychological Assessment Resources.

Kalverboer, A. F. (1971). Free-field behavior in preschool boys and girls. In G. B. Stoelinga & J. J. Van der Werff Tem Bosch (Eds.), *Normal and abnormal development of brain and behavior* (pp. 187–203). The Netherlands: Leiden University Press.

Keith, T. Z. (1987). Assessment research: An assessment and recommended interventions. *School Psychology Review, 16,* 276–289.

Kolb, B., & Whishaw, I. Q. (1980). *Fundamentals of human neuropsychology.* San Francisco: W. H. Freeman and Co.

Leavell, C., & Lewandowski, L. (1988). Neuropsychology in the schools: A survey report. *School Psychology Review, 17,* 147–155.

Lezak, M. D. (1983). *Neuropsychological assessment* (2nd Ed.). New York: Oxford University Press.

Luria, A. R. (1966). *Higher cortical functions in man.* Translated by B. Haigh. New York: Basic Books.

Luria, A. R. (1973). *The working brain.* New York: Basic Books.

McNutt, G. (1986). The status of learning disabilities in the states: Consensus or controversy? *Journal of Learning Disabilities 19,* 12–16.

Meier, M. J. (1981). Education for competency assurance in human neuropsychology: Antecedents, models, and directions. In S. B. Filskov & T. J. Boll (Eds.), *Handbook of clinical neuropsychology* (pp. 00–00). New York: Wiley-Interscience.

Parmalee, A. H., Beckwith, L., Cohen, S. E., & Sigman, M. (1983). Early Intervention: Experience with Preterm Infants. In T. B. Brazelton & B. M. Lester (Eds.), *New approaches to developmental screening of infants* (pp. 00–00). New York: Elsevier Science Publishing Company.

Parnas, J., Schulsinger, F., Teasdale, T., Schulsinger, H., Feldman, P., & Mednick, S. (1982). Perinatal complications and clinical outcome within the schizophrenia spectrum. *British Journal of Psychiatry, 140,* 416–420.

Pfeiffer, S. I., Dean, R. S., & Shellenberger, S. (1987). The school psychologist in medical settings. In T. Kratochwill (Ed.). *Advances in School Psychology* (Vol. 5) (pp. 177–202). New Jersey: Lawrence Erlbaum, Inc.

Pfeiffer, S. I., Heffernan, L., & Pfeiffer, C. (1985). The prediction of possible learning disabilities in high risk infants. *International Journal of Clinical Neuropsychology 7,* 49.

Public Law 94-142. (1975). The Education for All Handicapped Children Act of 1975. Washington DC: Federal Register.

Public Law 99-457. (1986). Education of the Handicapped Act Ammendments of 1986. Washington DC: Federal Register.

Rattan, G., & Dean, R. S. (1987). The neuropsychology of children's learning disorders. In J. M. Williams & C. J. Long (Eds.), *The rehabilitation of cognitive disabilities* (pp. 173–190). New York: Plenum Press.

Reed, H. B. C., & Reitan, R. M. (1963). Intelligence test performance of brain damaged subjects with lateralized motor deficits. *Journal of Consulting Psychology, 27* 102–106.

Reitan, R. M. (1964). Psychological deficits resulting from cerebral lesions in man. In J. M. Warren, & K. A. Akert (Eds.), *The Frontal granular cortex and behavior* (pp. 157–179). New York: McGraw–Hill.

Report of the INS - Division 40 Task Force on Education, Accreditation and Credentialing. (1987). *The clinical neuropsychologist, 1,* 29–34.

Report of the Task Force on Education, Accreditation and Credentialing. (1981). *The INS Bulletin,* 5–10.

Reynolds, C. R. (1988). Putting the individual into aptitude-treatment interaction. *Exceptional Children, 54,* 324–331.

Rosenberg, S. A., Robinson, C. C., Finkler, D., & Rose, J. S. (1987). An empirical comparison of formulas evaluating early intervention program impact on development. *Exceptional Children, 54,* 213–219.

Rourke, B. P. & Strang, J. D. (1983). Subtypes of reading and arithmetic disabilities: A neuropsychological analysis. In M. Rutter (Ed.), *Developmental neuropsychiatry* (pp. 141–169). New York: Guilford Press.

Rutter, M. (1982). Developmental neuropsychiatry: Concepts, issues, and prospects. *Journal of Clinical Neuropsychology, 4,* 91–115.

Rutter, M., Chadwick, O., Shaffer, D., & Brown, G. (1980). A prospective study of children with head injuries: I. Design and methods. *Psychological Medicine, 10,* 633–645.

Silverton, L., Finello, K., Mednick, S., & Schulsinger, F. (1985). Low birthweight and ventricular enlargement in a high risk sample. *Journal of Abnormal Psychology, 94,* 405–409.

Strom, D. A., Gray, J. W., Dean, R. S., & Fischer, W. E. (1987). The incremental validity of the Halstead-Reitan Neuropsychological Test Battery in predicting achievement for learning disabled children. *Journal of Psychoeducational Assessment, 2,* 157–165.

Taylor, M., & Abrams, R. (1984). Cognitive impairment in schizophrenia. *American Journal of Psychiatry, 141,* 196–201.

Taylor, M., Greenspan, B., & Abrams, R. (1979). Lateralized neuropsychological dysfunction in affective disorder and schizophrenia. *American Journal of Psychiatry, 136,* 1031–1034.

Torgeson, J. K. (1986). Learning disabilities theory: Its current state and future prospects. *Journal of Learning Disabilities, 19,* 399–407.

Tuma, J. M. (1982). *Handbook for the practice of pediatric psychology.* New York: Wiley-Interscience.

Woods, B. T., & Short, M. P. (1985). Neurological dimensions of psychiatry. *Biological Psychiatry, 20,* 192–198.

7

School Psychology in Residential Treatment Facilities[1]

RICHARD J. MORRIS
YVONNE P. MORRIS
University of Arizona

Although school psychologists are traditionally seen as working in the school setting, the breadth and depth of knowledge gained in school psychology training and practice qualifies school psychologists for employment in a wide variety of settings in which psychological knowledge in required (e.g., Bardon, 1982; Nagle, 1986; Phillips, 1986; Reynolds, Gutkin, Elliott, & Witt, 1984). Interestingly, however, surveys of school psychologists indicate that only a minority of them are employed in nonschool settings (e.g., Ramage, 1979) such as residential treatment facilities (e.g., those providing services to emotionally disturbed, mentally retarded, and/or adjudicated children and adolescents), business and industry, state and federal governmental agencies, mental health clinics, private practice, and general hospitals.

This is a surprising fact because many of these nonschool settings have operating goals that are consistent with the philosophies and standards regarding the provision of school psychological services of both the National Association of School Psychologists (NASP) and the Division of School Psychology of the American Psychological Association (APA) and, therefore, seem to be viable employment areas for psychologists

[1]This chapter is based on a paper presented as part of a symposium entitled, "Nontraditional activities for school psychologists," at the 95th annual meeting of the American Psychological Association, New York, New York, September, 1987. Portions of this chapter were prepared under research grant #G008730074 to the first author from the U.S. Department of Education, Office of Special Education and Rehabilitation Services.

who have been trained in school psychology (see, for example, Reynolds et al., 1984). In this chapter, we review the relevant literature pertaining to the work of school psychologists in residential treatment settings and critically discuss their role and function in such settings.

HISTORICAL BACKGROUND OF RESIDENTIAL TREATMENT SERVICES

The development of the residential treatment facility has been integrally tied to the social structure, values, and mores of the societies in which the concept of the institution emerged (Foucault, 1965). In the United States, for example, the development and growth of residential treatment facilities can be traced to the Jacksonian era (1820s–1830s). At that time the prevailing belief was that major social problems, including insanity, poverty, and crime, were caused or exacerbated by faulty social organization within the community (Rothman, 1971). Thus, by removing from society those persons who were mentally ill, paupers, or thieves, and placing them in the organized, regulated, and controlled environment of the asylum, it was assumed that these people would become rehabilitated and then be able to resume their place in society (Rothman, 1971).

Although specific assessment, educational, and/or therapeutic methods were sometimes used within the institutional setting, a major component of the total rehabilitative package involved the removal of a person from his or her home and community, and placing the person in the therapeutic milieu of the asylum—the assumption being that the very structured and predictable environment of the asylum would contribute substantially to the person's improvement. Institutions for the mentally ill, mentally retarded, and juvenile delinquent were established and operated in accord with this principle—again with the goal of returning the person to the community (e.g., Grob, 1973; Tyor & Bell, 1984).

A number of assessment and diagnostic instruments were developed under this early model of the residential treatment facility—with some of the instruments (e.g., *Vineland Social Maturity Scale;* Doll, 1935) being used today, albeit in revised format (see, for example, Sparrow, Balla, & Cicchetti, 1984). Moreover, the administrators of these early residential treatment facilities contributed—either directly or indirectly—to the development of several of our present day professional organizations and formed the basis for the establishment of several government sponsored research organizations that are today concerned with the provision of services to mentally retarded, mentally ill, and criminally adjudicated children and adolescents. For example, the American Association on Mental Deficiency evolved from the Association of Medical Officers of

American Institutions for Idiots and Feebleminded (Kanner, 1964). The National Institute of Mental Health evolved in part from the National Committee for Mental Hygiene, whose establishment in 1909 was largely attributable to the horrific conditions Clifford Beers encountered in his own psychiatric hospitalization (e.g., Beers, 1908). The Illinois Institute for Juvenile Research evolved from Chicago's Juvenile Psychopathic Institute (established in 1909)—an organization that was initially concerned with the fate of juveniles who were placed in prisons as a result of their criminal and/or antisocial acts (Morris & Kratochwill, 1983).

Residential treatment facilities have also played an important role in the education, training, and professional development of many contemporary psychologists whose primary clinical and research interests have focused on the psychological assessment and treatment of children (e.g., Gallagher, 1984; Kirk, 1984; Morse, 1984; Sarason, 1984; Zigler, 1984). In addition, several school psychologists who have gone on to work in school settings or in university-based school psychology training programs have recounted work experiences in residential treatment facilities as part of their educational or employment experiences (e.g., Crissey, 1983; Tindall, 1983). The significance of residential treatment facilities to the field of school psychology was aptly stated by Seymour Sarason (1983), whose work is associated with both mental retardation and school psychology. He stated that "the several years [I] spent at Southbury [State Training School] forged my identity as a school and educational psychologist. . . . [E]verything I have ever done or written has its origins in Southbury experience" (Sarason, 1983, p. 286).

THE ROLE OF THE SCHOOL PSYCHOLOGIST IN THE RESIDENTIAL TREATMENT FACILITY

The quest for the definitive list of roles played by school psychologists has proved to be virtually unending as well as controversial (e.g., Levy, 1986; Phillips, 1982, 1986; Reynolds et al., 1984; Rosenfeld, Shimberg, & Thornton, 1983). Surveys of practicing school psychologists (e.g., Farling & Hoedt, 1971; Ramage, 1979, 1986; Lacayo, Sherwood, & Morris, 1981; Smith, 1984; Benson & Hughes, 1985) suggest that there are broadly defined role categories that describe the activities engaged in by most school psychologists—for example, assessment, direct and indirect intervention with students and/or other clients, consultation with staff and parents, organizational development work, and research.

These broadly defined role categories are also consistent with the types of psychological services that are provided in various residential treatment facilities (see, for example, Baumeister & Butterfield, 1970; Crespi & Brennan, 1988; Whitman, Schibak, & Reid, 1983), and these facilities are therefore excellent potential employment settings for school psychologists. In fact, as Bergan (1985b) points out, "virtually any type of organization concerned with learning and adjustment may have a school psychologist on its staff" (p. 434). The doctoral level training of school psychologists is now sufficiently broad to prepare them to work in any residential treatment setting that emphasizes the role categories described previously (Conoley, 1987; Edwards, 1987; Lentz & Shapiro, 1987; Phillips, 1985).

Residential treatment facilities are today conceptualized as being short-to-intermediate term transitional care facilities aimed at assisting a client in returning to the community, i.e., natural home setting, group home, foster care facility, supervised apartment, etc. (Accreditation Council on Services for People With Developmental Disabilities, 1987; Crespi, 1987; Short, 1987; Steppe-Jones, 1987). This approach to residential treatment is consistent with the deinstitutionalization movement and the principle of normalization (e.g., Blatt, 1975, 1984; Wolfensberger, 1972). The exception to this viewpoint lies in the provision of services to severely and profoundly handicapped persons, the nature of whose handicap often necessitates long term or permanent care; however, even with these persons the philosophy underlying today's residential treatment facilities typically involves a commitment to the principle of normalization and providing each person with the least restrictive alternative services that are consistent with his or her needs. Although progress has been made over the past 10 to 15 years in the deinstitutionalization movement and in the establishment of the principle of normalization within residential facilities, more work is needed before the tenets of these concepts can be fully realized (e.g., Bercovici, 1983; Neufeld, 1979; Steppe-Jones, 1987).

With the advent of Public Law 94–142 ("Education for All Handicapped Children Act"), school psychologists became integrally tied to the concept of deinstitutionalization and the principle of normalization. Not only were school psychologists expected to perform necessary assessments of children and adolescents using culturally fair instruments, but they were directly or indirectly involved in the provision of least restrictive alternative services to clients in the school setting. School psychologists also began working with staff from residential treatment settings in terms of assisting students in generalizing changes in behavior from one setting to the other and in transitioning them from school into the work and community setting (e.g., Brunnquell, 1987; Crespi, 1987; Sabatino, 1981; Short, 1987).

Given the school psychologist's familiarity with P.L. 94–142, the deinstitutionalization movement, the principle of normalization, it would appear that he or she could take a position in a modern day residential treatment facility and feel quite comfortable with its goals and objectives.

Assessment and Diagnosis

The school psychologist working in a residential treatment facility is frequently part of a team concerned with the assessment and diagnosis of clients (and potential clients) of their organization. These activities cover the broad purposes of childhood behavior assessment outlined by Mash and Terdal (1981): (a) *diagnosis*—identifying the nature of the client's problem, (b) *design* —gathering data to aid in the development of a treatment program, and (c) *evaluation*—determining the efficacy of a treatment procedure. The child or adolescent recommended for placement in a residential treatment facility will often undergo an extensive assessment either prior to or immediately following arrival at the facility. For example, in the case of developmentally delayed persons, a multifaceted assessment process would take place that is consistent with the *Standards* established by the Accreditation Council on Services For People With Developmental Disabilities (ACDD, 1987). The assessment process would consist of evaluations that focused on both the person's physical condition as well as on his/her social-emotional, cognitive, educational, vocational, and developmental functioning. Besides assessing the developmentally delayed person, his or her family members, as well as relevant school personnel, would also be interviewed in order that the most comprehensive picture can be obtained of the person's: (a) presenting problems and disabilities, (b) developmental strengths and needs, (c) cognitive and emotional strengths and needs, and (d) the types of intervention and support services needed (ACDD, 1987).

This assessment approach is quite consistent with sound psychological assessment and service delivery practices taught in professional school psychology training programs (e.g., Phillips, 1985; Pryzwansky, 1982; Reynolds et al., 1984), and consistent with the standards for the provision of school psychological services as established by the National Association of School Psychologists (1985) and the American Psychological Association (1981). Thus, the professional training of school psychologists places them in a unique position for providing excellent psychological assessment services to persons placed (or under consideration for placement) in residential treatment facilities. The need for excellent assessment practices and psychological services is expected to increase in importance as more attention is focused on those individuals in residential treatment facilities who are dually diagnosed—such as those people who are diagnosed as being mentally retarded and mentally ill, or those who are juvenile offenders and also diagnosed as mentally ill and/or mentally retarded (e.g., Eaton & Menolascino, 1982; Reiss, 1982; Reiss, Levitan, & McNally, 1982).

School psychologists are not only trained in the assessment and diagnosis of children and adolescents, but also in the development of methodological approaches to evaluate the effectiveness of a particular intervention and/or other school psychological services program (e.g., Cancelli & Duley, 1985; Kratochwill & Bergan, 1978; Medway, 1985; Reynolds et al., 1984; Phillips, 1985). Because the research strategies, principles, and ethical concerns that underlie program evaluation work within the school setting are similar to those utilized within residential treatment settings, there is no reason why school psychologists could not apply their training and experience in program evaluation and methodology to the residential treatment setting. In fact, a fair amount of the early research on classroom management and behavior modification was conducted in residential treatment settings in either classroom environments or residential living units (see, for example, Baer, Peterson, & Sherman, 1967; Cohen, Filipczak, & Bis, 1967; Cotler, Applegate, King & Kristal, 1972; Kerr, Meyerson, & Michael, 1965; Lovaas, Berberich, Perloff, & Schaffer, 1966; Zimmerman & Zimmerman, 1962), and residential settings continue to be an important site for the conduct of behavioral treatment research (e.g., Morris, 1985). The knowledge gained in these settings continues to be applied in regular (nonresidential) school settings (e.g., Carroll, 1985; Morris, 1976, 1985; Morris & McReynolds, 1986; Sulzer-Azaroff & Mayer, 1986), and it should not be at all difficult for school psychologists to apply their knowledge of methodology and program evaluation in the residential treatment setting.

As part of their training, school psychologists are also informed of the importance of gathering assessment data from multiple sources to ensure the validity of any conclusions or diagnoses that are made (e.g., Cancelli & Duley, 1985; Elliott & Piersel, 1982; Reynolds et al., 1984). In addition, school psychologists are increasingly becoming aware of the importance of assessing the acceptability of a treatment procedure and whether the behavior change effected by the treatment resulted in socially important changes (e.g., Witt & Elliott, 1985). Specifically, we are finding an increasing amount of literature concerned with whether an intervention proposed or actually used with a child was judged as being acceptable to him or her, and whether the behavior changes resulting from an intervention procedure were judged by persons *not* connected with the intervention as being socially important/meaningful changes (e.g., Elliott, Witt, Galvin, & Peterson, 1985; Kazdin, 1977, 1980; Witt & Elliott, 1985; Witt & Martens, 1983). Developing assessment procedures along these dimensions within a residential treatment facility seems to be extremely important—especially with the current emphasis on deinstitutionalization—and it is clear that school psychologists working in such facilities could take a leadership role in ensuring that all interventions are not only acceptable but also socially valid.

Finally, given the emphasis on quantitative methods and tests and measurement procedures in school psychology training programs (e.g., Phillips, 1985; Reynolds, 1983), the school psychologist working in a residential treatment facility is in a unique position to be a valuable resource person to the administrators of the facility. Specifically, the school psychologist can evaluate the psychometric properties of the assessment instruments currently being used or considered for future use. The school psychologist can also make recommendations regarding the continued use of these instruments based on, for example, their respective reliability, validity, and norms, as well as develop psychometrically sound assessment instruments designed to meet the specific assessment and/or research needs that may arise within the residential setting.

Intervention Services

School psychologists can serve a direct and guiding role in establishing and implementing treatment programs as well as developing prevention programs for children and adolescents in residential treatment facilities. Their training in a variety of intervention strategies (e.g., Carroll, 1985; Medway, 1985; Mowder, 1983) helps form the foundation for the intervention work that is needed in residential treatment facilities. In addition, because of the emphasis in many school psychology training programs on coursework in classroom management, behavior modification, and principles of learning, school psychologists have the necessary background to implement intervention programs in residential facilities that often reflect a behavioral orientation (e.g., Kazdin & Frame, 1983; Matson & Andrasik, 1983; Matson & McCartney, 1981; Redner, Snellman, & Davidson, 1983; Schreibman, Charlop, & Britten, 1983; Whitman et al., 1983).

In school settings, school psychologists are often requested to consult with teachers in developing intervention programs, or to provide direct services themselves to students, for the reduction of disruptive behavior, the remediation of academic and behavioral deficits, the strengthening of low-frequency academic and social behaviors, or for the modification of behaviors that are under inappropriate stimulus control (e.g., Carroll, 1985, Medway, 1985; Phillips, 1982; Reynolds et al., 1984). Similar needs are also presented to psychologists who work in residential treatment facilities, where they are asked to provide direct intervention with a client and/or consult with staff in developing an intervention program. In fact, as can be seen from Table 7.1, behaviors that school psychologists are often confronted with in school settings involving, for example, developmentally disabled students are also found in many clients in residential treatment facilities—with a fair amount of the research that formed the foundation for this intervention literature again originating in work conducted with residential clients (see, for example, Lovaas, 1977; Lovaas & Bucher, 1974; Matson & Andrasik, 1983; Matson & McCartney, 1981; Redner, Snellman, & Davidson, 1983). By establishing programs to assist in the remediation of these target behaviors the school psychologist is contributing to the goal of having these clients live the most "normalized" lifestyle possible (Wolfensberger, 1972).

Several interesting treatment programs have been developed and implemented by psychologists who work with mentally retarded persons who are dually diagnosed. Among the problems that have been treated in persons who have this dual diagnosis are anxiety disorders, conduct disorders, childhood depression, psychosis, and autism (e.g., Jones, Favell, & Risley, 1981; Luiselli, 1977; Matson, DiLorenzo, & Andrasik, 1983). Recent attention has also been focused on the assessment and treatment of fears, phobias, and related anxieties in people who are mentally retarded (e.g., Jackson, 1983; McNally & Ascher, 1987; Morris, Green, & Kratochwill, 1987; Ollendick & Ollendick, 1982), using procedures that are consistent with those used for treating these behaviors in the school setting (see, for example, Morris & Kratochwill, 1983). Thus, school psychologists could easily transfer their knowledge and skills from a school setting into a residential setting.

The reason that there has been an upsurge in working with persons who have a dual diagnosis is that psychologists and other health care providers have discovered that many of the emotional disturbances that developmentally disabled persons experience can be successfully treated, and that a client's lack of verbal ability is no longer a reason for excluding him or her from intervention work (see, for example, Matson & Barrett, 1982; Morris et al., 1987; Reiss et al., 1982; Schreibman et al., 1983).

In correctional settings, psychologists have been involved in developing and implementing programs designed to teach a variety of social and living skills, as well as focusing on alternatives to aggression (e.g., Agee, 1979; Goldstein, Carr, Davidson, & Wehr, 1981; Phillips, 1968; Phillips, Fixsen, Phillips, & Wolf, 1979; Redner et al., 1983; Short, 1987). These programs have been developed with both residentially based children and adolescents, as well as with students in a classroom setting (e.g., Goldstein, Apter, & Harootunian, 1984), and can be utilized by the school psychologist working with aggressive and/or delinquent children and adolescents both in the classroom, as well as in the residential treatment setting.

TABLE 7.1
Selected Children's Behaviors Treated Using Behavior Modification Procedures

Behaviors Strengthened	*Behaviors Developed*	*Behaviors Reduced*
Assertiveness	Arm/leg movement	Bowel movement in pants
Attending to educational tasks/teacher	Color discrimination	Classroom disruption
Completion of educational tasks	Cooperative play	Climbing
Eating solid foods	Copying/tracing pictures	Constipation
Gross/fine motor skills	Echoing sounds	Crawling
Instruction/command following	Eye contact	Destroying objects
Math skills	Imitation (motoric and verbal)	Fears/phobias
Memory for spoken words	Independent dressing/undressing	Fecal smearing
Performing educational tasks	Independent walking	Fire setting
Personal hygiene skills	Letter discrimination	Gestures with fingers
Playing with toys	Making change	Hair pulling
Question answering/asking	Manual communication/use of signs	Headbanging
Reading	Name discrimination	Hitting others
Sitting	Naming objects	Hyperactivity
Social interaction	Pedestrian skills	Loud vocal utterances
Speech articulation	Reading	Mutism/selective mutism
Spontaneous speech	Self-feeding	Overeating
Talking to others	Shoe tying	Pinching, biting, kicking others
Toileting	Size discrimination	Refusing to eat
Use of eating utensils	Smiling	Rocking
Use of orthopedic devices for walking	Speech	Self-hitting/scratching
Use of particular arm/leg	Toilet training	Self-stimulation
Vocational/Prevocational skills	Tooth brushing	Stealing/grabbing food
Walking unaided	Tricycle/Bike riding	Stuttering/stammering
Writing skills	Using telephone	Tantrums, crying
	Washing face/hands	Throwing objects
	Word discrimination	Thumbsucking
		Tics
		Urinating in bed at night/urinating in day in pants
		Vomiting
		Yelling, screaming, hand-slapping

Adapted from Morris (1976) and Morris and McReynolds (1986).

Another area in which school psychologists can have a significant impact is in the area of vocational planning for adolescents in residential treatment settings (Sheldon & Prout, 1982; Timm, Myrick, & Rosenberg, 1982). Correctional facilities have focused on programs that enable residents to enter the labor force, due in part to such federal legislation as the Vocational Educational Amendments Act of 1975, the Vocational Rehabilitation Act of 1973 (sections 503 and 504), the Education of All Handicapped Children's Act of 1975, and the 1978 amendments to the

Comprehensive Employment and Training Act, in which career development for handicapped adolescents has been mandated.

The vocational school psychology literature suggests four components of career development that school psychologists can apply in their work in residential treatment settings: (a) increasing self-knowledge, (b) increasing occupational awareness, (c) facilitating job readiness and placement, and (d) facilitating adequate decision-making (Levinson, 1987). For school psychologists working in residential treatment settings, these career development components may involve vocational assessment of the client, as well as working with both parents and staff of the institution, school, and/or workplace, to help the client focus on career interests and develop the skills necessary for successful job placement. Paramount consideration, however, would involve matching job and social skills training to post-training job opportunities, and to continuing education and training for clients to ensure that job-related social and vocational skills are maintained and strengthened.

Consultation Services and Organization Development

Over the past 10 to 15 years, school psychologists have become increasingly involved in consultative practices (see, for example, Alpert, 1976; Alpert & Meyers, 1983; Alpert & Silverstein, 1985; Bergan, 1977; Conoley & Conoley, 1982; Meyers, Parsons, & Martin, 1979; Piersel, 1985). Although the concept of school consultation is not new (Meyers et al., 1979), its more central role in school psychology training programs and in the professional work of school psychologists is relatively new (Bergan, 1985a; Reynolds et al., 1984). In fact, among the various professional functions in which school psychologists are involved, some surveys (e.g., Benson & Hughes, 1985; Meacham & Peckham, 1978; Ramage, 1979) have reported that school consultation is ranked second highest.

Although a number of school consultation models have been discussed in the literature (e.g., Alpert & Silverstein, 1985; Bergan, 1977; Conoley & Conoley, 1982; Meyers et al., 1979), each of these approaches shares a common purpose—a collaborative problem-solving process between the consultant and consultee(s) with the emphasis on assisting the consultee(s) in providing psychological assistance to his or her client (Medway, 1979).

The use of consultation approaches in school psychology developed largely within the context of the community psychology movement and as a result of a growing disenchantment with traditional forms of school psychological services (e.g., Alpert & Silverstein, 1985; Piersel, 1985;

Reynolds et al., 1984). In particular, the growing dissatisfaction with the "school psychologist as tester" role and its strong emphasis on the testing-diagnosis-treatment model, led many writers and practitioners to search for other models of service delivery systems that: (a) were more ecologically relevant and appropriate for the school environment, (b) made more efficient use of the professional time of the school psychologist, (c) was increasingly responsive to the burgeoning literature on classroom management, (d) emphasized prevention, and (e) fit more appropriately with the least restrictive alternatives and mainstreaming concepts under P.L. 94-142 (e.g., Gibbins, 1978; Gutkin & Curtis, 1982; Meyers et al., 1979; Martin, 1983; Piersel, 1985; Reynolds et al., 1984).

Although consultation in the schools often encompasses many facets, its major emphases are (a) remediation of a presenting problem—for example, working with a teacher (consultee) regarding the management of a specific behavior problem of a student/client, and (b) prevention or teaching the consultee how to respond more effectively in the future—for example, to assist the consultee in improving his or her skills in order that she or he can more effectively deal with the same or similar behavior problems in the future (e.g., Martin, 1983; Reynolds et al., 1984; Stewart, 1986).

These emphases regarding consultation are also very appropriate for residential treatment facilities. Because the school psychology environment, as mentioned earlier, and the residential facility often share the same common goals and objectives with respect to assessment and treatment, it follows that such facilities would be supportive of this form of service delivery (see, for example, ACDD, 1987). Each of the major consultation models (i.e., mental health consultation, behavioral or ecological consultation, and organizational consultation) can be applied with little modification to a residential setting and some (e.g., behavioral consultation) have historical roots in residential treatment settings (e.g., Morris, 1985; Morris & McReynolds, 1986). In fact, some residential facilities have established consulting programs, called "technical assistance teams," whose major purpose is to consult with staff regarding intervention work with difficult-to-manage clients. Such consultation endeavors are clearly consistent with the work of school psychologists.

Two other school-based consultation activities of school psychologists would also fit into their work in residential settings, namely, parent consultation/training and inservice training/education. Findings from the survey research literature in school psychology (e.g., Lacayo, Sherwood, & Morris, 1981; Ramage, 1979; Smith, 1984) suggest that school psychologists spend approximately 5% to 10% of their time in these activities. Such activities are also desirable in residential treatment facilities (e.g., ACDD, 1987) and it would seem that school psychologists would be in an excellent position to provide this type of organizational consultative service. In fact, a fair amount of the parent training and inservice education literature (e.g., Bernstein, 1982; Dangel & Polster, 1984; O'Dell, 1985; Twardosz & Nordquist, 1987; Ziarnik & Bernstein, 1982) on which school psychologists base their consultative work involves target behaviors that are often found in children and adolescents in school, home, and residential treatment environments.

Organization development in residential treatment settings extends the notion of consultation as collaborative problem solving to the systems level, so that the focus is on consultation for organizational improvement rather than assisting the consultee in working with his or her clients. The assumption is that organizational culture influences both the ways in which the staff carry out their jobs and the level of staff satisfaction (Fullan, Miles, & Taylor, 1980; Schmuck, 1982; Schmuck & Runkel, 1985). In organizational development the school psychologist works with the organizational staff to develop and implement processes for: (a) identifying organizational (as opposed to individual) problems, (b) improving communication among organizational participants, and (c) devising strategies to solve both the problems that have been identified and future problems that might arise. In this capacity, the school psychologist can consult with organizational administrators (e.g., Snapp & Davidson, 1982), as well as consult with the entire organizational staff (e.g., Curtis & Metz, 1986). The types of problems that are dealt with are common to both school and residential settings and can range from issues of service delivery (the process by which clients enter the organization, receive treatment, and leave the organization) to implementing staff development and employee assistance programs to help combat staff burnout (Reynolds et al., 1984).

Research

As was mentioned earlier, residential treatment facilities have played an important role in the professional lives of psychologists whose clinical and research interests have focused on the psychological assessment and treatment of children and adolescents. The training of school psychologists in understanding and applying research findings, as well as in the design and conduct of scholarly research, suggests that school psychologists working in a residential treatment facility can make a significant contribution to the research literature in our field.

School psychologists, like other professional psychologists who are educated within the framework of a scientist-practitioner model, are trained in both research methodology and the conduct of psychological research. Thus, by the time they receive their doctoral degree, school psychologists are sufficiently familiar with all aspects of research methodology to be in a position to not only evaluate published research but also know how to formulate research questions and conduct experimental research to answer such questions.

The types of scientific research that are often conducted in school psychology are the following: historical research, descriptive research, passive observational methods (i.e., correlational and *ex post facto* research), randomized experimental group designs, quasi-experimental, and time series single subject experimental designs (e.g., Kratochwill, Schnapps, & Bissell, 1985). Each of these research methods can be appropriately used in the school setting, and each can be utilized within a residential treatment facility—assuming that the research meets ethical guidelines of the facility and of the American Psychological Association (APA, 1982).

Even if school psychologists working in a residential setting do not engage in research, they are in a unique position to effectively communicate research findings to residential staff and administrators, as well as critically evaluate the applicability of the research findings to their particular residential program. The school psychologist's familiarity with research design and methodology also provides the residential facility with a resource person to turn to when information is needed on the merits of a particular research proposal that is being proposed for implementation at the facility. Thus, as in the school setting, the school psychologist working in the residential treatment setting is also trained as a researcher, informed user of research findings, and as a communicator to others of the implication(s) of the research findings to the agency as a whole.

Ethical Practices

As part of their professional training, school psychologists are systematically exposed to the concept of ethics and ethical treatment practices as outlined by the American Psychological Association (e.g., APA, 1974, 1981, 1987) and the National Association of School Psychologists (e.g., NASP, 1985). In addition, often during their education, school psychologists are also exposed to the ethical statements of other professional organizations.

One such set of ethical guidelines is presented in Table 7.2 and reviews the position of the Association for the Advancement of Behavior Therapy regarding the provision of human services across populations, settings, and intervention procedures. The purpose of these guidelines, as well as other ethical practices statements, is to formulate an acceptable series of statements that members of an organization or a profession can subscribe to and agree to follow as they carry-out their daily professional duties (Morris, 1985; Morris & Brown, 1983).

Given the school psychologist's exposure to ethical practices in his or

TABLE 7.2
Ethical Issues for Human Services

The questions related to each issue have deliberately been cast in a general manner that applies to all types of interventions, and not solely or specifically to the practice of behavior therapy. Issues directed specifically to behavior therapists might imply erroneously that behavior therapy was in some way more in need of ethical concern than nonbehaviorally-oriented therapies.

In the list of issues, the term "client" is used to describe the person whose behavior is to be changed, "therapist" is used to describe the professional in charge of the intervention; "treatment" and "problem," although used in the singular, refer to any and all treatments and problems being formulated with this checklist. The issues are formulated so as to be relevant across as many settings and populations as possible. Thus, they need to be qualified when someone other than the person whose behavior is to be changed is paying the therapist, or when that person's competence or voluntary nature of that person's consent is questioned. For example, if the therapist has found that the client does not understand the goals or methods being considered, the therapist should substitute the client's guardian or other responsible person for "client," when reviewing the issues below.

A. Have the goals of treatment been adequately considered?
   1. To insure that the goals are explicit, are they written?
   2. Has the client's understanding of the goals been assured by having the client restate them orally or in writing?
   3. Have the therapist and client agreed on the goals of therapy?
   4. Will serving the client's interests be contrary to the interests of other persons?
   5. Will serving the client's immediate interests be contrary to the client's long-term interest?
B. Has the choice of treatment methods been adequately considered?
   1. Does the published literature show the procedure to be the best one available for that problem?
   2. If no literature exists regarding the treatment method, is the method consistent with generally accepted practice?
   3. Has the client been told of alternative procedures that might be preferred by the client on the basis of significant differences in discomfort, treatment time, cost, or degree of demonstrated effectiveness?
   4. If a treatment procedure is publicly, legally, or professionally controversial, has formal professional consultation been obtained, has the reaction of the affected segment of the public been adequately considered, and have the alternative treatment methods been more closely reexamined and reconsidered?
C. Is the client's participation voluntary?
   1. Have possible sources of coercion on the client's participation been considered?
   2. If treatment is legally mandated, has the available range of treatments and therapists been offered?
   3. Can the client withdraw from treatment without a penalty or financial loss that exceeds actual clinical costs?
D. When another person or an agency is empowered to arrange for therapy, have the interests of the subordinated client been sufficiently considered?
   1. Has the subordinated client been informed of the treatment objectives and participated in the choice of treatment procedures?

(*Continued*)

TABLE 7.2
(*continued*)

2. Where the subordinated client's competence to decide is limited, have the client as well as the guardian participated in the treatment discussions to the extent that the client's abilities permit?
3. If the interests of the subordinated person and the superordinate persons or agency conflict, have attempts been made to reduce the conflict by dealing with both interests?

E. Has the adequacy of treatment been evaluated?
1. Have quantitative measures of the problem and its progress been obtained?
2. Have the measures of the problem and its progress been made available to the client during treatment?

F. Has the confidentiality of the treatment relationship been protected?
1. Has the client been told who has access to the records?
2. Are records available only to authorized persons?

G. Does the therapist refer the clients to other therapists when necessary?
1. If treatment is unsuccessful, is the client referred to other therapists?
2. Has the client been told that if dissatisfied with the treatment, referral will be made?

H. Is the therapist qualified to provide treatment?
1. Has the therapist had training or experience in treating problems like the client's?
2. If deficits exist in the therapist's qualifications, has the client been informed?
3. If the therapist is not adequately qualified, is the client referred to other therapists, or has supervision by a qualified therapist been provided? Is the client informed of the supervisory relation?
4. If the treatment is administered by mediators, have the mediators been adequately supervised by a qualified therapist?

[Source: Association for Advancement of Behavior Therapy. Ethical issues for human services. *Behavior Therapy*. 1977, 8, v–vi. Reprinted with permission.]

her profession, this person is in a unique position to share this information with other professionals, as well as administrators. In addition, based on the school psychologist's familiarity with ethical practices statements and the assessment and intervention literature regarding children and adolescents, he or she is in a position to contribute to the development of a monitoring system to ensure that all assessment and intervention services that are provided clients are consistent with the ethical practices under which he or she is operating. Clearly, this approach to ethical practices can be instituted whether the school psychologist is working within a school setting or within a residential treatment facility.

An example of a monitoring system that was established in a residential treatment facility has been discussed by Morris, Barber, Hoschouer, Karrels, and Bijou (1979) and Morris (1985). The system was developed for a residential treatment facility providing services to developmentally disabled persons. Briefly, Morris and his associates (1979) established a two committee monitoring system for all intervention procedures planned for a particular person—whether the planned procedures involve positive or aversive programming.

The first committee that reviews the intervention proposal(s) is called the Program Review (PR) Committee. This committee does not function as an adversary group to the person(s) proposing to provide services to the client, but as a "helping" or advocacy committee in which the goal is to provide people with the best available advice about the adequacy and appropriateness of the proposed program plan(s). As such, the committee would base its approval or disapproval of a program plan on a number of factors—such as literature to support the effectiveness of the procedure(s) proposed, whether the plan is consistent with the overall individual program plan for the client, whether the plan involves the least restrictive or intrusive level of programming, and whether there are sufficient staff available (and trained to an agreed-upon criterion level) to implement the program in a consistent fashion.

The second committee is called the Human Rights and Ethics (HRE) Committee, and it provides independent and external monitoring of the maintenance of the rights of all children and adolescents receiving program plans. Thus, whereas the PR Committee's major purpose is the review of program plans regarding their technical feasibility and appropriateness, the HRE Committee's primary function is to serve as an external and independent group to assure that the rights of children are protected. Through the establishment of this committee, as well as the PR committee, we are not only being responsive to the ethical practices statements of those professional organizations with which school psychologists associate themselves, but we raise the overall level of awareness of other staff regarding the provision of the best possible services to those clients being served.

Training

The proliferation of specialty areas within the field of psychology has given rise to discussions about the nature of supervised training, and exposure to various conditions and clients, for graduate psychology students working with diverse client groups (Pfeiffer, Dean & Shellenberger, 1985). For those school psychologists working with severely handicapped children and adolescents, these discussions have focused on the ability to recognize behaviors associated with specific handicaps, and the training in specialized assessment procedures for assessing individuals with handicapping conditions (Sabatino, 1981). In this chapter we have tried to indicate the ways in which the doctoral level training of school psychologists is sufficiently diverse to prepare them to take a leadership role in the provision of psychological services to children and adolescents in such residential treatment settings as centers for developmentally disabled persons, psychiatric institutes, and juvenile training programs. State certification and licensure requirements for professional psychologists, and listing in the National Register of Health Service Providers in Psychology, requires at least one year of postdoctoral supervised experience (Toye & Pierce, 1987). School psychologists whose practicum and internship experiences have primarily been in the schools might want to broaden their professional experiences by working in a residential setting, and psychologists who have had a broad-based experiential background working in residential treatment settings should consider sharing their expertise by developing and advocating postdoctoral training at the residential setting where they are employed.

SUMMARY AND CONCLUSIONS

In this chapter, we have discussed the contribution and work of school psychologists in residential treatment facilities, and have critically examined their role and function. Based on this review, it seems clear, as Bergan (1985b) has indicated that school psychologists can fit into "virtually any type of organization concerned with learning and adjustment" (p. 434)—and residential treatment facilities are no exception. In addition, the school psychologist's (a) knowledge and sensitivity to the use of culturally-fair assessment instruments, (b) emphasis on a student's adaptive functioning, (c) experience in the use of and emphasis on least restrictive alternative services, and (d) training in the area of assessment and treatment of behavior disorders in children makes him or her a potentially excellent choice as a staff member in a residential treatment facility.

The specific roles and functions of school psychologists that we have examined in this chapter—namely, assessment and diagnosis, intervention services, consultation services and organizational development, the conduct of research, and maintenance of ethical practices—are all integrally-tied to the education and training that school psychologists receive (see, for example, Bergan, 1985c; Hynd, 1983; Reynolds et al., 1984; Thomas & Grimes, 1987). Interestingly, when one explores in detail the various role functions of school psychologists it becomes clear that the work of school psychologists in the school setting is not appreciably different from the activities in which they engage when working in residential treatment facilities. For example, in Table 7.3 we have adapted slightly the list of role functions of school psychologists as presented by

TABLE 7.3
Role Functions Ascribed to the School Psychologist Working in Residential Treatment Facilities*

1. Serve all children and adolescents in the residential treatment facility (RTF).
2. Work frequently with groups, rather than individual children, parents, and staff.
3. Act as an advisor to the total RTF, including program planning.
4. Apply findings from child development, learning, social, and physiological psychology.
5. Handle staffing and guidance committees and work through multidisciplinary or team approaches.
6. Assist staff educational and vocational programming and behavior management.
7. Deemphasize role in testing and classificatory diagnosis and emphasize diagnostic-intervention role.
8. Emphasize data-oriented problem solving and applied research.
9. Supervise psychology technicians and other personnel responsible for the implementation of program plans that have been established.
10. Assume responsibility for increased services to culturally disadvantaged children and adolescents.
11. Function as an expert in psychology and education.
12. Function as a consultant to program staff, administrators, and other RTF personnel.
13. Assume major role in preventive efforts.
14. Provide expertise in process of decision making in scientific endeavors and in helping relationships.
15. Facilitate interaction of the school and the RTF and coordinate all school and other service agencies with the RTF in referrals and follow-up.
16. Provide in-service education in child behavior and development and behavioral interventions.
17. Help administrative personnel establish and implement goals and behavioral objectives for program plans.
18. Deal adequately with ethical and value dilemmas encountered in assessing and modifying child, interpersonal, and organizational relationships.
19. Utilize effectively skills in social interaction and communication techniques.

*Derived from Hunter and Lambert (1974). Adapted from: Phillips, B. N. (1982). Reading and evaluating research in school psychology. In C. R. Reynolds & T. B. Gutkin (Eds.), *The handbook of school psychology* (pp. 24–47). New York: Wiley. Reprinted with permission.

Phillips (1982), and based on a study by Hunter and Lambert (1974). With only a few changes in the original wording, we have been able to apply Phillip's list to the role functions of school psychologists who work in residential treatment settings.

School psychologists are now in a position to make a meaningful contribution to the functioning of residential treatment facilities and we believe that they are fully prepared in their doctoral training programs to enter the job market in residential treatment facilities.

REFERENCES

Accreditation Council for People with Developmental Disabilities. (1987). *ACDD Standards*. Boston, MA: Author.

Agee, V. L. (1979). *Treatment of the violent incorrigible adolescent*. Lexington, MA: Lexington.

Alpert, J. L. (1976). Conceptual bases of mental health consultation in the schools. *Professional Psychology, 7*, 619–625.

Alpert, J. L., & Meyers, J. (Eds.). (1983). *Training in consultation: Perspectives from mental health, behavioral, and organizational consultation*. Springfield, IL: Charles C. Thomas.

Alpert, J. L., & Silverstein, J. (1985). Mental health consultation: Historical, present and future perspectives. In J. R. Bergan (Ed.), *School psychology in contemporary society: An introduction* (pp. 281–315). Columbus, OH: Charles Merrill.

American Psychological Association. (1974). *Standards for educational and psychological tests*. Washington, DC: Author.

American Psychological Association. (1981). Specialty guidelines for the delivery of services by school psychologists. *American Psychologist, 36*, 670–681.

American Psychological Association. (1982). *General guidelines for providers of psychological services*. Washington, DC: Author.

American Psychological Association. (1987). *Specialty guidelines for the delivery of services*. Washington, DC: Author.

Association for Advancement of Behavior Therapy. (1977). Ethical issues for human services. *Behavior Therapy, 8*, v-vi.

Baer, D. M., Peterson, R. F., & Sherman, J. A. (1967). The development of imitation for reinforcing behavioral similarity to a model. *Journal of the Experimental Analysis of Behavior, 10*, 405–416.

Bardon, J. I. (1982). School psychology's dilemma: A Proposal for its resolution. *Professional Psychology, 13*, 955–968.

Baumiester, A. A., & Butterfield, E. C. (Eds.). (1970). *Residential facilities for the mentally retarded*. Chicago: Aldine.

Beers, C. W. (1908). *A mind that found itself*. New York: Longmans.

Benson, A. J., & Hughes, J. (1985). Perceptions of role definitions in processes in school psychology: A national survey. *School Psychology Review, 14*, 64–74.

Bercovici, S. M. (1983). *Barriers to normalization*. Baltimore: University Park Press.

Bergan, J. R. (1977). *Behavioral consultation*. Columbus, OH: Charles E. Merrill.

Bergan, J. R. (1985a). School psychology: Science and profession. In J. R. Bergan (Ed.), *School psychology in contemporary society: An introduction* (pp. 3–24). Columbus, OH: Charles Merrill.

Bergan, J. R. (1985b). The future of school psychology. In J. R. Bergan (Ed.), *School psychology in contemporary society* (pp. 421–437). Columbus, OH: Charles Merrill.

Bergan, J. R. (Ed.). (1985c). *School psychology in contemporary society: An introduction*. Columbus, OH: Charles Merrill.

Bernstein, G. S. (1982). Training behavior change agents: A conceptual review. *Behavior Therapy, 13*, 1–23.

Blatt, B. (1975). Toward an understanding of people with special needs. In J. M. Kauffman & J. W. Payne (Eds.), *Mental retardation: Introduction and personal perspectives* (pp. 103–128). Columbus, OH: Charles Merrill.

Blatt, B. (1984). Biography in autobiography. In B. Blatt & R. J. Morris (Eds.), *Perspec-*

tives in special education: Personal orientations (pp. 263–307). Glenview, IL: Scott, Foresman & Company.

Brunnquell, D. (1987). Children and hospitalization. In A. Thomas & J. Grimes (Eds.), *Childrens needs: Psychological perspectives* (pp. 289–297). Washington DC: The National Association of School Psychologists.

Cancelli, A., & Duley, S. (1985). The role of assessment in school psychology. In J. R. Began (Ed.), *School psychology in contemporary society* (pp. 119–139). Columbus, OH: Charles Merrill.

Carroll, J. L. (1985). Strategies for behavioral interventions in school psychology. In J. R. Bergan (Ed.), *School psychology in contemporary society* (pp. 230–251). Columbus, OH: Charles Merrill.

Cohen, H. L., Filipczak, J. & Bis, J. (1967). A study of contingencies applicable to special education: Case I. In R. Ulrich, T. Stachnick, & J. Mabry (Eds.), *Control of Human Behavior* (Vol. II, pp. 51–69). Glenview, IL: Scott, Foresman & Co.

Conoley, J. (1987). "Dr. Future, we presume," said school psychology. *Professional School Psychology, 2,* 173–180.

Conoley, J. C., & Conley, C. W. (1982). The effects of two conditions of client-centered consultation on student teacher problem description and remedial plans. *Journal of School Psychology, 20,* 323–328.

Cotler, S. B., Applegate, G., King, L., & Kristal, S. (1972). Establishing a token economy program in a state hospital classroom: A lesson in training student and teacher. *Behavior Therapy, 3,* 209–222.

Crespi, T. D. (1987). Children and psychiatric involvement. In A. Thomas & J. Grimes (Eds.), *Childrens needs: Psychological perspectives* (pp. 451–460). Washington, DC: The National Association of School Psychologists.

Crespi, T. D. & Brennan, J. K. (1988). School psychologists in the correctional system: Preliminary exploration. *Professional Psychology, 19,* 239–240.

Crissey, M. S. (1983). School psychology: Reminisces of earlier times. *Journal of School Psychology, 21,* 163–177.

Curtis, M. J., & Metz, L. W. (1986). System level intervention in a school for handicapped children. *School Psychology Review, 15,* 510–518.

Dangel, R. F., & Polster, R. A. (1984). *Parent training: Foundations of research and practice.* New York: Guilford.

Doll, E. A. (1935). A genetic scale of social maturity. *The American Journal of Orthopsychiatry, 5,* 180–188.

Eaton, L. F., & Menolascino, F. J. (1982). Psychiatric disorders in the mentally retarded: Types, problems and challenges. *American Journal of Psychiatry, 139,* 1297–1303.

Edwards, R. (1987). Implementing the scientist-practitioner model: The school psychologist as a data-based problem solver. *Professional School Psychology, 2,* 155–161.

Elliott, S. N., & Piersel, W. C. (1982). Direct assessment of reading skills: An approach with links assessment to intervention. *School Psychology Review, 11,* 267–280.

Elliott, S. N., Witt, J. C., Galvin, G. A., & Peterson, R. (1985). Acceptability of positive and reductive interventions: Factors that influence teachers decisions. *Journal of School Psychology, 22,* 353–360.

Farling, W. H., & Hoedt, K. C. (1971). National, regional and state survey of school psychologists. Washington, DC: US Department of Health, Education and Welfare.

Foucault, M. (1965). *Madness and civilization: A history of insanity in the age of reason.* New York: Pantheon Books.

Fullan, F., Miles, M. B., & Taylor, G. (1980). Organizational development in schools: The state of the art. *Review of Educational Research, 50,* 121–183.

Gallagher, J. (1984). The evolution of special education concept. In B. Blatt & R. J. Morris (Eds.), *Perspectives in special education: Personal orientations* (pp. 210–232). Glenview, IL: Scott, Foresman & Company.

Gibbins, S. (1978). Public law 94–142: An impetus for consultation. *The School Psychology Digest,* Summer, 18–25.

Goldstein, A. P., Apter, S. J., & Harootunian, B. (1984). *School violence.* Englewood Cliffs, NJ: Prentice–Hall.

Goldstein, A. P., Carr, E. G., Davidson, W. S. II, & Wehr, P. (Eds.). (1981). *In response to aggression: Methods of control and prosocial alternatives.* New York: Pergamon.

Grob, G. N. (1973). *Mental institutions in America: Social policy to 1875.* New York: The Free Press.

Gutkin, T. B., & Curtis, M. J. (1982). School based consultation: Theory and techniques. In C. R. Reynolds & T. B. Gutkin (Eds.), *The handbook of school psychology.* New York: Wiley.

Hunter, C., & Lambert, N. M. (1974). Needs assessment activities in school psychology program development. *Journal of School Psychology, 12,* 130–137.

Hynd, G. W. (Ed.). (1983). *The school psychologist: An introduction.* Syracuse, NY: Syracuse University Press.

Jackson, H. J. (1983). Current trends in the treatment of phobias in autistic ane mentally retarded persons. *Australia and New Zealand Journal of Developmental Disabilities, 9,* 191–209.

Jones, M. L., Favell, J. E., Risley, T. R. (1981). *Socioecological programming of the mentally retarded.* New York: Plenum.

Kanner, L. (1964). *A history of the care and study of the mentally retarded.* Springfield, IL: Charles C. Thomas.

Kazdin, A. E. (1977). Assessing the clinical or applied significance of behavior change through social validation. *Behavior Modification, 1,* 427–452.

Kazdin, A. E. (1980). Acceptability of alternative treatments for deviant child behavior. *Journal of Applied Behavior Analysis, 13,* 259–273.

Kazdin, A. E., & Frame, C. (1983). Aggressive behavior and conduct disorder. In R. J. Morris & T. R. Kratochwill (Eds.), *The practice of child therapy* (pp. 167–192). New York: Pergamon.

Kerr, N., Meyerson, L., & Michael, J. (1965). A procedure for shaping vocalizations in a mute child. In L. Ullman & L. Krasner (Eds.), *Case studies in behavior modification* (pp. 366–370). New York: Hold, Rinehart & Winston.

Kirk, S. (1984). Introspection and prophecy. In B. Blatt & R. J. Morris, (Eds.), *Perspectives in special education: Personal orientations* (pp. 25–55). Glenview, IL: Scott, Foresman & Company.

Kratochwill, T. R., & Bergan, J. R. (1978). Training school psychologists: Some perspectives on a competency-based behavioral consultation model. *Professional Psychology, 9,* 71–82.

Kratochwill, T., Schnapps, A., & Bissell, M. (1985). Research design in school psychology. In J. R. Bergan (Ed.), *School psychology in contemporary society: An introduction* (pp. 58–91). Columbus, OH: Charles Merrill.

Lacayo, N., Sherwood, G., & Morris, J. (1981). Daily activities of school psychologists: A national survey. *Psychology in the Schools, 18,* 184–190.

Lentz, F. E., & Shapiro, E. S. (1985). Behavioral school psychology: A conceptual model for the delivery of psychological services. In T. R. Kratochwill (Ed.), *Advances in school psychology* (Vol. IV, pp. 191–222). Hillsdale, NJ: Lawrence Erlbaum Associates.

Lentz, F. E., & Shapiro, E. (1987). Training behavioral school psychologists: Development of a model. *Professional School Psychology, 2,* 181–190.

Levinson, E. M. (1987). Career development. In A. Thomas & Grimes, J. (Eds.), *Childrens needs: Psychological perspectives* (pp. 7–82). Washington, DC: The National Association of School Psychologists.

Levy, L. H. (1986). Reflections on "professionalism within school psychology". *Professional School Psychology, 1,* 35–39.

Lovaas, I. V. (1977). *The autistic child.* New York: Irvington Publishers.

Lovaas, I. O., Berberich, J. F., Perloff, B. F., & Schaeffer, B. (1966). Acquisition of imitative speech by schizophrenic children. *Science, 151,* 705–707.

Lovaas, O. I., & Bucher, B. (Eds.). (1974). *Perspectives in behavior modification with deviant children.* Englewood Cliffs: Prentice–Hall.

Luiselli, J. K. (1977). Care report: An attendant-administered contingency management programme for the treatment of a toileting phobia. *Journal of Mental Deficiency Research, 21,* 283–288.

Martin, R. P. (1983). Consultation in the schools. In G. W. Hynd (Ed.), *The school psychologist: An introduction* (pp. 269–292). Syracuse, NY: Syracuse University Press.

Mash, E. J., & Terdal, L. G. (1981). Behavioral assessment of childhood disturbance. In E. J. Mash & L. G. Terdal (Eds.), *Behavioral assessment of childhood disorders* (pp. 3–76). New York: Guilford Press.

Matson, J. L., & Andrasik (Eds.). (1983). *Treatment issues and innovations in mental retardation.* New York: Plenum.

Matson, J. L., & Barrett, R. P. (Eds.). (1982). *Psychopathology in the mentally retarded.* New York: Grune & Stratton.

Matson, J. L., DiLorenzo, T. M., & Andrasik, F. (1983). A review of behavior modification procedures for treating social skill deficits and psychiatric disorders of the mentally retarded. In J. L. Matson & F. Andrasik (Eds.), *Treatment issues and innovations in mental retardation* (pp. 415–454). New York: Plenum.

Matson, J. L., & McCartney, J. R. (Eds.). (1981). *Handbook of behavior modification with the mentally retarded.* New York: Plenum.

McNally, R. J., & Ascher, L. M. (1987). Anxiety disorders in mentally retarded people. In L. Michelson & L. M. Ascher (Eds.), *Cognitive-behavioral assessment and treatment of anxiety disorders* (pp. 74–98). New York: Guilford.

Meacham, M. L., & Peckham, P. D. (1978). School psychologists at three-quarters century: Congruence between training, practice, preferred role and competence. *Journal of School Psychology, 16,* 195–206.

Medway, F. J. (1979). How effective is school consultation: A review of recent research. *Journal of School Psychology, 17,* 275–282.

Medway, F. (1985). Direct therapeutic intervention in school psychology. In J. R. Bergan (Ed.), *School psychology in contemporary society: An introduction* (pp. 207–229). Columbus, OH: Merrill.

Meyers, J., Parsons, R. D., & Martin, R. (1979). *Mental health consultation in the schools.* San Francisco: Jossey Bass.

Morris, R. J. (1976). *Behavior modification with children: A systematic guide.* Boston: Little Brown.

Morris, R. J. (1985). *Behavior modification with exceptional children: Principles and practices.* Glenview, IL: Scott, Foresman & Company.

Morris, R. J., Barber, R. S., Hoschouer, R. H., Karrels, K. V., & Bijou, S. (1979). A working model for monitoring intervention programs in residential treatment settings: The peer review and ethics committees. *Rehabilitation Psychology, 26,* 155–156.

Morris, R. J., & Brown, D. K. (1983). Legal and ethical issues in behavior modification with mentally retarded persons. In J. L. Matson & F. Andrasik (Eds.), *Treatment issues and innovations in mental retardation* (pp. 61–96). New York: Plenum.

Morris, R. J., Green, R. H., & Kratochwill, T. R. (1987). *Treating fears, phobias and related anxieties in mentally retarded persons: A behavioral perspective.* Paper presented at the International Research Conference on the Mental Health Aspects of Mental Retardation, Chicago, Illinois.

Morris, R. J., & Kratochwill, T. R., (Eds.). (1983). *The practice of child therapy.* New York: Pergamon.

Morris, R. J., & McReynolds, R. A. (1986). Behavior modification with special needs children: A review. In R. J. Morris & B. Blatt (Eds.), *Special education: Research and trends* (pp. 66–130). New York: Pergamon.

Morse, W. C. (1984). Personal perspective. In B. Blatt & R. J. Morris (Eds.), *Perspectives in special education: Personal orientations* (pp. 101–124). Glenview, IL: Scott, Foresman.

Mowder, B. A. (1983). Assessment and intervention in school psychological services. In G. N. Hynd (Ed.), *The school psychologist: An introduction* (pp. 145–167). Syracuse, NY: Syracuse University Press.

Nagle, R. (1986). The doctoral program in school psychology at the University of South Carolina. *Professional School Psychology, 1,* 79–87.

National Association of School Psychologists. (1985). *Standards for the provision of school psychological services.* Washington, DC: Author.

Neufeld, G. R. (1979). Deinstitutionalization procedures. In R. Wiegerink & J. W. Pelosi (Eds.), *Developmental disabilities: The DD movement* (pp. 115–126). Baltimore: Brookes.

O'Dell, S. D. (1985). Progress in parent training. In M. Hersen, R. M. Eisler, & P. M. Miller (Eds.), *Progress in behavior modification* (Vol. 19, pp. 57–108). New York: Academic.

Ollendick, T. H., & Ollendick, D. G. (1982). Anxiety disorders. In J. Matson & R. Barrett (Eds.), *Psychopathology in the mentally retarded* (pp. 77–119). New York: Grune & Stratton.

Pfeiffer, S. I., Dean, R. S., & Shellenberger, S. (1985). The school psychologist in medical settings. In T. R. Kratochwill (Ed.), *Advances in school psychiatry* (Vol. V, pp. 177–202). Hillsdale, NJ: Lawrence Erlbaum Associates.

Phillips, B. N. (1982). Reading and evaluating research in school psychology. In C. R. Reynolds & T. B. Gutkin (Eds.), *The handbook of school psychology* (pp. 24–47). New York: Wiley.

Phillips, B. N. (1985). Education and training. In J. R. Bergan (Ed.), *School psychology in contemporary society: An introduction* (pp. 92–115). Columbus,OH: Merrill.

Phillips, B. N. (1986). School psychology at the University of Texas at Austin. *Professional School Psychology, 1,* 65–74.

Phillips, E. L. (1968). Achievement place: Token reinforcement procedures in a home-style rehabilitation setting for "predelinquent" boys. *Journal of Applied Behavior Analysis, 1,* 213–223.

Phillips, E. L., Fixsen, D. L., Phillips, E. A., & Wolf, M. M. (1979). The teaching-family model: A comprehensive approach to residential treatment of youth. In D. Cullinan & M. H. Epstein (Eds.), *Special education for adolescents: Issues and perspectives* (pp. 177–196). Columbus, OH: Merrill.

Piersel, W. J. (1985). Behavioral consultation: An approach to problem solving in educational settings. In J. R. Bergan (Ed.), *School psychology in contemporary society: An introduction* (pp. 252–280). Columbus, OH: Charles Merrill.

Pryzwansky, W. B. (1982). School psychology training and practice: The APA perspective.

In T. R. Kratochwill (Ed.), *Advances in school psychology* (Vol. II, pp. 19–39). Hillsdale, NJ: Lawrence Erlbaum Associates.

Ramage, J. (1979). National survey of school psychologists: Update. *The School Psychology Digest, 8,* 153–161.

Ramage, J. C. (1986). USA School psychologists: Characteristics, role and special education influence. *School Psychology International, 7,* 243–249.

Redner, R., Snellman, L., & Davidson, III W. S. (1983). Juvenile delinquency. In R. J. Morris & T. R. Kratochwill (Eds.), *The practice of child therapy* (pp. 193–220). New York: Pergamon.

Reiss, S. (1982). Psychopathology and mental retardation: Survey of a developmental disabilities mental health program. *Mental Retardation, 20,* 128–132.

Reiss, S., Levitan, G. W., & McNally, R. J. (1982). Emotionally disturbed mentally retarded people: An underserved population. *American Psychologist, 37,* 361–367.

Reynolds, C. R. (1983). Foundations of measurement in psychology and education. In G. W. Hynd (Ed.), *The school psychologist: An introduction* (pp. 47–66). Syracuse, NY: Syracuse University Press.

Reynolds, C. R., Gutkin, T. B., Elliott, S. N., & Witt, J. C. (1984). *School psychology: Essentials of theory and practice.* New York: Wiley.

Rosenfeld, M., Shimberg, B., & Thornton, R. F. (1983). *Job analysis of licensed psychologists in the United States and Canada.* Princeton, NJ: Educational Testing Service.

Rothman, D. J. (1971). *The discovery of the asylum: Social order and disorder in the new republic.* Boston: Little Brown & Company.

Sabatino, D. A. (1981). School psychology: An instrumental service for the handicapped. In T. R. Kratochwill (Ed.), *Advances in school psychology* (Vol. I, pp. 45–82). Hillsdale, NJ: Lawrence Erlbaum Associates.

Sarason, S. B. (1983). School psychology: An autobiographic fragment. *Journal of School Psychology, 21,* 285–295.

Sarason, S. B. (1984). Unlearning and learning. In B. Blatt & R. J. Morris (Eds.), *Perspectives in special education: Personal orientations.* Glenview, IL: Scott, Foresman & Company.

Schmuck, R. A. (1982). Organization development in the schools. In C. R. Reynolds & T. B. Gutkin (Eds.), *The handbook of school psychology* (pp. 829–857). New York: Wiley.

Schmuck, R., & Runkel, P. (1985). *The handbook of organization development in the schools* (3rd ed.). Palo Alto, CA: Mayfield Publishing Company.

Schreibman, L., Charlop, M. H., & Britten, K. R. (1983). Childhood autism. In R. J. Morris & T. R. Kratochwill (Eds.), *The practice of child therapy* (pp. 221–251). New York: Pergamon.

Sheldon, K., & Prout, H. T. (1982). Comprehensive vocational rehabilitation and the school psychologist. *The Journal for Vocational Special Needs Education, 4,* 21–22.

Short, R. J. (1987). Children and delinquency. In A. Thomas & J. Grimes (Eds.), *Children's needs: Psychological perspectives* (pp. 451–460). Washington, DC: The National Association of School Psychologists.

Smith, D. K. (1984). Practicing school psychologists: Their characteristics, activities, and populations served. *Professional Psychology, 15,* 798–810.

Snapp, M., & Davidson, J. L. (1982). Systems interventions for school psychologists: A case study approach. In C. R. Reynolds & T. B. Gutkin (Eds.), *The handbook of school psychology* (pp. 858–870). New York: Wiley.

Sparrow, S. S., Balla, D. A. & Cicchetti, D. V. (1984). *Vineland adaptive behavior scales.* Circle Pines, MN: American Guidance Service.

Steppe-Jones, C. (1987). Deinstitutionalization. In C. R. Reynolds & L. Mann (Eds.), *Encyclopedia of special education* (pp. 466–467). New York: Wiley.

Stewart, K. J. (1986). Innovative practice of indirect service delivery: Realities and idealities. *School Psychology Review, 15*, 466–478.

Sulzer-Azaroff, B. & Mayer, G. R. (1986). *Achieving educational excellence: Using behavioral strategies.* New York: Holt.

Thomas, A., & Grimes, J. (Eds.). (1987). *Children's needs: Psychological perspectives.* Washington, DC: National Association of School Psychologists.

Timm, F., Myrick, J., & Rosenberg, J. (1982). School psychologists in corrections: A new frontier. *The Journal for Vocational Special Needs Education*, *4*, 25–28.

Tindall, R. H. (1983). I didn't aspire to be a school psychologist: Reflections. *Journal of School Psychology, 21,* 79–89.

Toye, R. C., & Pierce, P. S. (1987). The forum. *Professional Psychology: Research & Practice, 10,* 3–4.

Twardosz, S., & Nordquist, V. M. (1987). Parent training. In M. Hersen & V. B. Vanhasselt (Eds.), *Behavior therapy with children and adolescents: A clinical approach* (pp. 75–105). New York: Wiley.

Tyor, P. L., & Bell, L. V. (1984). *Caring for the retarded in America: A history.* Westport, CT: Greenwood Press.

Whitman, T. L., Schibak, J. W., & Reid, D. H. (1983). *Behavior modification with the severely and profoundly retarded: Research and application.* New York: Academic Press.

Witt, J. C., & Elliott, S. N. (1985). The validity of assessing social validity and acceptability. In T. R. Kratochwill (Ed.), *Advances in school psychology* (Vol. IV, pp. 251–288). Hillsdale, NJ: Lawrence Erlbaum Associates.

Witt, J. C., & Martens, B. K. (1983). Assessing the acceptability of behavioral interventions used in classrooms. *Psychology in the Schools, 20,* 510–521.

Wolfensberger, W. (1972). *The principle of normalization in human services.* Washington, DC: National Institute on Mental Retardation.

Ziarnik, J. P., & Bernstein, G. S. (1982). A critical examination of the effects of inservice training on staff performance. *Mental Retardation, 20,* 109–114.

Zigler, E. (1984). A developmental theory on mental retardation. In B. Blatt & R. J. Morris (Eds.), *Perspectives in special education: Personal orientations* (pp. 173–209). Glenview, IL: Scott, Foresman & Company.

Zimmerman, E. H., & Zimmerman, J. (1962). The alteration of behavior in a special classroom situation. In L. P. Ullmann & L. Krasner (Eds.), *Case studies in behavior modification* (pp. 328–330). New York: Holt, Rinehart & Winston.

8
The Past, Present, and Future of School Psychology in Nontraditional Settings

RIK CARL D'AMATO
Mississippi State University

RAYMOND S. DEAN
Neuropsychology Laboratory, Ball State University
Indiana University School of Medicine

THE BIRTH OF NONTRADITIONAL SCHOOL PSYCHOLOGY

Lightner Witmer has often been credited with the underlying conceptualization of both school psychology and clinical psychology (Altmaier & Meyer, 1985; Brotemarkle, 1931; Eiserer, 1963; Magary, 1967; Reynolds, Gutkin, Elliott, & Witt, 1984). To understand his views, it is necessary to consider his background. Witmer's professional life began as an English and history teacher at Rugby Academy in Philadelphia (Brotemarkle, 1931). In this setting, Witmer was intrigued by the fact that some students did not learn despite the fact that they seemed motivated and bright (Brotemarkle, 1931; Collins, 1931; Gray, 1963; Witmer, 1907). It was this paradox that stimulated his study of psychology first at the University of Pennsylvania and later at the University in Leipzig. Under the direction of James Cattell and later Wilhelm Wundt, Witmer began to formulate his scientific approach to applied psychology (Boring, 1950; Brotemarkle, 1931; Garfield, 1985; McReynolds, 1987).

It is important to note that Witmer's empirical approach to applied psychology was a departure from the introspective focus of the times (Leahey, 1980; Woodworth, 1948). In light of Witmer's experimental training with Wundt, who is often credited with being the first experimental psychologist, it is surprising to find Witmer continuing in his commitment to an unquestionably practical psychology (e.g., children's problems; Leahey, 1980; Witmer, 1907, 1911). Indeed, early in this century the union of experimental and applied psychology created the kind of cross-fertilization Witmer (1896, 1897, 1907) had in mind. Without doubt, it was Witmer's seminal work in the Psychology Laboratory at the University of Pennsylvania that provided the foundation for what we have come to know as the scientist-practitioner model. Witmer's (1907) first cases were children with school-related difficulties. Specifically, one displayed difficulties with the English language (e.g., difficulties between verb tenses and missing word endings), and one had been labeled a chronic bad speller. From this description, these children would most probably be diagnosed as learning disabled. In a systematic fashion Witmer searched the literature and found that psychology had not investigated causes or treatments for these disorders. Witmer (1907) argued that there were no principles for him to follow and thus, he had to scientifically study these children before developing interventions.

In 1896, Witmer integrated his rather novel ideas about applied psychology in a paper entitled *The Clinical Method in Psychology and the Diagnostic Method of Teaching* at the Annual Meeting of the American Psychological Association (APA). This paper was an organizational plan for the role and structure of applied psychology (Witmer, 1896, 1897). The plan involved:

1. The investigation of mental development in children, as manifested by mental and moral retardation, by means of statistical and clinical methods.
2. A psychological clinic, supplemented by a hospital-training school, for the treatment of children suffering from all defects interfering with school progress.
3. The offering of practical applied work to those engaged in the professions of teaching and medicine, in the observation and training of normal and retarded children.
4. The training of students for a new profession—the expert, who would work with the school, or in connection with the practice of medicine, treating mentally retarded children. (Brotemarkle, 1931, reprinted from Witmer, 1907).

Apparently, the only response Witmer got from his audience of experimental psychologists was "a slight elevation of the eyebrows on the part of a few of the older members" (Collins, 1931, p. 5). Whatever the reaction, this paper portrayed a practical specialty that evolved into school psychology. Perhaps the most intriguing aspect of the role was that it stressed clinical *and* empirical methods for the understanding and treatment of children who displayed psychological and developmental deficits. The techniques offered involved the assessment of the disorder, the development of hypotheses concerning an appropriate intervention, and finally the provision and evaluation of the intervention. Training in Witmer's applied psychology was viewed as appropriate for professionals in varied careers (e.g., teachers, physicians, social workers), serving all types of children. Of interest to the present discussion, Witmer emphasized that psychologists trained as scientist-practitioners could expect to offer services in varied settings (Brotemarkle, 1931; Cutts, 1955; McReynolds, 1987). From its inception then, it is clear that what has come to be known as school psychology was meant to define the *problems* to be studied and *not* the setting.

Witmer (1907) viewed the psychological clinic as an institution for social and public service, for research and for the instruction of students in psychology. From this point of view, practitioners needed to train in the "psychology orthogenics" which included vocational, educational, corrective, hygienic, industrial and social guidance. To this end, instruction in applied psychology was seen as a broad based approach, reflecting backgrounds of a number of allied but related disciplines (Fernberger, 1931). Although much of this broad base is reflected in the common core psychology areas adopted by the APA, a number of elements (e.g., vocational, social guidance, etc.) are now also served by a multidisciplinary team approach (Brotemarkle, 1931; Reynolds, et al., 1984). Parenthetically, many of Witmer's notions seem in line with what has come to be called community psychology. However, few authors credit him with such a contribution (Spielberger & Stenmark, 1985).

The Clinical Psychology-School Psychology Split

Before World War II few distinctions were made between applied psychologists, however there seemed to be two rather distinct components of psychological services. These elements involved a psychotherapy-mental health focus or a more actuarial-psychometric component that stressed diagnosis (Gray, 1963). That is to say that prior to World War II, although psychologists would choose to emphasize one element over another, only *one* applied psychology existed. A great deal of evidence supports the hypothesis that World War II had a major impact on our current conception of psychological specialties (Altmaier & Meyer, 1985; Reynolds, et al., 1984). With war time stress came a considerable number of psychiatric casualties. However, few trained psychologists were available to meet these needs. In addition, because such a wide variety of psychological problems existed, the role of the service provider was quickly expanded to meet the needs of both diagnosis and ongoing treatment. To be sure, the needs of the Veterans Administration (VA) were instrumental in providing support for applied psychologists through both training grants and expanding employment opportunities immediately after the second world war. Indeed, the VA was the major employer of what are now seen as clinical psychologists. It was at this time that the notion of "clinical psychology" began to be considered. The subspecialty can be followed most directly to a 1947 APA committee on training in "clinical psychology" (see Committee on Training in Clinical Psychology, 1947).

The Boulder Conference in 1949 was a further attempt to refine the idea of "clinical psychology" (see Raimy, 1950). During this conference, the training model stressed for clinical psychology was that of a *scientist* (trained in the empirical tradition) linked with a *practitioner* (competent in dealing with psychopathology). Of interest here, is the fact that this mix had been previously detailed by Witmer (1907). Activities at this conference included the development of goals and policies for clinical psychologists, established by university trainers. In general, these factors solidified the role of the *clinical psychologist* and moved "clinical psychology" further away from Witmer's early interpretation of applied psychology. So too, with this move clinical psychology became identified with the diagnosis and treatment of severe psychopathology. Clinical psychology's move from child/family oriented services to more severe psychiatric disorders has been well detailed (see Garfield, 1985; Harris, 1980). Harris (1980) argues that school psychology is the applied specialty that "stayed at home" while clinical psychology "moved on to new neighborhoods" (p. 15). It seems obvious that applied psychologists working with children and families in community clinics, hospitals, and schools are far closer to Witmer's original notions that to what today is generally thought of as clinical psychology.

The public schools exerted an influence comparable to that of the VA on applied psychology. In the middle to late 1800s schools began to utilize special teachers in programs to serve children with learning and behavior problems. One attempt in 1871 occurred in New Haven, Connecticut where classes provided for children "who were running wild on the street and becoming a public nuisance" (Fein, 1974, p. 2). Because programs of this type were developing rapidly, specialists were in demand to identify students who would benefit from these special programs. The public school movement quickly adapted a psychometric emphasis, which followed in the wake of Alfred Binet and Theophile Simon's pioneering of standardized intelligence testing in Europe (Fein, 1974; Reynolds, et al., 1984). It has been well established that the use of these tests, in the placement of deficient children, was well received by the public schools. This interpretation is consistent with the fact that the 1916 Stanford Revision of the Binet-Simon Intelligence Scale became the most popular test in the United States during the next 25 years (Fein,

1974). This instrument did much to crystallize the role of what was to become applied psychology in the schools.

Still another wave of the tide of psychology in the schools came with the mental hygiene/mental health movement. In this case, the applied psychologist working in the schools was seen as a good ally for providing mental health services to children (Magary, 1967; Tindall, 1964). Because this movement stressed prevention and early intervention services, the public schools became the ideal institution on which to focus (Cutts, 1955). For some, schools appeared to have the potential of becoming what we view today as community mental health centers (Tindall, 1964). In some ways, this role ran counter to the more test-oriented psychometrist, who saw their role as diagnosing and placing "backward" children. As expected, even during this time period, the diagnostic-remedial activities of psychologists in the schools often took precedence over more preventive mental health oriented activities. From even a brief review of literature, it is evident that the practice of psychology in the public schools happened haphazardly, rather than developing from rational arguments of how psychology could be best applied to the educational enterprise.

The Practice of Psychology in the Schools

The demand for applied psychologists to provide services in the schools intensified after World War II (Eiserer, 1963). This need was related to the countries' turn to domestic needs, the post-war baby boom and notions of progressive, quality education for all children. During this period, it also became clear that many school children needed *individualized* instruction if they were to succeed in the traditional educational environment (Bardon & Bennett, 1974). Consequently, psychologists contributed to these efforts by providing psychoeducational assessment and mental health services (Bower, 1955; Herron, Green, Guild, Smith, & Kantor, 1970; Reger, 1965). However, due to the limited number of trained applied psychologists and the needs of the schools, the number of school psychologists was limited. In tandem with this shortage came questions about how to best meet the psychological needs of school-age children. With the Boulder Conference as a backdrop, some school psychologists (e.g., Newland, 1970) began arguing for a similar conference to outline elements of training and practice with school-age children (Cutts, 1955; Reynolds et al., 1984; Ysseldyke & Schakel, 1983).

These concerns led to a conference that was held at the Thayer Hotel in West Point, New York in 1954. The objective of the Thayer Conference was to address the roles, goals, functions, and training of school psychologists, encourage the development of new training programs, and continue training psychologists as scientists/practitioners. Role definition issues were also addressed in an effort to establish school psychology as a distinct specialty in the APA. Although specific roles were detailed concerning the development and adjustment of children though assessment, consultation, remedial programming, research and the like, the conference proceedings stressed a rather broad definition of school psychology services:

> There are innumerable ways in which the school psychologist can apply his knowledge. The details of what he does and of how he does it will depend on the particular situation in which he finds himself, on the special needs for his service inherent in the situation, and upon this training and qualifications. (Cutts, 1955, p. 172)

With the definition of a specialty in mind, individual states were encouraged to set credentialing requirements, and the title *school psychologist* was thought to be best reserved for doctoral level psychologists. But the need for two-year graduate training programs were seen as a necessary service component, although no title was agreed on for this level of training (Gray, 1963). Without a strong role statement, these two distinct levels of service (subdoctoral and doctoral) called for in this conference began, at once, to drift into a *single* level of service. Basically, in the shadow of the Boulder Conference, the Thayer Conference established school psychology as a separate and viable specialty within applied psychology. At this point in time, school psychology rested on a well documented foundation, albeit the foundation was built predominantly on *school property*.

Not surprisingly, little changed after the conference. Psychologists who practiced in the schools in the 1960s reported concerns about the efficacy and efficiency of their work, dissatisfaction with roles and relationships, problems developing multidisciplinary teams, few consultation opportunities, limited time for individual counseling and dissatisfaction with time for research (Bower, 1955; Eiserer, 1963; Gray, 1963; Hirst, 1963; Reger, 1965; Valett, 1963). It appears that some doctoral psychologists were inadequately prepared for the restricted school role and over prepared for the daily public education routine (Bardon, 1981; Gray, 1963; Hynd, 1983; Mullen, 1981; Newland, 1981).

THE CURRENT ROLE OF THE SCHOOL PSYCHOLOGIST

Concomitant with needs in the applied setting has come growth in programs that train school psychologists. Fagan (1985a, 1985b, 1985c, 1986a) reports that there are approximately 20,000 school psychologists at present, with approximately 12,000 holding membership in the National Association of School Psychologists and about 2,500 belonging to the American Psychological Association's School Psychology Division 16. Moreover, training in school psychology is accomplished through 79 doctoral training programs and 254 subdoctoral training programs (Brown & Minke, 1984; Brown, Sewall, & Lindstrom, 1977; Fagan, 1985b, 1985c). Thirty-six of the doctoral programs are accredited by the APA and 53 are accredited by the National Council for Accreditation of Teacher Education/National Association of School Psychologists (NCATE/NASP) (American Psychological Association, 1987, National Council for Accreditation of Teacher Education, 1986-1987; Fagan, 1985c, 1986a). So too, NCATE/NASP has accredited 67 specialist's and 103 master's programs (Bardon & Wenger, 1974; National Council for Accreditation of Teacher Education, 1986-1987).

It is apparent that the psychologist who practices in the schools has the potential of providing a unique view to the educational enterprise. By virtue of training and focus, the school psychologist brings the technical insight of the science of psychology to bear on problems that may hinder the full development of school-age children. While these services could be provided in a variety of settings, schools continue to dominate the employment picture. Although we are far from consensus on the specific role the school psychologist should play, there seems to be general agreement among educators that the application of psychological principles and techniques in the educational setting is important to pedagogic pursuits (Conoley & Gutkin, 1986; Senft & Snider, 1980). Unfortunately however, assessment activities continue to cloud the original vision of school psychology (Bardon, Davis, Howard, & Myrick, 1982; Bennett, 1970, 1985; Benson & Hughes, 1985; Conoley & Conoley, 1982; Goldston, 1986; Stewart, 1986).

Although a wide variety of functions have been offered as appropriate for the school psychologist, numerous factors have combined to impede the growth of the specialty beyond an individual assessment focus. Owing, perhaps, to the fact that psychological personnel have been employed at only one level in the schools, the duties of the school psychologist have revolved around individual diagnostic assessments as a precursor to special class placement (e.g., D'Amato & Dean, 1987). Debate has continued for at least four decades concerning whether this is the proper role for the psychologist; however, it remains the primary function of most practicing school psychologists (e.g., Dean, 1980; Meacham & Peckham, 1978; Sattler, 1988). This expression of the specialty has been reemphasized by Federal legislation (e.g., P.L. 94-142) which has mandated even greater emphasis on formal child evaluation services by the public schools. With special education reimbursements tied to rather strict procedures in determining children's initial and continuing eligibility and the fact that the bulk of the child assessment procedures are provided by psychological personnel, the school psychologist's role has become further solidified within the schools (Solly & Hohenshil, 1986). Therefore, although legislation has expanded the need for school psychological personnel, it has continued to narrow services to individual child assessment.

Doctoral versus Subdoctoral Training and Levels of Service

Confusion concerning the level of training necessary for entry into the profession has existed for some time. Unlike other applied psychology specialties, state standards for licensure, certification, and those offered by professional organizations are often at odds with each other in school psychology. A case in point is the APA, which has continued to advocate that minimal competence as a psychologist, in any setting, can only be maintained at the doctoral level. Although this position has rarely been seriously challenged by other applied psychological specialties, it has led to controversy in school psychology (Dimond, Havens, Rathrow, & Colliver, 1977; Hilke & Brantley, 1982; Korman, 1974; Smith & Soper, 1978). The position of less than a doctorate for entry into school psychology, although favored by some, is rather disturbing to many who feel that psychological practice in the schools is as demanding in sophistication as any other applied specialty in psychology, regardless of the present reality of practice (Bardon, 1982; Dean, 1982a; Hilke & Brantley, 1982; National Association of School Psychologists, 1984). Historically, the interest in individual assessment and relatively few trained psychologists may have been responsible for the early entry, growth, and certification of paraprofessionals who served as *testers* and *gatekeepers* for special education entry (Cutts, 1955; Hall, 1949; Kennedy, 1971). This seems a benchmark, because this practice apparently is the antecedent of the certification of psychological personnel for work in the schools by the educational community (Bennett, 1985; Hall, 1949). Although the role frequently espoused for school psychology has been an expansion beyond diagnosis-placement functions (e.g., Alpert, 1985; Bergan, 1979), the profession has clearly remained dependent on this function and hence on public education for direction (Gilmore & Chandy, 1973; Hartshorne & Johnson, 1985). Such dependency is in sharp contrast to more broad-based service notions offered early on for school psychology (Cutts, 1955; Fernberger, 1931; Witmer, 1896, 1897, 1907, 1911).

Although this assessment emphasis may well be appropriate for subdoctoral-trained specialists, doctoral-level psychologists usually have expanded training that widens the scope of their skills and understanding (Fagan, 1985c, Matarazzo, 1987). In fact, some authors have argued for a distinction between doctoral and subdoctoral-level psychological personnel, with names reflecting their level of training and expertise (Bardon 1982, 1983, Chapter 1). Thus, subdoctoral practitioners would be "school psychologists," whereas doctoral-level psychologists would function under a title recognizing that they have the potential to offer services in a wider variety of settings (e.g., family service psychologists or applied educational psychologists). Although these settings may include the schools, such applied psychologists would not be restricted to public education. After considering the level of services provided in most schools, some have questioned the need for doctoral-level training in school psychology. In theory, it seems that additional training should enable psychologists to perform functions not possible with less training. Obviously, different levels of training enable psychologists to perform varied types of activities. Although such service models have been articulated (e.g., see Dean, 1982a), their application has not been realized in the schools. In essence, most doctoral-level school psychologists perform duties *identical* to subdoctoral level school psychologists when they practice in the schools (Dean, 1982b; French & McCloskey, 1980; Gilmore & Chandy, 1973; Meacham & Peckham, 1978; Reynolds et al., 1984).

From this point of view, one wonders if acceptance of subdoctoral training as the level of entry may well serve as a tacit acceptance of the services presently offered as "school psychology". In other words, are we prepared as a profession to accept psychological services now provided in the schools as being *school psychology?* Another question concerns the extent to which we are willing to accept the solidification of school psychology from forces outside of psychology? However, congruent with any argument counter to considering psychological services presently offered in the schools as being *school psychology* must come the resolve that the parameters of the profession should be defined by forces within the profession.

In what seems to be an effort to extend the role of the school psychologist or to concretize role gains, a number of papers have appeared calling for expanded services (e.g., Alpert, 1985; Fagan, 1986b; National School Psychology Inservice Training Network, 1984). These papers have come in the wake of other noteworthy attempts (e.g., Spring Hill and Olympia), to direct the future of school psychology (see Brown, Cardon, Coulter, & Meyers, 1982; Oakland, 1986; Ysseldyke & Weinberg, 1981). In each case, authors have portrayed the school psychologist as a provider of a full gamut of services. This position stands in sharp contrast to current training statements, which stress or at least accept subdoctoral level-training. With this in mind, one must wonder if it is possible to accept a call for an *increased* role while retaining a subdoctoral entry level. Interestingly however, authors that have argued for an expanded role pay relatively little attention to how such additional elements could be integrated into training (Alpert, 1985; National School Psychology Inservice Training Network, 1984). Although it is impossible to draw a line clearly separating appropriate services for doctoral and nondoctoral-level psychological personnel, common sense establishes that we cannot continually expand services while advocating for less than doctoral level training. Evidence suggests that implicit in this role extension must come the need for doctoral level training (Bardon, 1982, 1983).

School Psychology's Link to Education

In general, school psychology has remained intrinsically tied to a single institution—the school (Bennett, 1985; Dean, 1982b). This is not as hackneyed a view as it would appear; for the ramifications of this fact may well be responsible for innumerable obstacles to our development as a profession. This is not meant to paint public education with a brush of sinister motives, but rather a consideration of those factors which have shaped school psychology. Bardon (1982, 1983) has articulated a stance that recognizes our failure to fully develop as a field within the schools. Indeed, Bardon (1982, 1983, Chapter 1) like many others, has questioned the heuristic value of the APA's Division 16 as defining itself as school psychology when that entity has been associated with psychological applications which fall short of a distinct specialization within American Psychology. Bardon's position, although rather disturbing to some, succinctly portrays the view held by many, that school psychology as presently practiced in the schools drastically lacks the sophistication envisioned for the specialty (Gray, 1963; Fernberger, 1931; Holt & Kicklighter, 1971; Hall, 1949; Witmer, 1907; White & Harris, 1961).

The situation that exists is hardly surprising because as psychologists who owe their existence to the schools, we are bound by the same political and economic forces which shape that institution. In fact, the many difficulties of the educational system have been well publicized (Education Commission of the States, Task Force on Education for Economic Growth, 1983; Goodlad, 1979; National Commission on Excellence in Education, 1983; National School Psychology Inservice Training Network, 1984). Although a variety of problems have plagued public education, Hyman (1979a) succinctly portrays the overall picture:

> In fact, rather than accumulating wisdom and prestige, American education constantly appears to be deteriorating as it flaps and flutters in the changing winds of political and economic uncertainty. And the interface between psychology and education, whether it be at the experimental or the professional level, can never provide a solid base for improvement in many children's lives until schooling becomes less susceptible to the whims of the many forces affecting it. (p. 1026)

Overall then, because certification, initial employment, and the ability to structure the role of psychological services are controlled by the educational community, acceptance by the APA of the practice of school psychology seems more a recognition of the realities of the specialty as practiced than a reconceptualization of school psychology (Sewall & Brown, 1976). Hyman (1979a, 1979b) argues that the lack of effective contact between psychology and education is a problem of social policy and planning. Whatever the reason, a sad admission, indeed, is the fact that the influence the APA has enjoyed in the practice of school psychology is at best indirect and at worst illusionary.

NONTRADITIONAL SCHOOL PSYCHOLOGY AND THE FUTURE

School psychology would seem to have matured to the point where the specialty offers marketable nonredundant skills that are in demand in a variety of settings (Levy, 1986). However, this fact is often obscured because of the institutional affiliation that the school psychology name designates. Indeed, a number of authors have argued convincingly that school psychologists have long utilized psychological skills that are appropriate in numerous settings (D'Amato, Dean, Hughes, Harrison, McCloskey, Pryzwansky, & Hartlage, 1987; Giebink & Ringness, 1970; National Association of School Psychologists, 1986; Reynolds & Gutkin, 1982). By training, school psychologists are able to provide an understanding of the factors that influence children's cognitive and emotional functioning notwithstanding settings (Alpert, 1985; Meacham & Peckham, 1978; National School Psychology Inservice Training Network, 1984). Table 8.1 displays some of the nontraditional settings where school psychologists have successfully practiced. As reviewed above, the roots of school psychology in settings other than the schools can be traced back to the very founding of the field (Fernberger, 1931; Witmer, 1896, 1897, 1907, 1911). With the expansion of psychology into new areas, a variety of alternative roles have continued to evolve for school psychologists. This approach stresses matching client needs with appropriate services—while paying little attention to the settings in

TABLE 8.1
Nontraditional Settings Advocated for School Psychologists

Evaluation Centers	Brantley (1971)
University Clinics	Witmer (1907)
	Hughes & Benson (1986)
Private Practice	Harries (1982)
Medical/Family Clinics	Pfeiffer, Dean, & Shellenberger (1986)
Developmental Pediatric Centers	Hartlage & Hartlage (1978)
Neurology Departments	D'Amato & Dean (1988)
Neuropsychology Clinics	Dean (1982a)
Residential Treatment Facilities	Witmer (1897)
Community Mental Health Centers	Granowsky & Davis (1974)
	Klosterman (1974)

which the services are offered. Figure 8.1 displays the dynamic relationship between settings, services, and clients. Clearly, most services can be offered to a variety of clients in many different settings.

In general, the last eight decades have revealed two distinctive dimensions of applied service applications which have evolved after melding clients, services, and settings. These two approaches seem to characterize the overall practice of school psychology in nontraditional settings. In fact, these two service dimensions were displayed rather dramatically before the clinical-school psychology split.

Consulting Family-Service Psychology. The first orientation is that of a consulting family-service psychologist. This specialist offers a wholistic view of the child who is interacting with the educational system in light of the functioning of their family, peers, and community. Early on, anthropologists argued the importance of the relationship between individuals and their environment (e.g., Mead, 1961). Since that time others have advocated for similar child/family services with data suggesting both the effectiveness of this perspective and the scarcity of service providers (Hannah & Midlarsky, 1985; Hobbs, 1964, 1968, 1976; Montgomery & Paul, 1982; President's Commission on Mental Health, 1978; Pryzwansky, 1986; Rappaport, 1977; Smith & Hobbs, 1966). From this ecological perspective, the psychologist is seen to interface, negotiate, and intervene after evaluating the needs of the client and the system/family (Lewin, 1936; Nelson, 1976). The state of affairs at present supports such an interactional/ecological view, in light of the forces that influence children and families on a daily basis (National School Psychology Inservice Training Network, 1984). Moreover, this community-family-based approach to psychological services would seem to blend well

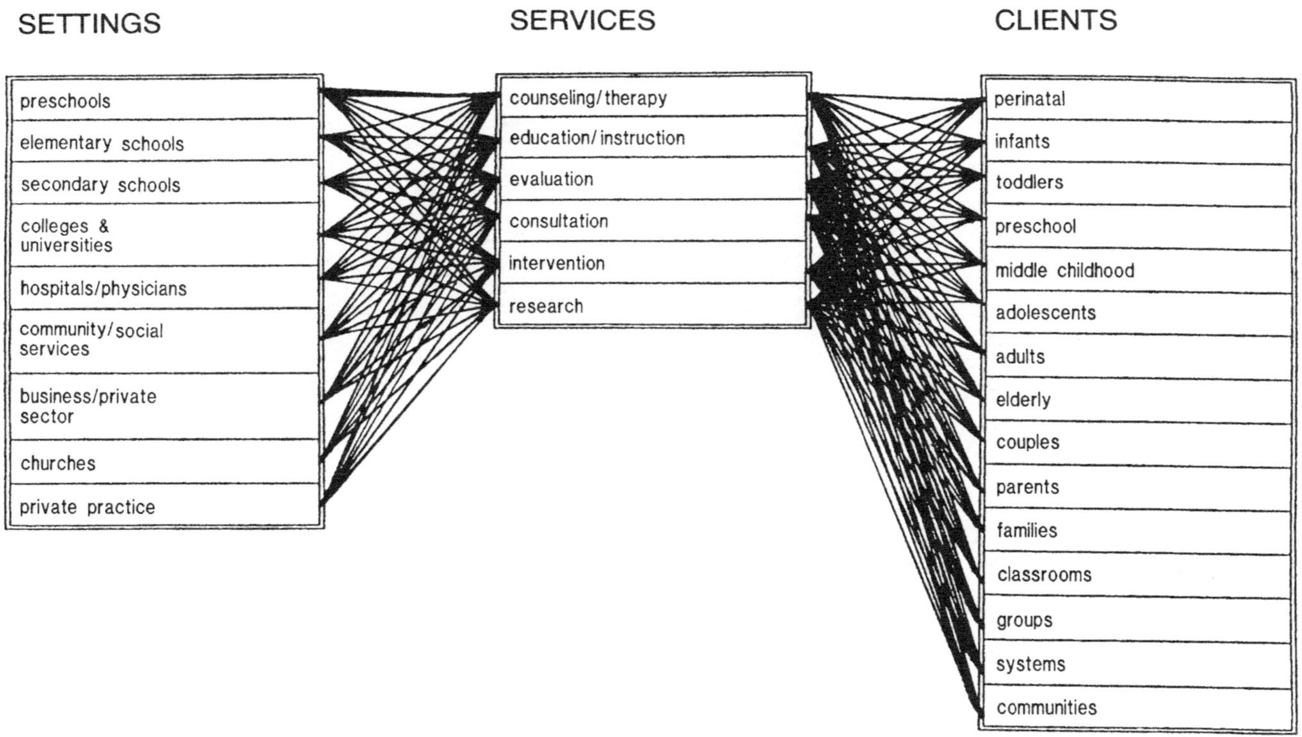

FIGURE 8.1. Graphic portrayal of the interactions which are possible between settings, services and clients.

with the more preventive mental health and social adjustment needs of school-age children (Alpert, 1985; Bardon, 1982, 1983; Conoley & Conoley, 1982; Hughes & Benson, 1986; Mearig, 1982; Packard, 1983; Ruckhaber, 1970; Scarr, 1979; Spielberger & Stenmark, 1985). Services in this area may include educational activities for parents and children (e.g., parent training, marriage enrichment, self-concept development, communication classes), individual and family counseling and therapy (Conoley, Chapter 2), behavioral programming and management (Morris & Morris, Chapter 7) and support groups (e.g., assertiveness training, single parenting). The general focus of this area is on clinical services to children and families, with little consideration provided to the fact that these services are offered outside of the educational enterprise (Pryzwansky, Chapter 3). From a theoretical view, this wider service model makes both conceptual and practical sense and is a good fit with the school psychologist's training and experiences.

Actuarial and Rehabilitation Psychology. In contrast, other authors have stressed psychodiagnostic and/or rehabilitation aspects of functioning in nontraditional settings (Anastasi, 1988; Cohen, Montague, Nathanson, & Swerdlik, 1988; Dean, 1982a; Sattler, 1988). For decades it has been argued that school psychologists have training and expertise that enables them to serve as assessment and remedial experts (Bardon, 1982; Bardon & Bennett, 1973; Bower, 1955; Gray, 1963; Reger, 1965; White & Harris, 1961; Valett, 1963). Although a number of these evaluative activities (e.g., standardized testing, patient/family interview) are similar to the traditional school assessment process (Reynolds et al., 1984; Sattler, 1988), when practiced in alternative settings, a greater number of evaluative techniques are utilized and the resulting data are interpreted quite differently (e.g., see Dean, 1982a). As would be expected, this actuarial approach (Cronbach, 1957; Meehl, 1954), finds easy expression outside of the public school system (Dean, 1982a; D'Amato & Dean, 1988). From this conceptualization, school psychologists may be involved in settings where comprehensive assessments are required (Wodrich & Pfeiffer, Chapter 4), or they could work in the development and planning of rehabilitation programs (Stone, Gray, & Dean, Chapter 6). With a psychometric background, school psychologists would also seem well positioned to spearhead test and product development and serve as research and personnel consultants (Harrison & McCloskey, Chapter 5).

For the most part, both service dimensions have the potential to contribute significantly to settings outside of the schools (Bardon, 1982; Cummings, 1979; Hobbs, 1968, 1976, 1978; Pfeiffer, Dean, & Shellenberger, 1986). When one considers the political and economic forces that influence education, it is evident that school psychologists working outside of the educational enterprise may operate in a fashion as consistent with their training as psychologists providing services in the schools. It would also seem possible for the school psychologist working in nontraditional settings to offer a level of psychological services that authors have long argued to be an integral part of the school psychologist's role (Alpert, 1985; Brantley, 1971; D'Amato, Dean, Hughes, Harrison, McCloskey, Pryzwansky, & Hartlage, 1987; Granger & Campbell, 1977; Granowsky & Davis, 1974; Hartlage, 1971; Hohenshil, 1974; Klosterman, 1974; Lambert, 1973; National School Psychology Inservice Training Network, 1984; Reilly, 1973, 1974; Singer, Whiton, & Fried, 1970). To be sure, with employment in a number of nontraditional settings has come the opportunity to practice and hone many school psychology skills that are rarely applied in educational settings (Table 8.2). Apparently, the number of school psychologists attracted to alternative settings has grown geometrically since opportunities outside of the public schools seem to be increasing (D'Amato, Dean, Hughes, Harrison, McCloskey, Pryzwansky, & Hartlage, 1987; D'Amato, Dean, & Holloway, 1987).

TABLE 8.2
School Psychology Services Which Find Easy Application to Nontraditional Settings

Assessment (Goh, 1977; Stewart, 1986)	Neuropsychology (Dean, 1982a)
Consultation (Pryzwansky, 1986; Ramage, 1979)	Community Services (Brantley, Reilly, Beach, Cody, Fields, & Lee, 1974; Granowsky & Davis, 1974)
Research (Dean, 1982b; Gray, 1963)	Instruction (National School Psychology Inservice Training Network, 1984)
Counseling & Therapy (Hartshorne & Johnson, 1985)	Mental Health Services (Klosterman, 1974)
Systems Development (Dean, 1982b; Gray, 1963)	Vocational Evaluations & Programing (Hohenshil, 1974, 1979)
Behavioral Management (Gray, 1963)	Multicultural Activities (Gray, 1963)
Group Testing (Stewart, 1986)	Personnel Development (National School Psychology Inservice Training Network, 1984)
Individual Program Planning (Stewart, 1986)	Program Evaluation (Granger & Campbell, 1977)

Nontraditional School Psychology Training and Practice

It is appropriate to ask if school psychology training provides psychologists with the skills necessary to practice in nontraditional settings. However, after a review of training requirements in school psychology doctoral programs, the breadth of the specialty becomes clear (Fagan, 1985c; Goh, 1977; Reynolds, et al., 1984; Pfeiffer & Marmo, 1981). Similar to other applied psychology specialities, school psychology training requires core course work in the biological, social, individual difference, and cognitive-affective bases of behavior, as well as work in the general areas of assessment, interventions, consultation and remediation (Fagan, 1985c; Goh, 1977; Pfeiffer & Marmo, 1981). Specialized practicum and internship opportunities in clinical settings with children and families are also common training elements (National Association of School Psychologists, 1972, 1984; Pryzwansky, 1971). In essence, it would appear that this training offers a solid foundation that could be applied across settings.

It has been argued that the distinctive forces that previously shaped applied specialties are no longer evident (Bardon, 1983; D'Amato, Dean, & Holloway, 1987; Goldstein & Krasner, 1987; Levy, 1984, 1986). For example, school psychologists often practice family therapy, clinical psychologists provide vocational assessment, and counseling psychologists are involved with psychotherapy in state hospitals (Altmaier & Meyer, 1985; Bardon, 1983; Cummings, 1979; Fitzgerald & Osipow, 1986; Levy, 1984, 1986; Trickett, 1984). Further developing this notion, Matarazzo (1987) claims there is *one* psychology, with no specialties but many applications. Stated differently, Levy (1984, 1986) has argued that the traditional specialties, as once conceptualized, are in danger of extinction. They are so blurred that although current names remain (e.g., clinical psychology), the coherence and distinctiveness that may once have characterized these major areas is now absent (Levy, 1984, 1986; Fox, 1982; Trickett, 1984). This interpretation is consistent with the notion that clinical psychology, counseling psychology, and school psychology have all emphasized role and guild issues in place of concerning themselves with an empirical foundation for training and practice (D'Amato & Dean, 1988; Fox, 1982; Levy, 1986; Oakland, 1986; Routh, Schroeder, & Koocher, 1983). The issues within these specialty areas are further separated by distinct divisions within the APA. In place of integrated psychology services we seem to have hybrids of specialty areas (e.g., clinical child psychology, pediatric psychology). Keeping abreast of recent developments across related human service fields becomes a quandary.

With this patchwork as a backdrop, Levy (1984) has argued convincingly for a merger of applied specialties into human services psychology. This reconceptualization would defined applied psychology "so as to include all professional psychology knowledge concerned with the treatment and prevention of psychological and physical disorders" (p. 490). The rationale here is to provide a wide band of services by clinically trained practitioners, which is, of course, consistent with Witmer's notions (Bardon & Bennett, 1974; Gray, 1963; Witmer, 1907). In concert with Levy's (1984) notion of human services psychology, recent occupational and employment analysis has shown the growth and development of some rather specialized areas (e.g., clinical neuropsychology, behavioral medicine) that cross traditional clinical, counseling, and school psychology boundaries in training and application (D'Amato, in press; Dean, 1982a, 1986; Routh, Schroeder, & Koocher, 1983). A case in point is the considerable interest shown recently in clinical neuropsychology. Not only has there been growth in professional ororganizations, publications, and related training, but a concomitant increase has occurred in available positions (D'Amato & Dean, 1988; D'Amato, Dean, & Holloway, 1987; Dean, 1982a, 1986). Of interest here, is the fact that training in clinical neuropsychology can be found in clinical, counseling and school psychology programs. Thus, it seems that currently the applied psychology specialities find it difficult to adapt *differently* to the unique needs of both individuals and systems. For example, Fagan (1985c) reported data from school psychology doctoral programs which offer specialization areas (e.g., behavioral medicine, clinical psychology, therapeutic intervention, research, organizational development) that would seem more closely aligned to programs in clinical or counseling psychology than with school psychology. Such confusion emphasizes either the need for further specialization areas within applied psychology, which focus on applied services in specific areas, or the need for a more general approach in the training of applied service psychologists.

Cross-fertilization between traditional specialities (school, counseling, clinical) and other specialization/concentration areas would seem to offer a stronger applied psychology in general. It can be readily seen that growth in subareas like rehabilitation psychology and neuropsychology offers promise for the development of effective school programs for students with emotional, physical, and learning disabilities. These skills would add much to the school psychologist's functioning. It would seem that applied psychology could first offer generic training for all human service psychologists, followed by more highly specialized training in specific areas. Stated differently, students could be trained in an Applied Psychology PhD program and then would specialize in a single focal area. These areas could relate to age groups (e.g., perinatal/early childhood psychology, child/adolescent psychology, adult psychology, geriatric psychology), specific areas of study (neuropsychology, behavioral medicine, rehabilitation psychology, health psychology), and/or areas of practice/application (family psychology, community psychology, substance abuse psychology). Such distinctions would clarify which services psychologists would be trained to offer and be applicable to a variety of settings. Interestingly, a similar resolution stressing training in the general field of psychology and then specialization appropriate to the students' career goals was recently approved by the National Conference on Graduate Education in Psychology (1987). Such an approach to applied psychology training is consistent with what has been conceptualized as school psychology in nontraditional settings.

Conclusions

School psychology in this chapter has been defined as a specific approach to solving problems and not as a setting specific service. As such, it seems apparent that school psychology is a viable specialty notwithstanding environmental settings. Support for this conclusion comes from the fact that numerous school psychologists have successfully demonstrated how to apply their skills in various nontraditional settings. So too, the original definition and vision for the field encompassed a full gamut of settings. That is not to say that school psychology does not hold promise for the future of education, but only that it is an appropriate specialty both in and out of the schools. In sum, little has changed since Gray (1963) issued a challenge to the field a quarter of a century ago, asserting that school psychologists "today often find themselves in a morass of unmet demands for service, but they may look beyond it to a future that will not be easy, but that is full of broad possibilities for the creative and productive use of psychology . . ." (p. 388). Today, more than ever before, individuals in society are displaying needs at an immeasurable rate, and the educational enterprise is in desperate need of leadership. These needs, taken together with recent advances in the science of psychology, suggest the paramount role that school psychologists should play both in the present and future. For this to happen, school psychologists will need to go well beyond the schools in order to facilitate the emotional and educational adjustment of all individuals in our problem-saturated society.

REFERENCES

Alpert, J. L. (1985). Change within a profession: Change, future, prevention, and school psychology. *American Psychologist, 40,* 1112–1121.

Altmaier, E. M., & Meyer, M. E. (Eds.). (1985). *Applied specialties in psychology.* New York: Random House.

American Psychological Association. (1987). APA-accredited doctoral programs in professional psychology: 1987. *American Psychologist, 42,* 1107–1113.

Anastasi, A. (1988). *Psychological testing* (6th ed.). New York: Macmillan.

Bardon, J. I. (1981). A personalized account of the development and status of school psychology. *Journal of School Psychology, 19,* 119–210.

Bardon, J. I. (1982). *Psychology applied to education: A professional specialty in search of an identity.* Address presented at the Annual Convention of the American Psychological Association, Washington, D.C.

Bardon, J. I. (1983). Psychology applied to education: A speciality in search of an identity. *American Psychologist, 38,* 185–196.

Bardon, J. I., & Bennett, V. C. (1974). *School psychology.* Englewood Cliffs, NJ: Prentice–Hall.

Bardon, J. I., Davis, L. T., Howard, C., & Myrick, C. C. (1982). Raising standards of practice in school psychology through the use of field-based training. *Journal of School Psychology, 20,* 86–85.

Bardon, J. I., & Wenger, R. D. (1974). Institutions offering graduate training in school psychology: 1973–74. *Journal of School Psychology, 12,* 70–83.

Bennett, V. C. (1970). Who is a school psychologist? (and what does he do?). *Journal of School Psychology, 8,* 166–171.

Bennett, V. C. (1985). School psychology. In E. M. Altamier & M. E. Meyer (Eds.), *Applied specialties in psychology* (pp. 129–144). New York: Random House.

Benson, A. J., & Hughes, J. (1985). Perceptions of role definition processes in school psychology: A national survey. *School Psychology Review, 14,* 64–74.

Bergan, J. R. (1979). *Behavioral consultation.* Columbus, Ohio: Charles E. Merrill.

Boring, E. G. (1950). *A history of experimental psychology.* New York: Appleton-Century-Crofts, Inc.

Bower, E. M. (1955). *The school psychologist.* Sacramento, CA: California State Department of Education.

Brantley, J. C. (1971). Psycho-educational centers and the school psychologist. *Psychology in the Schools, 8,* 313–318.

Brantley, J. C., Reilly, D. H., Beach, N. L., Cody, W., Fields, R., & Lee, H. (1974). School psychology: The intersection of community, training institution and the school system. *Psychology in the Schools, 11,* 28–32.

Brotemarkle, R. A. (Ed.). (1931). *Clinical psychology: Studies in honor of Lightner Witmer to commemorate the thirty-fifth anniversary of the founding of the first psychological clinic.* Philadelphia: University of Pennsylvania Press.

Brown, D. T., Cardon, B. W., Coulter, W. A., & Meyers, J. (Eds.). (1982). The Olympia Proceedings, [Special issue]. *School Psychology Review, 11.*

Brown, D. T., & Minke, D. M. (1984). *Directory of school psychology training programs.* Washington, D.C.: National Association of School Psychologists.

Brown, D. T., Sewall, T. J., & Lindstrom, J. P. (1977). *The handbook of certification/licensure requirement for school psychologists.* Washington, D.C.: National Association of School Psychologists.

Cohen, R. J., Montague, P., Nathanson, L. S., & Swerdlik, M. E. (1988). *Psychological testing: An introduction to tests & measurement.* Mountain View, CA: Mayfield Publishing.

Collins, J. (1931). Lightner Witmer: A biological sketch. In R. S. Brotemarkle (Ed.), *Clinical Psychology: Studies in honor of Lightner Witmer to commemorate the thirty-fifth anniversary of the founding of the first psychological clinic* (pp. 3–9). Philadelphia: University of Pennsylvania Press.

Committee on training in clinical psychology, American Psychological Association. (1947). Recommended graduate training program in clinical psychology. *American Psychologist, 2,* 539–558.

Conoley, J. C., & Conoley, C. W. (1982). *School consultation: A guide to practice and training.* Elmsford, NY: Pergamon Press.

Conoley, J. C., & Gutkin, T. B. (1986). Educating school psychologists for the real world. *School Psychology Review, 15,* 457–465.

Cronbach, L. J. (1957). The two disciplines of scientific psychology. *American Psychologist, 12,* 671–684.

Cummings, N. (1979). The undoing of clinical psychology. *APA Monitor, 2.*

Cutts, N. E. (Ed.). (1955). *School psychologists at mid- century.* Washington D.C.: American Psychological Association.

D'Amato, R. C. (in press). A neuropsychological approach to school psychology or pediatric-school neuropsychology. Professional School Psychology.

D'Amato, R. C., & Dean, R. S. (1987). Psychological reports, individual education programs, and daily lesson plans: Are they related? *Professional School Psychology, 2,* 93–101.

D'Amato, R. C., & Dean, R. S. (1988). School psychology practice in a department of neurology. *School Psychology Review, 18,* 416–420.

D'Amato, R. C., Dean, R. S., & Holloway, A. F. (1987). A decade of employment trends in neuropsychology. *Professional Psychology: Research and Practice, 18,* 653–655.

D'Amato, R. C. (Chair), Dean, R. S., Hughes, J. N., Harrison, P., McCloskey, G., Pryzwansky, W. B., & Hartlage, L. C. (1987). Non-traditional activities for school psychologists. *Proceedings of the National Association of School Psychologists 19th Annual Convention,* (pp. 96–97). New Orleans, LA. The National Association of School Psychologists.

Dean, R. S. (1980). A comparison of preservice and experienced teachers' perceptions of the school psychologist. *Journal of School Psychology, 18,* 283–289.

Dean, R. S. (1982a). Neuropsychological Assessment. In T. Kratochwill (Ed.), *Advances in School Psychology (Vol. 2)* (pp. 171–201). Hillsdale, NJ: Lawrence Erlbaum Associates.

Dean, R. S. (1982b). Providing psychological services to school-age children. In G. D. Miller (Ed.), *Human Support Services for Children* (pp. 98–123). St. Paul, Minnesota: State Department of Education.

Dean, R. S. (1986). Perspectives on the future of neuropsychological assessment. In. B. S. Plake & J. C. Witt (Eds.), *Buros—Nebraska series on measurement and testing: Future of testing and measurement* (pp. 203–244). Hillsdale, NJ: Lawrence Erlbaum Associates.

Dimond, R. E., Havens, R. A., Rathrow, S., & Colliver, J. A. (1977). Employment characteristics of subdoctoral clinical psychologists. *Professional Psychology, 8,* 116–121.

Education commission of the states, Task force on education for economic growth. (1983). *Action for excellence: A comprehensive plan to improve our nation's schools.* Denver, CO: The Commission.

Eiserer, P. E. (1963). *The school psychologist.* Washington, D.C.: Center for Applied Research in Education.

Fagan, T. K. (1985a). Sources for the delivery of school psychological services during 1890–1930. *School Psychology Review, 14,* 378–382.

Fagan, T. K. (1985b). The quantitative growth of school psychology programs in the United States. *School Psychology Review, 14,* 121–124.

Fagan, T. K. (1985c). Best practices in the training of school psychologists: Considerations for trainers, prospective entry-level and advanced students. In A. Thomas & J. Grimes (Eds.), *Best practices in school psychology* (pp. 125–141). Kent, Ohio: The National Association of School Psychologists.

Fagan, T. K. (1986a). The historical origins and growth of programs to prepare schools psychologists in the United States. *Journal of School Psychology, 24,* 9–22.
Fagan, T. K. (1986b). School psychology's dilemma: Reappraising solutions and directing attention to the future. *American Psychologist, 41,* 851–861.
Fein, L. G. (1974). *The changing school scene: Challenge to psychology.* New York: Wiley.
Fernberger, S. W. (1931). History of the Psychological Clinic. In R. A. Brotemarkle (Ed.), *Clinical Psychology: Studies in honor of Lightner Witmer to commemorate the thirty-fifth anniversary of the founding of the first psychological clinic* (pp. 10–36). Philadelphia: University of Pennsylvania Press.
Fitzgerald, L. F., & Osipow, S. H. (1986). An occupational analysis of counseling psychology: How special is the specialty? *American Psychologist, 41,* 535–544.
Fox, R. E. (1982). The need for a reorientation of clinical psychology. *American Psychologist, 37,* 1051–1057.
French, J. L., & McCloskey, G. (1980). Characteristics of doctoral and nondoctoral school psychology programs: Their implications for the entry-level doctorate. *Journal of School Psychology, 18,* 247–255.
Garfield, S. L. (1985). Clinical psychology. In E. M. Altmaier & M. E. Meyer (Eds.), *Applied specialties in psychology* (pp. 19–44). New York: Random House.
Giebink, J. W., & Ringness, T. A. (1970). On the relevancy of training in school psychology. *Journal of School Psychology, 8,* 43–47.
Gilmore, G. E., & Chandy, J. M. (1973). Educators describe the school psychologist. *Psychology in the Schools, 10,* 397–403.
Goodlad, J. I. (1979). Can our schools get better? *Phi Delta Kappan, 60,* 342–347.
Goh, D. S. (1977). Graduate Training in school psychology. *Journal of School Psychology, 15,* 207–218.
Goldstein, A. P., & Krasner, L. (Eds.). (1987). *Modern applied psychology.* New York: Pergamon.
Goldston, S. E. (1986). Primary prevention: Historical perspectives and a blueprint for action. *American Psychologist, 41,* 453–460.
Granger, R. C., & Campbell, P. B. (1977). The school psychologist as program evaluator. *Journal of School Psychology, 15,* 174–183.
Granowsky, S., & Davis, L. T. (1974). Three alternative roles for the school psychologist. *Psychology in the School, 11,* 415–421.
Gray, S. W. (1963). *The psychologist in the schools.* New York: Holt, Rienhart and Winston.
Hall, M. E. (1949). Current employment requirements of school psychologists. *American Psychologist, 4,* 519–525.
Hannah, M., & Midlarsky, E. (1985, April). *Assessing the child-classroom "fit"—An ecological approach to measurement.* Paper presented at the 17th Annual convention of the National Association of School Psychologists, Las Vegas, NV.
Harries, J. T. (1982). Perspectives on the private practice of school psychology. In C. R. Reynolds & T. B. Gutkin (Eds.), *The handbook of school psychology* (pp. 688–720). New York: Wiley.
Harris, J. (1980). *The evolution of school psychology.* Arizona State University, unpublished manuscript.
Hartlage, L. C. (1971). A look at models for the training of school psychologists. *Psychology in the Schools, 8,* 304–306.
Hartlage, L. C., & Hartlage, P. L. (1978). Clinical consultation to pediatric neurology and developmental pediatrics. *Journal of Clinical Child Psychology, 7,* 52–53.
Hartshorne, T. S., & Johnson, M. C. (1985). The actual and preferred roles of the school psychologist according to secondary school administrators. *Journal of School Psychology, 23,* 241–246.

Herron, W. G., Green, M., Guild, M., Smith, A., & Kantor, R. E. (1970). *Contemporary school psychology*. Scranton, PA: Intext Educational Publishers.
Hilke, J. L., & Brantley, J. C. (1982). The specialist-doctoral controversy: Some realities of training, practice, and advocacy. *Professional Psychology, 13,* 634–638.
Hirst, W. E. (1963). *Know your school psychologist*. New York: Grune & Stratton.
Hobbs, N. (1964). Mental health's third revolution. *American Journal of Orthopsychiatry, 34,* 822–833.
Hobbs, N. (1968). Reeducation, reality and community responsibility. In J. W. Carter (Ed.), *Research contributions from psychology to community mental health*. New York: Behavioral Publications.
Hobbs, N. (1976). *Mental health, families, and children*. Austin: Hogg Foundation for Mental Health.
Hobbs, N. (1978). Families, schools, and communities: An ecosystem for children. *Teachers College Record, 79,* 756–766.
Hohenshil, T. H. (1974). The vocational school psychologist - A speciality in quest of a training program. *Psychology in the Schools, 11,* 16–18.
Hohenshil, T. H. (1979). Adulthood: New frontier for vocational school psychology. *School Psychology Digest, 8,* 193–198.
Holt, F. D., & Kicklighter, R. H. (1971). *Psychological services in the schools: Readings in preparation, organization and practice*. Dubuque, IA: Wm. C. Brown.
Hughes, J. N., & Benson, A. J. (1986). University clinics as field placements in school psychology: A national survey. *Professional School Psychology, 1,* 131–142.
Hyman, I. A. (1979a). Psychology, educational and schooling: Social policy implications in the lives of children and youth. *American Psychologist, 34,* 1024–1029.
Hyman, I. A. (1979b). Will the real school psychologist please stand up? A struggle of jurisdictional imperialism. *School Psychology Digest, 8,* 174–180.
Hynd, G. W. (1983). *The school psychologist: An introduction*. Syracuse University Press.
Kennedy, D. A. (1971). A practical approach to school psychology. *Journal of School Psychology, 9,* 484–489.
Klosterman, D. (1974). The role of the school psychologist in a community mental health center. *Psychology in the Schools, 11,* 269–274.
Korman, M. (1974). National conference on levels and patterns of professional training in psychology: The major themes. *American Psychologist, 29,* 441–49.
Lambert, N. M. (1973). The school psychologist as a source of power and influence. *Journal of School Psychology, 11,* 245–250.
Leahey, T. H. (1980). *A history of psychology*. Englewood Cliffs, NJ: Prentice–Hall.
Lewin, K. (1936). *Principles of topological psychology*. New York: McGraw–Hill.
Levy, L. H. (1984). The metamorphosis of clinical psychology: Toward a new charter as human services psychology. *American Psychologist, 39,* 486–494.
Levy, L. H. (1986). Reflections on "Professional school psychology". *Professional School Psychology, 1,* 35–39.
Magary, J. F. (1967). *School psychological services: In theory and practice*. Englewood Cliffs, NJ: Prentice–Hall.
Matarazzo, J. D. (1987). There is only one psychology, no specialties, but many applications. *American Psychologist, 42,* 893–903.
McReynolds, P. (1987). Lightner Witmer: Little-known founder of clinical psychology. *American Psychologist, 42,* 849–858.
Meacham, M. L., & Peckham, P. D. (1978). School psychologists at three-quarters century: Congruence between training, practice, preferred role and competence. *Journal of School Psychology, 16,* 195–206.
Mead, M. (1961). *Cooperation to competition among primitive peoples*. Boston: Beacon Press.

Mearig, J. S. (1982). Integration of school and community services for children with special needs. In C. R. Reynolds & T. B. Gutkin (Eds.), *The handbook of school psychology* (pp. 748–773). New York: Wiley.

Meehl, P. E. (1954). *Clinical versus statistical prediction: A theoretical analysis and a review of the evidence.* Minneapolis: University of Minnesota Press.

Montgomery, M. D., & Paul, J. L. (1982). Ecological theory and practice. In J. L. Paul & B. C. Epanchin (Eds.), *Emotional disturbance in children* (pp. 213–241). Columbus, OH: Merrill.

Mullen, F. A. (1981). School psychology in the USA: Reminiscenses of its origin. *Journal of School Psychology, 19,* 103–119.

National Association of School Psychologists. (1972). *Guidelines for training programs in school psychology.* Akron, Ohio: NASP.

National Association of School Psychologists. (1984). *Standards for Training and Field Placement Programs in School Psychology.* Washington, D.C.: NASP.

National Association of School Psychologists. (1986). *16th annual convention call for papers: Emphasis on non-traditional roles and practice.* New Orleans, LA.

National Commission on Excellence in Education. (1983). *A nation at risk: The imperative for educational reform.* Washington, DC: U. S. Government Printing Office.

National Conference on Graduate Education in Psychology. (1987). Resolutions approved by the National Conference on Graduate Education in psychology. *American Psychologist, 42,* 1070–1084.

National Council for Accreditation of Teacher Education. (1986–1987). *NCATE thirty-third annual list.* Washington, D.C.: National Council for Accreditation of Teacher Education.

National School Psychology Inservice Training Network. (1984). *School psychology: A Blueprint for training and practice.* Minneapolis, MN: National School Psychology Inservice Training Network.

Nelson, E. (1976). Interactional psychology. In D. Magnusson & N. Endler (Eds.), *Personality at the crossroads: Current issues in interactional psychology* (pp. 99–111). Hillsdale, NJ: Lawrence Erlbaum Associates.

Newland, T. E. (1970). The search for the new: Frenzied, faddish, or fundamental? *Journal of School Psychology, 8,* 242–244.

Newland, T. E. (1981). School psychology - observations and reminiscence. *Journal of School Psychology, 19,* 4–20.

Oakland, T. D. (1986). Professionalism within school psychology. *Professional School Psychology, 1,* 9–27.

Packard, V. (1983). *Our endangered children: Growing up in a changing world.* Boston: Little Brown.

Pfeiffer, S. I., Dean, R. S., & Shellenberger, S. (1986). The school psychologist in medical settings. In T. Kratochwill (Ed.), *Advances in School Psychology (Vol. 5)* (pp. 177–202). Hillsdale, NJ: Lawrence Erlbaum Associates.

Pfeiffer, S. I., & Marmo, P. (1981). The status of training in school psychology and trends toward the future. *Journal of School Psychology, 19,* 211–216.

President's Commission on Mental Health. (1978). *Report to the president* (Vol. 1). Washington, D.C.: Government Printing Office.

Pryzwansky, W. B. (1971). Practicum training in the school setting. *Psychology in the Schools, 15,* 307–313.

Pryzwansky, W. B. (1986). Indirect service delivery: Considerations for future research in consultation. *School Psychology Review, 15,* 479–488.

Raimy, V. C. (Ed.). (1950). *Training in clinical psychology.* Englewood Cliffs, NJ: Prentice–Hall.

Ramage, J. C. (1979). National survey of school psychologists: Update. *School Psychology Digest, 8,* 153–161.

Rappaport, J. (1977). *Community psychology: Values, research and action.* New York: Holt, Rinehart & Winston.

Reger, R. (1965). *School psychology.* Springfield, IL: Charles C. Thomas.

Reilly, D. H. (1973). School psychology: View from the second generation. *Psychology in the Schools, 10,* 151–155.

Reilly, D. H. (1974). A conceptual model for school psychology. *Psychology in the Schools, 11,* 165–170.

Reynolds, C. R., & Gutkin, T. B. (Eds.). (1982). *The handbook of school psychology.* New York: Wiley.

Reynolds, C. R., Gutkin, T. B., Elliott, S. N., & Witt, J. C. (1984). *School psychology: Essentials of theory and practice.* New York: Wiley.

Routh, D. K., Schroeder, C. S., & Koocher, G. P. (1983). Psychology and primary health care for children. *American Psychologists, 38,* 95–98.

Ruckhaber, C. J. (1970). An elementary school mental health program: The stark school model. *Journal of School Psychology, 8,* 197–201.

Sattler, J. M. (1988). *Assessment of Children* (3rd ed.). San Diego, CA: Jerome M. Sattler Publisher.

Scarr, S. (Ed.). (1979). Psychology and children: Current research and practice [Special Issue]. *American Psychologist, 34.*

Senft, L. B., & Snider, B. (1980). Elementary school principals assess services of school psychologists nationwide. *Journal of School Psychology, 18,* 276–282.

Sewall, T. J., & Brown, D. T. (1976). *The handbook of certification/licensure requirements for school psychologists.* Washington, D.C.: National Association of School Psychologists.

Singer, D. L., Whiton, M. B., & Fried, M. L. (1970). An alternative to traditional mental health services and consultation in school: A social systems and group process approach. *Journal of School Psychology, 8,* 172–179.

Smith, M. B., & Hobbs, N. (1966). The community and the community mental health center. *American Psychologist, 15,* 113–118.

Smith, R. G., & Soper, W. B. (1978). A survey of master's level staffing patterns and clinical roles. *Professional Psychology, 9,* 9–15.

Solly, D. C., & Hohenshil, T. H. (1986). Job satisfaction of school psychologists in a primarily rural state. *School Psychology Review, 15,* 119–126.

Spielberger, C. D., & Stenmark, D. E. (1985). Community psychology. In E. M. Altmaier & M. E. Meyer (Eds.), *Applied Specialties in psychology* (pp. 75–98). New York: Random House.

Stewart, K. J. (1986). Innovative practice of indirect service delivery: Realities and idealities. *School Psychology Review, 15,* 466–478.

Tindall, R. H. (1964). Trends in development of psychological services in the school. *Journal of School Psychology, 3,* 1–12.

Trickett, E. (1984). Toward a distinctive community psychology: An ecological metaphor for the conduct of community research and the nature of training. *American Journal of Community Psychology, 12,* 261–279.

Valett, R. E. (1963). *The practice of school psychology: Professional problems.* New York: Wiley.

White, M. A., & Harris, M. W. (1961). *The school psychologist.* New York: Harper & Row.

Witmer, L. (1896). Practical work in psychology. *Pediatrics, 2,* 462–471.

Witmer, L. (1897). The organization of practical work in psychology (Abstract of APA paper), *Psychological Review, 4,* 116–117.

Witmer, L. (1907). Clinical psychology. *The Psychological Clinic, 1,* 1–9.

Witmer, L. (1911). *The special class for backward children.* Philadelphia: Psychological Clinic.

Woodworth, R. S. (1948). *Contemporary schools of psychology.* New York: The Ronald Press.

Ysseldyke, J. E., & Schakel, J. A. (1983). Directions in school psychology. In G. W. Hynd (Eds.), *The school psychologist: An introduction* (pp. 3–26). Syracuse, NY: Syracuse University Press.

Ysseldyke, J. E., & Weinberg, R. A. (Eds.). (1981). The future of psychology in the schools: Proceedings of the Spring Hill Symposium. *School Psychology Review, 10.*

Author Index

H

J

K

Subject Index

V

W

For Product Safety Concerns and Information please contact our EU representative GPSR@taylorandfrancis.com Taylor & Francis Verlag GmbH, Kaufingerstraße 24, 80331 München, Germany

Batch number: 10758214

Printed by Printforce, the Netherlands